2- 15-90

THE MYTH OF THE HYPERACTIVE CHILD

THE
MYTH OF THE HYPERACTIVE CHILD

And
Other Means of Child Control

by
Peter Schrag and Diane Divoky

PANTHEON BOOKS

A Division of Random House, New York

Library of Congress Cataloging in Publication Data

Schrag, Peter.
    The Myth of the Hyperactive Child.

    Bibliographical note: pp. 239–40
    Includes index.
    1. Hyperactive Children--United States.
2. Behavior modification. I. Divoky, Diane, 1939–
joint author. II. Title.
HQ773.S32 1975   371.9′3   75–10359
ISBN 0–394–49555–1

Manufactured in the United States of America

First Edition

Grateful acknowledgment is made to the following for permission to
reprint previously published material:

Philadelphia Inquirer: For permission to reprint an excerpt from the
article "Secret Dossiers vs. Parents' Right to Know" (*Philadelphia Inquirer,* March 13, 1972, page 11). Copyright © 1972 by *Philadelphia Inquirer.*

Providence Sunday Journal: For permission to reprint an excerpt from the
article "Drugs for Children—Miracle or Nightmare?" by Randall Richard
(*Providence Sunday Journal,* February 6, 1972, page 1). Copyright © 1972,
Providence Sunday Journal.

The Sterling Lord Agency, Inc.: For material from the article, "To Keep
the Kid Quiet" by Roger Rapoport. Copyright © 1971 by Roger Rapoport.
Article reprinted from *West Magazine, The Los Angeles Times,* April 25,
1971.

For David

Acknowledgments

We are grateful to countless individuals and organizations for their assistance, among them Nat Hentoff, Roger D. Freeman, Jerome Miller, Diane Bauer, Peter Bull, Susanne Martinez, Peter Sandman, Fred Nader, William Laurie, James Robison, John Roemer, Henry L. Lennard, Mae Churchill, Carol S. Kennedy, Leon J. Whitsell, Norman E. and Margaret C. Silberberg, Stanley Murphy, Lee Coleman, Nicholas Hobbs, Ned Opton, Diane Wilson, Sarah C. Carey, James H. Collier, Carol Crowther, Mary C. Howell, Allen S. Berman, Bruce Burt, Juliana Rousseau, Carol L. McCabe, James Shoettler, Leo Summer, Frank McCulloch, Vivian Stewart, John I. Meier, Caroline Rodriguez, Joseph Rosenthal, J. William Rioux, Morton Malkofsky, Lawrence Smith, Patricia Peterson, Wallace Roberts, Mark L. Stewart and Daniel Safer. We are also indebted to the American Civil Liberties Union, the New York Civil Liberties Union, the Maryland Civil Liberties Union, the National Committee for Citizens in Education, the Children's Defense Fund, the San Francisco Youth Law Center, the American Orthopsychiatric Association, the American Academy of Pediatrics, the Association for Children With Learning Disabilities, the California Association for Neurologically Handicapped Children, the Juvenile Department of the Los Angeles Public Defender's Office, the Council for Exceptional Children, the California Council for Criminal Justice, the Wheaton (Illinois) Social Service Bureau, the Bell Gardens (California) Youth Services Bureau, the Rhode Island Youth Services Bureau, the Law Enforcement Assistance Administration, the National Institute of Mental Health, the Institute for Behavioral Research, the National Council on Crime and Delinquency, the Youth Development and Delinquency Prevention Administration, the Russell Sage Foundation, *Academic Therapy,* the *Journal of Learning Disabilities, Learning,* the National Council of Juvenile Court Judges, Public Service Systems, Inc., the Bucks County Public Schools (Intermediate Unit, No. 22), the Delaware Community School Corporation (Muncie, Indiana), the Waterloo (Maryland) School, the Massachusetts Department of Mental Health, and the Medical Committee for Human Rights.

CONTENTS

Introduction

In the past five years there has been a profound shift in the way Americans and American institutions treat children. The shift is pervasive, yet so subtle and complex that no simple label is adequate. Drawing on hard medical evidence that a small percentage of the population suffers from brain damage or other neurological or emotional problems, schools, doctors and juvenile authorities have begun to attribute similar or related "ailments" to millions of children who suffer from no scientifically demonstrable ailments but whose behavior is regarded as troublesome to adults. At the same time—and partly as a result—traditional methods of management and control (threats, punishment, school suspensions) have been replaced by an accumulation of psychosocial and psychochemical techniques and by an ideology of "early intervention" which regards almost every form of undesirable behavior, however benign, as a medical ailment requiring treatment. Among the components are the prescription of psychoactive drugs to make children manageable in the classroom; the growing fashion for giving ordinary children ill-defined or meaningless pseudo-scientific labels like "learning disabled," "hyperkinetic," "behaviorally dysfunctional" or "predelinquent" and using them to justify segregation in special programs; the proliferation of mandatory screening and testing of schoolchildren to identify those with emotional or neurological "problems" or learning "handicaps," many of them more imagined than real; the growing popularity of "behavior modification" and other means of "scientific" behavior control, particularly in schools and juvenile detention homes; the use of records and dossiers as instruments of institutional control; the growth of social and psychological "treatment" projects to deal with those who may, in the view of teachers, school administrators or juvenile authorities, become academic or social deviants in the future; the erosion of individual privacy through questionnaires, tests, screens and records; the increasing collaboration of physicians, psychologists, educational authorities, social workers and the police in managing and "treating" children; and, most significantly, the dramatic growth of an ideology which sees almost all nonconformity as sickness and which, in the name of prevention, imposes increasingly narrow limits on what it will accept as tolerable behavior.

We are not talking about isolated cases:

• A well-intentioned movement to provide adequate schooling for truly handicapped youngsters has turned into a comprehensive screening and sorting game in which new categories of problems and new labels are continually being created, and in which children are being found to fit them. Between 1971 and 1974, thirty states passed special education laws and more are doing so each year; many of these mandate the screening of entire school populations not only for defective vision and hearing, for malnutrition and bad teeth, but for "oedipal conflicts," "ego disturbances" and "normalcy" in "impulse control," "withdrawal" and "social behavior." Such screening is now common, even for four-year-olds.

• By early 1975 between 500,000 and 1,000,000 American children and adolescents were taking amphetamine-type drugs and other psychostimulants by prescription, but since their numbers have been doubling every two or three years, the total may well exceed 1,000,000 before the end of 1975. A small percentage of those children suffer from some diagnosable medical ailment sufficiently serious to warrant chemotherapy. Most do not; they are being drugged, often at the insistence of schools or individual teachers, to make them more manageable.

• Hundreds of thousands of children are being placed in special classes or programs on the basis of those screens and labels, despite their vagueness and their lack of validation. Others are being drugged, and still others are being watched as potential "predelinquents." In some communities, five-year-olds have been enrolled in "predelinquency" projects sponsored by the federal government. In others, students are placed in "motivational" projects or behavior modification programs to correct "attitudes" and "deficient citizenship." The basis of those placements is usually nothing more than a test or the judgment of a teacher that the child has a "problem." In many places parents are never told what those placements mean or why their children are included.

• Personal, political and psychological data about children and their parents have been accumulating at an increasing rate in school files and in a growing number of data banks maintained by schools, health departments, the police and other public agencies. These data, often shared among agencies, are more accessible to the police, juvenile authorities, employers and the federal government than they are to the parents and children. Within schools, the information is used to intimidate students, to rationalize pedagogical failure and to justify the segregation of children into dead-end programs. Outside the schools—and despite assurances and regulations which purport to protect confidentiality—adolescents are denied jobs on the basis of those records; others are harassed by the police, and still others, if they are ever arrested, are sentenced to extended terms of "treatment" in juvenile homes even though they have never committed a serious crime.

• A growing research establishment supported by pharmaceutical firms, the federal government and other agencies is working hard to develop and test more powerful techniques of identifying and treating children described as "violence prone," "learning disabled," "predelinquent" or otherwise deviant. The studies include work on new drugs, psychosurgery, chromosome anomalies, neophrenological tests (e.g., physical deformities as indicators of violent tendencies), brain implantations, hormone and chemical imbalance and all forms of behavior modification. In many instances the subjects are ordinary schoolchildren, many of whose parents are never fully informed of their participation.

There are scores of examples and hundreds of illustrative horror stories: stories about children who grow bone thin and zombie-like from the effects of the drugs they take; stories of parents who are told to have their children started on medication if they don't want them expelled from school or placed in a "special" class; cases where parents have found themselves described in their children's school records as "radicals," "militants" or alcoholics or as unfit to raise children; instances where the police or the schools routinely inform employers about old and unsubstantiated charges against adolescent job applicants; communities which require children to furnish extensive personal information about their parents; and, at the extreme, cases where doctors perform psychosurgery on seven-year-old "hyperactive" children to make them docile. But what appears most significant is that all these examples are part of a phenomenon in which the whole is far greater than the sum of the parts, a spreading ideology of "early intervention" and "treatment" in which the language and, often, the techniques of medicine are used extensively to serve the purposes of social control. That ideology is not the particular province of any single set of institutions, nor is it limited to certain sections of the country; increasingly it pervades all the major institutions dealing with the young: schools, probation departments, clinics, the federal government and that growing scientific and corporate establishment conducting research in the proliferating "syndromes" and "diseases" of nonconformity.

There are hundreds of such "syndromes" and almost every week others are "discovered." Few, if any, have any validation in science or medicine; most simply reflect behavior that some adult doesn't like, but they are nonetheless discussed and attributed to individual children as if they were medically demonstrable organic ailments. As a consequence, millions of children are no longer regarded as part of the ordinary spectrum of human personality and intelligence—children who are quieter or brighter than the average, children who are jumpy, children who are slow—but as people who are *qualitatively* different from the "normal" population, individuals who, as a consequence of "minimal brain dysfunction," "hyperactivity" or "functional behavior disorders" constitute a distinct and separate group. There is no way to estimate how many children now carry such labels, or have been assigned to special classes, or have been taught that they are somehow different, but their number clearly runs into the millions and is growing every year. These are not sick children or people with obvious physical or psychological handicaps: they are healthy children—poor, affluent, bright, slow, black, white—who come from an ordinary spectrum of homes, live in ordinary towns and go to ordinary schools.

This book is about these new methods of child control— and, for comparison, occasionally about some old ones—and about the ideology and mystiques with which they are associated. With a few exceptions, it is restricted to the world of ordinary children; we have not tried to deal with juvenile prisons or mental hospitals (which obviously are subjects in themselves), nor have we dealt much with the proliferating literature and practices of child manipulation in the home. Although related, these also strike us as separate issues. We have tried to consider only the politics, practices and ideology that operate on this side of formal commitment to residential institutions and, in general, outside the private child-rearing practices of individual families. On the surface, that appears to be a simple subject, but when one goes beyond the horror stories and the absurdities and stupidity of daily practice one confronts something much more subtle and complex. It is not merely the labels, the drugs and the screens which make up this new world, it is a set of techniques and assumptions which affect almost all children and parents and which are likely to have profound effects in the future. We are, among other things, raising the first American generation whose records include not only the commonplace data of education (grades, test scores and anecdotes about character) but also extensive psychological information, material on family relationships, income, sexual habits and, among other things, conjectures by psychologists and social workers about the psyches and personalities of millions of individuals. Equally important, even those not segregated in special programs as a consequence of these screens and labels, those not drugged or otherwise "treated," are likely to be conditioned by their chilling effects: if they don't conform, they too may be placed in one of those classes or be labeled as "maladaptive." Everyone has a record, and everyone is subject to the tests and procedures which assign only a minority to the special categories. All are being taught that it is normal to be watched, tested and treated, that deviance is disease, and that punishment, which used to be direct and overt, is now meted out furtively in the guise of therapy.

It is a gradual, subtle and seductive process, but the political and social consequences are enormous. When the impositions come in the name of diagnosis and treatment ("for the benefit of the child"), not in the name of punishment and control, otherwise arbitrary institutional procedures begin to look reasonable and the power to manipulate is immeasurably enhanced. This is science talking, it is the natural order of things; what we are doing to you has nothing to do with the arbitrary decisions of school administrators or cops or the social bias of the community. As a consequence it becomes increasingly hard to resist, increasingly tempting to go along, and increasingly difficult for the individual—parent or child—even to know exactly what is happening or why. What is certain is that the new ideology and the associated techniques—screens, drugs, behavior modification, special programs—all serve the purpose of legitimizing and enlarging the power of institutions over individuals. In every instance it is argued that for this individual case, the "treatment" is preferable to the alternatives. But such arguments, even in the rare instances where they are reasonable, invariably disregard the larger social and political consequences of the things the new methods of control are teaching children (and often parents) about the power and legitimacy of institutions, about the right to resist, and about the possibilities of asserting themselves as independent, healthy human beings. An entire generation is slowly being conditioned to distrust its own instincts, to regard its deviation from the narrowing standards of approved norms as sickness and to rely on the institutions of the state and on technology to define and engineer its "health." In enhancing the power of the state, and in destroying even the ability to imagine the alternatives and understand the liberties which might once have been exercised in defending them, the impact of that conditioning is almost incalculable.

THE MYTH OF THE HYPERACTIVE CHILD

ONE

The
Hutschnecker Memo

The request, dated December 30, 1969, went from the President through his domestic affairs advisor, John D. Ehrlichman, to the Secretary of Health, Education and Welfare. Attached was a 1,600-word memorandum from a New York physician named Arnold A. Hutschnecker proposing, among other things, that "the Government should have mass testing done on all 6–8 year old children . . . to detect [those] who have violent and homicidal tendencies."[1] The President was soliciting the Secretary's opinion "as to the advisability of setting up pilot projects embodying some of these approaches."

Dr. Hutschnecker, who had once treated Richard M. Nixon for a medical problem when the latter was vice-president and who was now engaged in the practice of psychotherapy, also proposed that children identified as showing "delinquent tendencies" be subject to "corrective treatment" —counseling, day care centers and, for "the young hard-core criminal," enrollment in special camps. Dr. Hutschnecker was certain that there were already studies which demonstrated that "future delinquent tendencies" could be predicted in nine out of ten cases. Although he agreed that there was a desperate need for urban reconstruction, especially in the inner cities, he was confident that an effective way to attack the problem of violent crime, particularly among juveniles, was to focus on "the criminal mind of the child" and "to prevent a child with a delinquent character structure from being allowed to grow into a full-fledged teenage delinquent or adult criminal."

Toward the middle of February, after six weeks of study, Dr. Stanley F. Yolles, the director of the National Institute of Mental Health, drafted a reply for the Secretary's signature. There were, he said, no tests of sufficient reliability which would make possible the mass testing and intervention that Dr. Hutschnecker proposed:

> Predictions aimed at events which have relatively low frequencies (e.g. violent crimes and homicides), almost invariably have rather high rates of erroneous predictions. Such errors are of two types: those predicted to be violent who in fact do not later display such behavior (false positives), and those predicted to be not violent who in fact later display violent behavior (false negatives). Thus, while some devices . . . do pick out high proportions of youngsters who may actually become delinquent, they do this at the cost of having a rather high rate of "false positive" errors.[2]

In addition to these drawbacks, said Dr. Yolles, there were "some obvious social policy and Constitutional questions about intervening in the lives of youngsters who are *predicted* to be violent but have not yet displayed such behavior." He therefore recommended that plans for corrective treatment "and other related interventions" might best be introduced at the point where "the child begins to display discernible problems in his behavior." That would represent a more realistic, feasible and desirable strategy, he thought, and would not raise "the aforementioned Constitutional and social policy questions." Dr. Yolles, however, did not reject the

Hutschnecker proposals out of hand. Along with the development of Comprehensive Community Mental Health Centers, "small residential treatment and rehabilitation camps and centers located in or close to the community would appear very worthy of pilot testing and development." Although the "present state of technological advancement" did not appear adequate for effective "mass testing of young children," Yolles pointed out that NIMH was supporting a number of studies "aimed at the development of more accurate and efficient instruments for predicting deviant behavior."

Early in April 1970, someone at HEW leaked the Hutschnecker memo to the press, generating several weeks of vigorous denunciation by most of the psychiatric and sociological establishment. Walter Barton, medical director of the American Psychiatric Association, told reporters that Dr. Hutschnecker was not certified as a specialist in psychiatry, "nor, to the best of our knowledge, does his proposal have any support whatsoever within the profession." Dr. Hutschnecker, said a spokesman for the American Psychological Association, "shows a complete lack of understanding as to what psychological tests can or cannot do or even what they were meant to do." Hutschnecker replied that he had received some support from such experts as Dr. Louise Bates Ames, associate director of the Gesell Institute of Child Development in New Haven. By October, almost six months after the leak, Hutschnecker claimed that "officially the President has not as yet rejected my plan." He was preparing a project to be financed by a private foundation which he hoped would convince the government of the effectiveness of this style of crime prevention.

On April 14, 1970, a week after the Hutschnecker proposal became public, the late James E. Allen, Jr., then Assistant Secretary for Education, and U.S. Commissioner of Education, spoke before the annual convention of the National School Boards Association. Dr. Allen was generally regarded as a liberal—later, as a result of his public opposition to the Vietnam war, he would be forced to resign. He was proposing a program "which may be considered by some as revolutionary in concept" and which had, as its base, "the continuing prescription of individualized programs of education, health and welfare for every child" in every school district in America:

> Under the plan, there would be available in the school district a Central Diagnostic Center to which, at age 2 1/2, a child would be brought by his parents or guardian. The purpose of the Center would be to find out everything possible about the child and his background that would be useful in planning an individualized learning program for him. This would be accomplished through an educational diagnosis, a medical diagnosis, and home visits by a trained professional who would in effect become the child's and family's counsellor. By the time the tests and home visits were completed, the Center would know just about everything there is to know about this child—his home and family background, his cultural and language deficiencies, his health and nutrition needs, and his general potential as an individual.[3]

The information gathered would be fed into a central computer, whence it would be analyzed and transmitted to a team of trained professionals whose job it would be to write "a detailed prescription for the child and, if necessary, for his home and family as well." The prescription for the home, Allen said, would be "every bit as important as the prescription for the child himself. If the home is contributing negatively to the child's development, it too should receive attention and aid." Allen visualized the establishment of Good Start Centers where children would learn how to get along with children of different backgrounds, and the creation of a "central academy" which would function as a "nerve center for academic control, instructional supervision, pupil auditing, and specialized help." Continuing evaluations would be made until the child was through school—every few weeks between the ages of two-and-a-half and six, and every six months thereafter—and these evaluations would also be analyzed through the computer and used to revise, as necessary, the individual's "prescription," which "would be filled by the Board of Education and the City Health Department or the family doctor . . . plus whatever other health, education and welfare agencies have jurisdiction over the services needed." His proposal was far more sweeping than Hutschnecker's, more intrusive into the private lives of children and their families, and indicative of a much greater faith in the possibilities of tests and treatment. The Commissioner was a liberal, a man with a certified record of concern for children. He wanted to prescribe and cure, not to punish. How could one quarrel with his intent?

Clearly something was in the wind. The two proposals had little immediate impact on policy. Allen's was scarcely noticed at the time it was made, though it would be noticed later; Hutschnecker's disappeared into a fog of government rhetoric. But they nonetheless indicated a profound change in ideology and practice—despair, on the one hand, with the proposals for social reform of the sixties, and a mushrooming faith, on the other, in the possibilities of screening, diagnosing and treating individuals. They signaled the beginning of what would, in effect, constitute a new era in the social and psychological control of children in America. Within three years of delivery, Allen's speech would be pulled from apparent oblivion and used as the basis of a proposal by the San Francisco Unified School District for a city-wide program to test and "treat" all children beginning at the age of three. Within two years of their submission, Hutschnecker's ideas would be embodied in projects to identify "predelinquents" in Southern California and children with "maladaptive tendencies" in Baltimore. Concurrently, the state of Illinois would plan and begin to institute a state-wide program of medical and psychological testing, the state of Maryland would establish a central computer data bank with a complete record of every child who had ever received special medical or psychological services or who had any other sort of "handicap," and across the country between 500,000 and 1,000,000 young children would be taking psychoactive drugs by prescription, often at the behest of their schools, to enable them to sit still and concentrate in the classroom.[4] By 1974, the spirit, and often the substance, of the Hutschnecker and Allen proposals would be institutionalized in research programs, teacher training courses, experiments in behavior modification, conferences on delinquency and learning disabilities, and in thousands of programs involving millions of children.

On the surface, the two proposals appeared as different as night and day—Hutschnecker's resonant with overtones of Prussian heavy-handedness and intimations of the concentration camp, Allen's growing Dewey-eyed from the social service ideology of the preceding decade. Allen himself conceded that he was not suggesting anything that hadn't already been proposed or tried in discrete projects; he was only recommending that a lot of separate ideas—nutritional, educational and medical—be systematically combined with a program of diagnosis and prescription to cover every significant aspect of a child's life. It was, Allen explained, a way of making real "the education revolution so hopefully envisioned in the late fifties." But the target of reform had changed radically since the late fifties, there had been a shift from institutions to individuals, a replacement of the language of sociology with the metaphors of medicine, and an emphatic change from reform of "conditions" to the "treatment" of patients. A "mass program of Prevention of Crime," Hutschnecker had said, answering the recommendations of the Eisenhower Commission on Violent Crime, "could begin almost immediately, without the need to wait for the slow agonizing process of improving living conditions and the elimination of hunger." Allen seemed to be answering Hutschnecker by trying to go him one better; he would, in the interest of the children, write prescriptions for everyone, beginning at the age of two-and-a-half.

The coincidence between the two proposals went beyond the timing. There were the medical language and metaphors —prescription, diagnosis, treatment. ("In medicine," Hutschnecker had written, "we seek preventive measures: we vaccinate, we quarantine, we immunize.") There was the view of the child as patient coupled with the supreme confidence in the ability of "trained professionals" to write accurate "prescriptions" and offer effective remedies. Finally, there was the overriding expectation that social ills, however defined, could be eradicated by reforming individuals rather than institutions. It was hardly a new idea; its roots were twisted around two millennia of Western history—inquisitions, witch trials, tests of loyalty, tests of fitness, tests that would predict fidelity, religious orthodoxy and chivalric honor, psychological tests, measures of cranial capacity, intelligence and criminal tendencies. For hundreds of years demonology and medicine, sometimes indistinguishable, alternated as the bases for theoretical explanations of deviance (which, in some medieval texts, included every affliction from mental illness to impotence, sterility and poor harvests). The modern version, however, can be traced most conveniently to the rise of the social sciences and the growing faith that there could be a science of society as rigorous and positivist as physics and chemistry. In the last generation of the nineteenth century, an Italian criminologist named Cesare Lombroso, drawing on a mix of earlier phrenological and anthropological studies, had proposed a program of "preventive isolation" of born criminals. Lombroso, a liberal in his time, opposed hard punishment of occasional criminals, favored separating young delinquents from hardened criminals, and believed in the application of psychology in child guidance and reform. "The child," he wrote, "ought to be persuaded without being constrained by violence. We should prevent, rather than encourage, as many do, the association of ideas between bad actions and punishment, on account of which, when the surveillance of parent or teacher is removed, children no longer fear to do wrong." He was

confident, however, that his proposal for "preventive isolation" of born criminals was feasible, having been "considerably facilitated by new advances in anthropology."[5] They
could easily be identified:

> The characteristics of physiognomy and cranium, taken
> together with biological characteristics and the excess of
> tendencies to evil-doing, assist powerfully in distinguish-
> ing the dominant and always increasing criminality of the
> born criminal from that which is found temporarily in the
> case of all children. . . . The isolation of the born criminal,
> in these cases, prevents his perfecting himself in evil, and,
> what is more important, prevents fruit, congenitally rot-
> ten, from tainting hundreds that are sound.[6]

Lombroso's book, *Crime: Its Causes and Remedies,* was published in the United States in 1911 under the sponsorship of
a committee of attorneys, law professors and sociologists,
among them Roscoe Pound of Harvard, Ernst Freund of the
University of Chicago and John H. Wigmore of Northwest-
ern. They introduced Lombroso's book by pointing out that
crime, like disease, had "natural causes" and that the "individualization of disease, in cause and treatment, is the
dominant truth of modern medical science." What was required, they believed, was the individualization of "penal
treatment." Although they refused to accept all of Lombroso's conclusions—Lombroso himself had modified his
original belief that every "born criminal" was an atavistic
throwback to a primitive human type—they accepted his
"analogies" between "moral imbecility," epilepsy and "congenital criminality." They also seemed to accept the list of
physiological characteristics and "psychic anomalies" which
Lombroso associated with criminals, epileptics and "ata-
vism" and which, in spirit, and sometimes in detail, would
anticipate hypotheses of the 1970s concerning "learning
disabilities," delinquency and other forms of social and academic deviance. (Among others, Lombroso listed left-handedness and ambidexterity; cranial capacity too large or too

small, and "physiopsychic hyperexcitability."[7])

The interest never faded. Several major studies were conducted in the twentieth century to examine the relationship between delinquency and physical characteristics, and to determine whether that relationship could be used to predict or prevent delinquent behavior. Dr. William H. Sheldon of Columbia University made extensive measurements on boys in a state training school in Massachusetts and concluded (1949) that sharp deviations in certain physical characteristics were found in a disproportionate number of the delinquents.[8] Similar studies were conducted by Sheldon and Eleanor Glueck of Harvard, who developed the delinquency prediction tables that Hutschnecker hoped to use and who observed (in a book called *Physique and Delinquency* published in 1958[9]) that there were twice as many mesomorphs ("relative predominance of muscle, bone and connective tissue") among delinquents as among nondelinquents, that the proportion of ectomorphs ("predominance of linearity and fragility") was even in both groups, and that there were fewer endomorphs ("soft roundness throughout the various regions of the body") among the delinquents. The Gluecks were careful to warn against belief in any "unitary cause or theory of delinquency" but they pointed out that certain factors, acting in combination, "are found to occur so frequently in the constitution and developmental history of delinquents . . . that we may legitimately conclude that the weight they contribute to the causal scales is excessive."

> The cause of delinquency . . . is the totality of conditions sufficient to produce it. Thus many boys may be very close to delinquency, yet not experience sufficient internal and external pressure to be thrust across the line of customary and legal prohibitions. This, incidentally, indicates how enormously important it is to develop instruments for the detection of potential delinquents early enough in life, in order so to accommodate the internal and external situa-

tion of a child as to counterpoise an almost dominant tendency to commit crime.[10]

The Gluecks' predictive tables did not include physical characteristics; they relied primarily on psychological tests, family relationships ("supervision of boy by mother," "discipline of boy by father") and "personality traits." The data in the study of physical characteristics did suggest, however, that "trait-disharmony" ("traits which seemingly create an internal disharmony in a particular body type to which they are normally alien") tends "to find an outlet in delinquency."

Lombroso's book crossed the Atlantic during the first great American awakening to the possibilities of educational and psychological testing, ethnic exclusion in immigration, and eugenics, which, from their first beginnings, tended to travel similar paths. The pioneers of the testing movement in America, H. M. Goddard, Lewis M. Terman, and Edward L. Thorndike, among others, were certain that moral capacity was associated with intelligence ("all feeble-minded are at least potential criminals," Terman wrote in 1916, and "every feeble-minded woman is a potential prostitute"), and all were involved in the growing eugenics movement during the first decades of the twentieth century.[11]

Goddard, who had translated the Binet-Simon scale from the French in 1908 and used it to identify the "feeble-minded" at a training school in New Jersey, went on to write *The Kallikak Family,* which purported to trace the history of three generations of "paupers, criminals, prostitutes and drunkards." Terman, who would observe that the racial stocks "most prolific of gifted children are from Northern and Western Europe, and the Jewish [while] the least prolific are the Mediterranean races, the Mexicans and the Negroes," served as a leader of the California Human Betterment Foundation which was credited with 6,200 sterilizations in the 1920s. As late as 1939, Thorndike would talk about the "substantial positive correlation between intelligence and morality." "One sure service (about the only one) which the inferior and vicious can perform is to prevent their genes from survival."[12] What was required was selective breeding, selective immigration and selective placement of personnel in positions of responsibility. "It has been figured," Terman told a convention of the National Education Association in 1923, "that if the present differential birth rate continues, 1,000 Harvard graduates will at the end of 200 years have but 50 descendants, while in the same period 1,000 South Italians will have multiplied to 100,000."[13]

The prime function of the tests was to predict how the subject would perform in tasks similar to those being tested —meaning, usually, the prediction of success within the school system and in corporate society generally. In the process, as many critics have pointed out, the tests became instruments justifying the system, were used, in other words, to teach the losers that their failures, low status, poor grades, bad schools and dirty jobs had been determined by their own lack of ability and were, if not deserved, at least part of the natural order of things.[14] In the past half-century, and particularly in the past decade, a vast literature has accumulated about what tests do and don't do, how they discriminate and how they have been used to support status and racial bias. But there has been, in addition, an ideological element dating from the introduction of the first intelligence tests, and running through the history of testing, that is now likely to have implications far more significant than those usually debated by the critics. The test enables the "trained professional" to know something about the client that the client does not know about himself and that will enable the professional, like a good physician, to prescribe for the client's own good. But where people like Terman and Thorndike merely assumed that they could associate certain social and moral conclusions with test scores on a specific item (e.g., feeble-mindedness with "potential criminal"), the proliferation of tests in recent years began to suggest that science now enabled the "professional" to test for everything directly, that one could, in other words, design scales to determine criminal or violent "tendencies" without inferential detours, and that through batteries of tests one could understand the essence of the individual's psyche, abilities and personality in purely scientific terms. The individual thus came to be regarded as a cluster of physical characteristics and "behaviors"—the noun had gone plural—to be examined and discussed *as if* by some means—counseling, drugs, behavior modification or other "therapy"—they were subject to revision or cure. More important, the instrument came to be used not merely to justify placement in existing programs or school grades or, more generally, to test for characteristics which, however vague, had some prior independent conceptual existence (e.g., "intelligence") but to create entirely new categories and labels which had no base other than the test itself. In the guise of creating tests for diseases, the diagnosticians created diseases for the tests.

As a consequence, a whole new demonology has sprung into existence: the predelinquent, the learning disabled, the minimally brain damaged. Since a small percentage of children could be shown, through medical tests, to be organically brain damaged, a substantial number of other children who had trouble learning to read and who showed some, though not all, of the same "behavior syndromes" were labeled "minimally brain damaged" (or MBD) even though no one could find any sign of organic damage and all tests showed that there was none.[15] Subsequently MBD was further broadened to mean, among other things, "minimal brain dysfunction" and invoked to explain everything from learning difficulties to divorce and homicide. Dr. Camilla M. Anderson, a circuit-riding psychiatrist who became a favored speaker at conferences on learning disabilities in the early 1970s, told her audiences that MBD was the cause of far too much social pathology to be treated simply as a cause of learning problems and far too pervasive to be eradicated by anything less than eugenic means: the only social solution was to keep those who carried it from breeding. What was required, she said, was

to have a commitment to do whatever is necessary to see
to it that people who cannot either manage or sustain their
own lives and cannot understand the responsibilities of
parenting are not permitted to procreate. We have failed
to challenge the assumption of people's inalienable right
to procreate. . . . We should be ready to admit that the
poverty pockets of our nation are the prime source of this
handicap (MBD); it's time we faced up to the implications. If this position makes you squeamish, spend a few
years in prison or the ghettoes, which exist even in
sparsely populated areas. You will find that whereas slums
make people, the basic truth is that people make slums;
they cannot do otherwise. Their deficits and their lack of
equipment make it inevitable that they will create a sham-
bles. They ought not be permitted to bring children into
the world to perpetuate their own misery and inner and
outer poverty. Training them for jobs in this competitive
society is no answer except for a few. We already know
what needs to be done. There will still be plenty of children with MBD born to more normal and adequate parents to keep all of the rehabilitation programs busy and
going strong.[16]

After sixty years of research, the theory appeared to have
come full circle to the point where it had begun with Goddard, Terman and Thorndike.

Anderson, however, represented an extreme. The liberal
mainstream shuddered at suggestions of eugenics, psychosurgery and aversive therapy, the practice of using a
series of painful electric shocks to modify "maladaptive behavior" among children and adults.[17] The response, in juvenile justice, in education and in medicine, was treatment and
"early intervention." As a consequence there sprang up, almost overnight, a new and professedly humane generation of
preemptive labels and anticipatory syndromes. In order to
spare the individual the invidiousness and embarrassment of
school failure or the characterization of "delinquent," and to
identify potential problems early, there would be tests,
screens and diagnoses to discover learning disabilities, delin-

quent tendencies or any of a hundred other problems indicating likelihood, possibility or "proneness." Symptoms were escalated into syndromes and syndromes into diseases: delinquents spawned predelinquents and predelinquents were anticipated by those prone to delinquency; hyperkinesis spawned "pseudo-hyperkinesis."

The syndromes were associated with observed behavior covering the whole spectrum of juvenile activity: children who were jumpy, who couldn't sit still ("hyperactive"), who sat still too much ("hypoactive"), who couldn't learn to read as expected ("dyslexic"), who repeated themselves ("perseverative"), or who twiddled their hair or played with their genitals or talked too much or were distracted too easily.[18] Sometimes the labels were merely tautological or Latin or Greek forms of common English words, sometimes they expressed obvious and possibly serious problems which required attention (and which were, therefore, probably evident without tests), but in all instances they imputed to the syndrome or disease an aura of scientific precision and considered judgment. If invidiousness was thus reduced, it was done at the expense of creating labels and distinctions that sounded far more legitimate, precise and definitive than the casual characterizations of parents or teachers which they replaced: they converted what had been the observations of admittedly fallible human beings ("the kid can't sit still") into disease ("hyperkinesis"). Most significantly, where the old labels, by their very nature, had a kind of perishability and usually expired with maturity, the new ones implied a permanence that the individual might never outlive. Bad boys grew into something else, usually responsible men, but minimal brain dysfunction sounds like it will be forever. And despite an extensive literature on the self-fulfilling effects of labels—if you call someone a poor learner or a delinquent you increase his chances of becoming one—the labeling went on, often in the name of avoiding labels. The new labels, after all, did not represent the opinions of particular individuals sitting in judgment; they were the expressions of an overarching, cosmic and impersonal science.

II

With the exhaustion of faith in the New Frontier, the Great Society and the social and institutional reform they promised, the focus shifted to the management, adjustment and treatment of individuals. Within a five-year period beginning in 1969, the country suffered a veritable epidemic of "learning disabilities" affecting, in the view of the field's leading scholars, between 10 and 20 percent of the juvenile population; at the same time, sociologists and social workers and penologists were speaking of an eruption in juvenile delinquency and other juvenile pathology, and seeking new means to "treat" those infected by them. But now it was the system that was given, legitimate and permanent, and the individual who had to be transformed if he was unable to live within it. If there was a controversy between liberals and conservatives it was not about that assumption, but only about the means: the adjusters against the spankers. The developing dialectic of the seventies offered three options: punishment, psychoactive drugs or counseling and "behavior modification." With the exception of the handful of people who were trying to create "alternative institutions" at the social fringes (often using the same means), no other option was offered. Although the practitioners in the fields of juvenile justice, education and mental health, as individuals, often sensed that the system (or the school or the teacher) helped cause the problem, the *ideology* admitted no such possibility. It was, in that sense, quite totalitarian.

What remained of the liberalism of the sixties was the assumption that the state, meaning the social service system, had a major responsibility in generating reform and producing change. But where, in the sixties, the ostensible prime objective was society itself—ghettoes, schools, jobs—it now became the client. In its new application, the liberal ideology would provide individualized treatment for all, with the state playing the role of physician, thereby accelerating the century-old shift of the burden of responsibility from the individual to the system. With the passage of the Omnibus Crime Control and Safe Streets Act in 1968, the establishment of the Law Enforcement Assistance Administration, and the drying up of federal funds for poverty programs, Model Cities and educational experimentation, the emphasis and the funds in the social service sector tended not only to reinforce the status quo—which was presumably the intent of the policy—but to be directed quite consciously to the control and management of deviance. The Law Enforcement Assistance Administration, which did not exist in 1967, was spending $1 billion a year by 1974, about a fifth of it on juvenile delinquency prevention and diversion; concurrently, while there developed a national surplus in teachers and social workers, the areas dealing with special forms of pathology, and particularly the field of learning disabilities, found themselves desperately shorthanded. By 1973 it was not uncommon to find veterans of Model Cities or Office of Economic Opportunity projects running police youth bureaus and delinquency prevention programs funded by LEAA or the Youth Development and Delinquency Prevention Administration of HEW, or one-time proponents of open schools and other educational options taking crash courses in learning disabilities and behavior modification. They had started to redo society and were now learning to redo people.

The techniques proposed to cure the diagnosed illnesses were more diverse than the diagnoses themselves, but most of the practitioners behaved as if science was, at the very least, capable of finding solutions, if, indeed, it had not already found them. The invention of the new syndromes, the rediscovery of old and nearly forgotten ones, and the availability of research funds from the new federal programs, the drug companies and other sources produced an explosion of studies on the cure of learning disabilities, behavior modification, delinquency prevention, hyperkinesis, mental retardation and scores of other ailments, real and mythical. The best known of the new apostles of the "science" of human behavior was B. F. Skinner, the Harvard psychologist who proposed to redesign the whole culture through operant conditioning—the creation of an environment that would reinforce the kind of behavior that he assumed would assure the survival of that culture. Skinner argued that all human behavior could be explained, and therefore shaped, through environmental reinforcement, "contingencies" that rewarded certain kinds of behavior and not others. Through a proper understanding of these contingencies, the idea of autonomous man would become as passé as the explanation that physical objects were propelled by a force called "impetuosity." The outlines of a technology to shape the culture, Skinner said, "are already clear."[19]

> A science of behavior is not yet ready to solve all our problems, but it is a science in progress, and its ultimate adequacy cannot now be judged. When critics assert that it cannot account for this or that aspect of human behavior, they usually imply that it will never be able to do so, but the analysis continues to develop and is in fact much further advanced than its critics usually realize.

Most of the practitioners in the field of child management were far more modest than Skinner, not only about their ambitions but, in many cases, about the state of their technology. Yet Skinner's assertion was nonetheless paradigmatic in its expression of the desire to find the appropriate technology. "Ten years hence," said Harold and June Shane in the official magazine of the National Education Association in January 1969, "it should be more accurate to term [the teacher] a 'learning clinician.' This title is intended to convey the idea that schools are becoming 'clinics' whose purpose is to provide individualized psychosocial 'treatment' for the students."[20] While people like Hutschnecker were casting envious eyes at "Pavlovian methods" which had been "used effectively in the Soviet Union," the more moderate practitioners of behavior control were arguing that "learning behaviors are related to their consequences, and that, by establishing specific learning procedures, environmental controls and appropriate consequences for performance, these learning behaviors can be developed, maintained, and extended."[21] The pure behaviorists were not interested in internal states, psychic or physical disorders or their diagnoses, but rather in finding the proper "contingencies" to shape and reinforce the desired behavior. Some theorists suggested that all problems were essentially physical in nature—most delinquents, said a university psychologist, suffer from "hyperkinetic impulsive disorder," a neurological incapacity to control their own actions—but they all believed fervently in the possibilities, if not the power, of their own science. In the five years after 1969, "behavior modification" became an all-purpose phrase which was applied to everything from the prescription of drugs and the use of electroshock to the institution of "token economies" which rewarded appropriate behavior with candy bars, soft drinks or free time in the school playground. That many of these forms of intervention were ineffective, however, was not nearly as significant as the purposes for which they were instituted or the faith which the practitioners invested in them. "Behavior modification" seemed to explain itself.

It is hardly surprising that there was, in many instances, more scientism than science. The studies that poured out of the universities, the special child study centers, the youth bureaus and the schools tended to be flawed not merely by inadequate statistical methods, skewed population samples (usually ghetto blacks), minuscule control groups and an almost total absence of long-range followup, but also by an almost totally arbitrary set of definitions which in many cases represented nothing more than the bias of teachers or cops translated into scientific jargon. Long before most of the experiments of the seventies were launched, for example, there existed a voluminous literature indicating that juvenile delinquency depended, more than anything, on social definitions—arbitrary decisions by the police, judges, probation officers and communities as to what constituted delinquent conduct—and that behavior regarded as benign in one town might be regarded as criminal in the next. Nonetheless, most of the proliferating delinquency projects and "treatment" centers of the seventies made extensive (and usually unsuccessful) attempts to demonstrate their effects on juvenile crime and recidivism: precise definitions were never attempted and reasonable statistical procedures were rarely employed. Similarly, the attempt to study MBD or "learning disabilities" frequently evaporated into a fog of uncertain definitions: in 1966, one of the inventors of MBD listed 99 symptoms of the disease in children and concluded that some combination of the most frequently cited created a single syndrome."[22] (Someone would later call it "a sophisticated statement of ignorance.") When Noam Chomsky wrote his elegant attack on Skinner's thesis about the possibilities of behavioral technology, the argument applied equally to the more limited and ostensibly precise theories of the new generation of child testers and therapists. "There exists no behavioral science incorporating nontrivial, empirically supported propositions that apply to human affairs or support a behavioral technology," Chomsky concluded, and there was no evidence that one would ever be developed.[23] The notion that batteries of tests and diagnoses analyzed through computers in central diagnostic centers, and a panoply of separate cures for ostensibly discrete ailments, social or medical, could collectively accomplish the same thing was equally unfounded.

The important thing, however, was the wish. Because it stemmed largely from essentially political, not scientific, motives, the desire to develop the technology was almost immune to the effects of its limitations. There were, of course, real forms of pathology with demonstrable symptoms— hearing and speech problems, problems of coordination, organic brain damage, mental retardation—which required special attention—compensatory treatment by teachers, parents or doctors, or other forms of intervention. The very existence of these demonstrable disorders, however, furnished a convenient and plausible rationale for the creation of others which were essentially social, not medical, in nature. There were problems that occurred in a small percentage of the population—for example, hyperactivity so severe that the child was a danger to himself or others—which had been stretched by definition to include large numbers of other individuals whose handicap, at worst, was social (e.g., irritating the teacher) and where intervention was merely a matter of institutional convenience. There were others—many instances of "learning disabilities," for example—which simply reflected a gap between arbitrary institutional expectations and performance. In one Midwestern school system, the definitions had intentionally been stretched to the point where a system-wide screening procedure would turn up some "disability" for every student.[24] The real ailments had thus become models not only for synthetic diseases invented in behalf of social institutions to medicalize behavior antithetical to efficient management and shrinking norms of acceptable conduct but also for indications that such behavior might show up in the future. Since most children fell under a normal curve in most categories, and since nearly every individual showed "soft signs" of something, it was relatively easy to draw the line between pathology and normality anywhere the institution desired.

Ironically, though quite logically, the extension of rudimentary due process rights to juveniles, largely through judicial decisions, spurred the development and spread of the medical model. The decision of the U.S. Supreme Court in the *Gault* case (1967)[25] which, for the first time, gave children the right to be represented by counsel and to have an adversarial proceeding in juvenile court, was perhaps the most important single stimulus for the establishment of delinquency prevention programs, youth bureaus and other efforts to deal with the potential offender before he came to court—to deal with kids, in other words, before they could demand their rights. Similarly, the imposition of due process requirements in placing students in special classes (for slow learners, behavior problems or whatever), or in suspending them, put additional pressure on schools to find informal remedies for academic or behavioral difficulties—real or imagined—and to deal with them through academic or medical therapy rather than expulsion or segregation. A general liberalization of attitudes regarding overtly coercive means to maintain order, including restrictions on corporal punishment, reinforced the due process decisions in generating a new search for modes of control which appeared more humane, reasonable and "scientific" and which would circumvent the need for formal institutional action. If the school couldn't paddle the child, or throw him out, it might at least encourage, or force, his parents to find a doctor who would prescribe the appropriate medication.

I I I

The attempts to develop new modes of control in the educational and juvenile justice fields now follow similar and often identical paths connected by ideology, medical typology, and a growing number of studies suggesting that problems in one area are problems in the other. "A hyperactive child," a California psychiatrist told us, "is a predelinquent," and in Rhode Island a psychologist named Allen Berman who conducted studies in a boys' training school declared that the majority of the delinquents there owed their problems to neurological learning disabilities which should have been treated in school. Such observations reinforce the folklore that school failure inevitably leads to delinquency and crime. The critic Alfred Kazin anticipated a considerable body of contemporary "science" in recalling that, during his school days in the twenties, he was certain that any classroom transgression, however small, would set him on the path to Sing Sing.[26]

> The dangers of going bad were constantly impressed upon
> me at home and in school in dark whispers of the "reform

school" and in examples of boys who had been picked up for petty thievery, rape, or flinging a heavy inkwell straight into a teacher's face. Behind any failure in school yawned the great abyss of a criminal career. Every refractory attitude doomed you with the sound "Sing Sing." Anything less than absolute perfection in school always suggested to my mind that I might fall out of the daily race . . . or—dared I think of it?—fall back into the criminal class itself.

The contemporary refinement of that mythology has been purged of its moralistic content and reduced to speculations about the cumulative effects of disease. But however the disease is labeled, and however precise the diagnosis pretends to be, there remains a tendency to focus simply on undifferentiated deviance. The system may define all sorts of things, and may attach all sorts of names, but what it is concerned about is acceptable behavior: the issue is not a child's silent agony but those things about him which tend, either now or later, to make him a nuisance or a menace. There are, says the jacket blurb of a fashionable book on learning disabilities,

> about eight million American children who suffer from a single or multiple form of physiological impairment that prevents them from achieving the usual, ordinary goals expected of them. (These are *not* mentally retarded or visibly deformed youngsters; and, initially, they are not psychologically disturbed.) They have average or better intelligence—all the mental potential for learning and growing.
>
> Yet, due to some subtle, often difficult-to-diagnose physical impairments, most of which can be overcome or compensated for when recognized early and treated properly, the majority of these children fail to learn, and through that failure become behavioral misfits, psychological problems, and frequently subjects of tragedy to themselves, to their families, to their teachers, and even to society.[27]

The logical consequence of such reasoning is to bring increasing numbers of clients into a network of special controls at increasingly earlier ages. In the delinquency area it is often called "outreach"—sending cops into the schools, for example, to counsel, teach or identify problem children before the trouble hits the streets; in education it is generating growing acceptance of the idea that children require attention long before they reach school age and, in some circles, before they are even born. (We know of at least one experiment in "behavioral genetics" designed to identify the "gene" which causes "learning disabilities." Presumably a fetus so diagnosed could then be aborted if the mother didn't want to deal with learning disabilities.[28]) The ultimate ideal of such a search is rarely, if ever, expressed in terms of control; the rationalization scrupulously avoids anything that smacks of politics or overt manipulation, but it is not hesitant about suggesting a vision of an antiseptic state which has been cleansed of scruffy individuals and all forms of behavior which stand in the way of the happy management of a culture and its institutions. Its ideology has little place for conflict or cantankerousness or idiosyncracy, and none for the risks of nonconformity. It thus turns "individualization" on its head: individualization is the starting point, the word that precedes "diagnosis" or "treatment," but rarely, if ever, the objective of the process. Health becomes a social obligation, a prime duty of state and citizen. It is a vision of a sterilized world.

The practices of early intervention and preventive social medicine, combined with the rapid development of data systems centralizing information on all aspects of a child's personal, medical, psychological and social history, creates, at the very least, the illusion of control not only among the practitioners but also among the clients. Even if the data are subject to the most scrupulous standards of confidentiality—which they usually are not—and even if the technology is generally weak in diagnosis and treatment—which it usually is—they enhance the mystical powers ascribed to the tester, the therapist and the institution. They tend, among other things, to confirm institutional legitimacy by reinforcing the corresponding illusion that there are legitimate, universally accepted norms underlying the practice. The teacher may be capricious, brutal and stupid, but if you test the child with the most difficulties for MBD, or if you test all children, you reinforce the assumption that the teacher, the school and the system are functioning properly. The frequent argument that test data will enable the system to make proper adjustments (to individualize instruction, for example) is simply a self-serving argument about its own flexibility and universality and therefore another point for legitimacy. As long as the ideology focuses on diagnosis and treatment it tends to confirm the belief that the system can know and do things which the individual cannot know and do for himself: the individual who fails or cannot adjust requires further treatment.

The power of such systems does not depend on results any more than did the power of the witch doctor or the priest; the larger the armamentarium of routines, the greater the mystification. What paint and feathers and mumbo-jumbo did for the shaman, screens, computers and syndromes can do for the diagnostician. Part of the object of the process, after all, is the confirmation of its own legitimacy. Where the process is limited in objective to relatively finite characteristics—intelligence, say, or reading ability—its effects are likely to be circumscribed; they may even suggest that whatever is being measured isn't so important after all. But where it goes to broader and more fundamental matters, MBD or the child's psychological "health" or the chances that he will become a criminal, the process leaves little room for escape. The more sweeping it becomes, the more total the effect.

The differences between new and traditional modes of control is that the traditional modes tended to be self-mitigating. Usually they left no question about who was doing what to whom: the teacher paddled the kid, the principal threw him out, the police told him to stop hanging around the corner. In that sense the system was personal and overt, and it left the individual at least a chance to determine that the actor, or the system in general, had motives, passions, biases and limitations. Equally important, it tended to act on the basis of what someone had done and not on elusive assumptions about what he might do or what he showed propensities to do. Most significantly, it recognized him as a person with free will who was responsible for his acts; even when it operated unjustly or with obvious bias it did something more than regard the subject as a collection of neurons, syndromes and dysfunctions. In that sense, which is the literal sense, it never completely dehumanized him.

The most common defense of the new modes of control invokes two related arguments: that they are more effective and that they are more humane. Isn't behavior modification or even the prescription of psychoactive drugs better than punishment or failure? Isn't it better to identify and treat problems of social adjustment before they ripen into full-blown delinquency? Who has the right to deprive a child of a chance for treatment and thereby increase his risk of subsequent failure and more serious problems? Each of these questions assumes that it is the system's prerogative to define failure and determine punishment; each assumes that there exists a connection between present diagnosis and future behavior, and that the remedies provided will be at least as effective as no intervention at all; each assumes that description of a problem as essentially medical or psychological is less invidious and punitive than the overtly negative consequences, if any, of the behavior which the therapist hopes to prevent. Collectively, the questions posit the ideal of a hygienic state purged as much as possible of social friction; they define the client as the problem and advocate techniques which teach him that something external is the source of his health and effectiveness; in many instances they suggest that his own will is somehow beyond his control. (In a number of cases, for example, young children have complained to their parents that they were bad in school that day because someone had forgotten to give them their pill.) If the technology is to be powerful, it will invest the system which operates it with extensive means of control and manipulation; if it is to be weak, then it will be an ineffective and arbitrary imposition on the client: Would the country be in better shape if the tests and remedies Allen and Hutschnecker recommended were totally effective? In either case, the application of the technology and the supporting ideology teach the individual that his ability to cope by himself is limited. That idea is barely defensible within a narrowly circumscribed medical system which the individual enters voluntarily; within a social system, and particularly in an educational system with powers of legal coercion, it is a travesty. "Man's consciously lived fragility, individuality and relatedness," wrote Ivan Illich, "make the experience of pain, of sickness and of death an integral part of his life. The ability to cope with this trio in autonomy is fundamental to his health. To the degree to which he becomes dependent on the management of his intimacy he renounces his autonomy, and his health *must* decline."[29]

The new modes of control, like the old, are directed primarily at children. Unlike the traditional modes, however, there is nothing inherent in them that limits them to the young. (The common progression in the application of behavioral technology begins with rats and pigeons, goes on to mental patients and prisoners, and then to schoolchildren.) Not only can most of the techniques be applied to adults— the diagnostic tests, the drugs, the behavior modification— but their application in childhood is likely to teach the client to accept similar treatment as an adult. A student who has been tested all his life and who accepts as normative an uninterrupted series of questions about his private life, his family, and the state of his emotional health is not likely to be terribly troubled when he is forced to answer similar questions from credit companies, employers or the federal government. A child who knows or suspects that his file is open to teachers, counselors and psychologists is not likely to find it all that unusual or troubling if it is later available to the police. An individual who learns to seek solace from the social service system as a child or to regard drugs, however nonaddictive, as a means of supporting socially acceptable behavior is a fair candidate for social or pharmacological tranquilizing as an adult.

The arguments for the new technology have an elusive, seductive quality. It is often easier to "treat" than to suffer the nuisance, easier to "prevent" than to cure, easier to sedate than to shackle. (Similarly, the defenders of electric shock therapy and psychosurgery always insist that their treatment saves people with severe emotional disturbances from their own self-destructive acts or from the necessity of tying them down.) What the arguments always conceal is the assumption that the problem is worse than the remedy, an assumption that may be correct in some cases but which always leaves the definition of "worse" to the person who proposes the treatment. The ideology itself works as a political sedative because it regards nonconformity as a medical problem and therefore tends to strip the individual not only of the political possibilities of confronting the system but also of the personal possibilities, however risky, of asserting himself. By converting social problems into medical cases or into subjects for "behavior modification," the ideology obviates legal and institutional due process and encourages the individual to surrender his right to confront, question and challenge, however rudimentary that right may be. And by blurring the line between poor performance, crime and disease, the ideology tends to create an entirely new category of crime and unacceptable behavior, this time without the protection of courts, legal counsel or the right to confront the accuser. The accuser will be "science" masquerading as the friend of the victim.

TWO

The Invention
of a Disease

In less than a decade, the ailment spread from virtual obscurity to something well beyond epidemic proportions. It has no single name, no universally accepted symptoms, and no discernible anatomical or biochemical characteristics which can be diagnosed in a clinic or a laboratory, yet it is said to afflict as many as 40 percent of all American children, to reflect an organic or chemical dysfunction of the brain or the nervous system and to be the cause of most, if not all, pediatric problems in learning and behavior. Its most common name, not surprisingly, is "learning disabilities" (LD) but it is also associated, sometimes synonymously, with "minimal brain dysfunction" (MBD), "hyperkinesis," "impulse disorder" and a substantial number of other conditions and "syndromes." Before 1965 almost no one had heard of it, but by the beginning of the seventies it was commanding the attention of an armada of pediatricians, neurologists and educational psychologists, and by mid-decade, pedagogical theory, medical speculation, psychological need, drug company promotion and political expediency had been fused with an evangelical fervor to produce what is undoubtedly the most powerful movement in—and beyond—contemporary education. Learning disabilities, according to some "authorities" in the field, account for nearly all school failure, most juvenile delinquency, a large proportion of broken marriages, and some part of virtually every other social affliction in modern life.

In the annals of socially fashionable ailments—melancholia, gout, consumption, polio—few have ever been as pervasive and none as politically significant. By 1974 a growing number of states were planning to screen their entire school populations for learning disabilities, mandating in-service training for all teachers in remediation techniques, and developing professional certification requirements for LD specialists; the U.S. Office of Education was promoting fifteen learning disabilities programs among the 107 model education projects selected for national emulation; the Association for Children with Learning Disabilities (ACLD), which was not founded until 1964, was attracting 5,500 participants to its annual convention to hear 480 speakers, the newly formed American Foundation for Learning Disabilities, supported by funds raised at a national tennis championship, was launching a public information campaign and instituting a computer-based retrieval system at the Massachusetts Institute of Technology where parents could call for quick information about LD evaluation centers, programs and professionals in their local communities; the members of the National Association of Elementary School principals were anxiously exchanging ideas at their annual convention on how to set up LD programs in a hurry; and the *Journal of Learning Disabilities,* founded in 1967, had grown from a circulation of 7,500 in 1970 to a subscriber list of more than 15,000. Within a single week in 1974, hyperactivity, the most widely discussed of those partly synonymous ailments, was the subject of an interview on the NBC Today Show, a five part series on the CBS radio network, hearings of the California Legislature, and of countless meetings and seminars sponsored by local school systems and learning disabilities groups. On the daytime radio talk shows, mothers were exchanging information on their children's diagnoses and comparing notes on neurologists and medications: one calls in to ask an allergist if feeding her infant Jello will make him hyperactive; another confesses that her LD child is breaking up her marriage; a third asks whether her son's two daily Ritalin pills might be more than necessary to make him sit still in school.

There are few reliable figures for the amount of money, the number of teachers, special classes and programs, or the percentage of children who have actually been designated as learning disabled. Between 1966 and 1972 the funds spent on public school programs for the "handicapped" tripled, reaching some $2 billion, and the figure has probably doubled again since then; a majority of states now provide substantial assistance to local districts for special classes, including classes for the learning disabled. Yet no one knows how much money goes specifically for LD programs. The vagueness of the ailment itself defies specific categorization: funds come from a variety of sources—existing budgets for the handicapped, special education budgets, federal programs for the retarded or the emotionally disturbed, state and local allocations for "exceptional children," and a growing number of federal grants for specific learning disabilities projects regarded by the U.S. Office of Education as models for all systems. In practical terms, moreover, the figure may not make much difference; in many states, "learning disabilities" is simply part of a grab bag of handicaps. Children are labeled, counted and often segregated, but they are not necessarily "treated." The labeling itself is often enough to get the money, to put the stigma on the child, and to rid the classroom teacher of a person she considers a nuisance. (In some places the "learning disabled," the "emotionally handicapped" and the "educable handicapped" are indiscriminately thrown together: the point is to get them out of the classroom and to get the money.) There are indications, however, from estimates based on the growing number and membership of some eight hundred local and state learning disabilities organizations, the dramatic increase in LD training programs for teachers, the avalanche of popular books issued by commercial publishers, and the torrent of journal articles appearing in medical and educational periodicals. In the mid-sixties, no more than a handful of children were taking psychoactive drugs for LD or hyperkinesis; since then, according to all available estimates, the number has doubled every two or three years. In the mid-sixties there were no LD training programs in schools of education, no inservice training, no summer workshops; by 1974, there were hundreds. In the mid-sixties, journal articles on learning disabilities and related ailments appeared at a rate of perhaps three or four a year; by 1973–1974 they were appearing at a rate of three or four a week, the product of scores of research projects conducted at nearly every major university in America and supported by an estimated $10 million a year in federal and private grants.[1] In a "Forecast for the 1970s" published in 1969, the official magazine of the National Education Association predicted that by the end of the decade "educators will assume a formal responsibility for children when they reach the age of two. We will work with parents of young children [and] offer such services as medical-dental examinations and followup, early identification of the handicapped and deprived, attacks on nutritional needs, and—of major importance—early referral to cooperating social agencies for treatment of psychobehavioral problems."[2] In the past couple of years, said Jean Peterson at the national ACLD office in Pittsburgh, "it's really taken off."

Officially, according to a report from the National Institute on Neurological Diseases and Stroke, children with learning disabilities are those who "exhibit a disorder in one or more of the basic psychological processes involved in understanding or using spoken or written languages. These may be manifested in disorders of listening, thinking, talking, reading, writing, spelling or arithmetic. They include conditions which have been referred to as perceptual handicaps, brain injury, minimal brain dysfunction, dyslexia, developmental aphasia, etc. They do not include learning problems which are due primarily to visual, hearing or motor handicaps, to mental retardation, emotional disturbance or to environmental disadvantage."[3] Learning disabilities, in other words, is a disease by default, the medical ailment which can be ascribed to those children who have no other problems but who don't learn to talk or read as their elders think they should. They are the children who are not mentally retarded, physically handicapped or sufficiently "disturbed" emotionally to be assigned to conventional "special education" classes but are difficult enough, nonetheless, to frustrate the routine of the ordinary school program. Since there are two fundamental requirements in that program, acceptable academic performance and compliant behavior, there are also two basic categories of learning-disabled children. Those who, despite a background in model, middle-class homes and despite adequate IQ scores, defy pedagogical expectations by performing poorly in one or more academic areas get the pure LD labels—dyslexia, dysgraphia, aphasia, agnosia—depending on what the system regards as the specific problem area. Those who bother teachers with generally unacceptable classroom behavior are labeled "hyperactive" or "hyperkinetic." If they are children who simply persist in annoying conduct—wiggling in their seats, repeatedly asking the same question, tapping a foot—the description may be more discrete: "short attention span," "impulsivity," "distractibility," "perseveration." Those who show a number of those symptoms will usually get the broader labels, the special classes, or the suggestion from a teacher or school psychologist that they be taken to a doctor for medication. Sometimes the two categories overlap, although at least one study, conducted at the University of California at Berkeley, indicates that "hyperactive" children fall in the normal range of achievement scores in reading and mathematics, with almost a third in the top quartile in reading.[4] Despite such findings, "hyperactive" children often get low grades as a consequence of their behavior. They also get the label: every annoying habit has now been honored with a pseudo-scientific designation. In most instances, the label becomes part of the permanent record.

Given the profusion of labels, diagnoses and ailments, and the vagueness of the terms, it is hardly surprising that there is no agreement on the number of children who are said to suffer from learning disabilities. Estimates range from a negligible 3 percent to better than 40 percent—something in excess of 15 million individuals—and the figures are rising. A 1969 prevalence study sponsored by the federal government and often cited by authorities in the field put the figure at 15 percent.[5] In 1972 Eric Denhoff, a pediatric neurologist and learning disabilities spokesman, reported that "at least ten percent" of children from middle-class homes are learning disabled, and "with children from lower socioeconomic families, the percentage is much higher." Denhoff noted that there "are clear indications that the numbers of children with learning problems are increasing,"[6] and by 1974, local chapters of the Association for Children with Learning Disabilities and LD clinics like Chicago's Educational Facilities Center were saying one out of every five children is learning disabled. In the meantime, the incidence of hyperkinesis, which is emerging as the most common of the "learning disabilities," has enjoyed a comparable boom. In 1971, a report from the U.S. Department of Health, Education and Welfare on stimulant drugs estimated that 3 percent of the school age population suffered from moderate or severe hyperkinesis. By 1974, other quasi-official estimates placed the figure at 15 percent.[7] Whichever figure is used, and some are considerably higher than 15 percent, there is general agreement that boys outnumber girls by something like four to one. The explanations for that disproportion are as uncertain as the definition of the ailment itself: boys are neurologically more immature; they are genetically different; they are more active. The possibility that all this may be culturally determined does not appear to be a sufficiently serious possibility to lead the estimators to reexamine their premises.

There is nothing new about teachers and parents complaining that children are difficult to teach or control. Teachers have traditionally assumed that between a fourth and a third of their students would be academic losers, and mothers have always complained that their children can't sit still. In 1958, for example, a study of a representative group of mothers found that half regarded their own children as overactive, and ten years later a survey of the entire school system in Des Moines, Iowa, showed that teachers believed that 53 percent of the boys and 30 percent of the girls were having problems associated with too much activity.[8] What is new, however, is the increasingly fashionable attribution of common problems to neurological abnormalities, and the increasingly common description of "these affected children" as victims of a clearly defined medical syndrome. In Cranston, Rhode Island, the Harringtons get a note from their son's elementary school teacher warning them that if Danny is not given medication for his hyperactivity, the boy will be expelled from school. On the advice of the family pediatrician, who thinks drugs are unnecessary, the Harringtons reply that Danny is on medication—though in fact he is not. A week later, a note comes back from the teacher thanking the family for their cooperation and explaining that Danny's behavior is much improved. In another community, the parents get a note from the school nurse: "Your son is hyperactive. He doesn't sit still in school. Please see a physician." The parents send the child to another school with another teacher, and the "problem" is never mentioned again. In Oakland, California, a mother explains that her son has been on medication through his entire elementary school career, with the exception of the fourth grade where, she says, "he had a good teacher." In Baltimore, a group of children are referred to a clinic for treatment of their hyperkinetic conditions; the team of doctors and psychologists who examine the children are unable to agree, however, that 87 percent of the children so designated by their schools are, in fact, hyperkinetic. And in a suburb of Cleveland, a boy referred to a class for the learning disabled performs even worse, in the judgment of the teachers, than he did in the regular classroom; in desperation, they send him to another regular classroom, and he begins to read. Since there are no clear definitions, no standard symptoms, no guidelines for diagnosis, there is no ceiling on the incidence of affliction. Any estimate is as good as any other. Gerald D. LaVeck, director of the National Institute of Child Health and Development, noted at a national medical conference on learning disorders that half of the school population of Newark, New Jersey, suffers from some form of learning disability. Among Spanish Americans and inmates in federal prisons, he reported, the figures are even higher.[9]

I I

The learning disabilities movement takes its doctrine from a primitive body of medico-educational theory, updated and extended to meet the political and social necessities of an age searching desperately for an explanation to a classic problem and for a scientific replacement for the golden rule and the hickory stick. Until World War II, children who didn't behave in school were almost universally regarded as defective in will and character: they were bad, lazy or shiftless, or, if they worked hard and still failed, they were euphemistically described as slow. In the 1950s, the schools discovered Freudian psychology and psychoanalysis, hired staff psychologists, and began to attribute failure to "emotional handicaps," "reading blocks," or overbearing fathers. In the sixties, after they began to discover the poor and the black, they attributed failure to the effects of discrimination and "cultural disadvantage," and prescribed compensatory education as a remedy. By the middle of the sixties, however, the problems of failure among particular groups of children had been absorbed in what became—in rhetoric, if not in fact—a nearly universal movement of reform. Spurred by pressure from minority groups, radical critics, parental uprisings and student revolt, and stimulated by a sudden flow of federal funds from the Elementary and Secondary Education Act (ESEA) and from the Office of Economic Opportunity, the entire educational establishment began to discuss experimentation and plan reform—reform for the bright, the slow, the middle class, the poor, the handicapped: open schools, storefront schools, schools without walls, collaborative learning, peer group teaching, multidisciplinary projects, team teaching, nonauthoritarian teaching, multimedia curricula, individualized instruction. There would be a program hospitable to every conceivable minority and a system of education flexible enough to accommodate every style, attitude and interest. Most significantly, it was the system, not the individual, that was the target of remediation.

By the end of the decade, it was all over. The national mood had changed, school bond issues and tax increases were voted down, and the federal money began to run out. The same parents who had once demanded relevant curricula and better teachers complained about disruption and violence; the administrators who had talked bravely—if reluctantly—about reform were trying to balance budgets, meet a renewed demand for order and discipline, and answer a new set of attacks from parents asking why, after all those promises and all that money, their children still couldn't read. The pressure, in community after community, was for business as usual: hold down the budget, keep the kids in line and teach the basics.

That, however, turned out to be difficult. Although the programs of the sixties were being modified or phased out altogether, the criticism of the previous decade had permanently discredited the rhetoric and ideology of the traditional school: in most systems corporal punishment, though often permitted, was regarded with suspicion, rote learning remained ineffective for many children, the courts had started to impose rudimentary due process standards for school transfers and suspensions, and nineteenth century conservatism, though it appeared in pure form in a number of schools, remained unpalatable to the majority of parents. The search was on for something more modern, more scientific, something that might replace character judgments (which reflected on parents and on race) with something more clinical, something less individious.

The solution evolved almost organically from the experience of the sixties. The arguments for Head Start and early childhood programs had themselves been based on the assumption that intervention was most effective in the earliest years of a child's life. The various studies conducted within those programs seemed to demonstrate that a large proportion of minority group children suffered from a variety of medical and dental conditions which had never before been diagnosed and which, in some instances at least, affected their ability to function in school. Before the end of the decade, plans had been developed to screen large segments of the population not only for tuberculosis, malnutrition and tooth decay but for a variety of neurological defects which might have been caused by inadequate prenatal care or by insufficient medical attention in the first years of life. At the same time, middle-class parents who resented the attribution of their children's school difficulties to emotional problems began to press for a more satisfactory and (it was hoped) more useful diagnosis. The designation of learning disabled appeared to be an almost ideal solution: it implied no stigma on either the child or his parents, carried no racial overtones, and suggested an ailment that was the metaphorical corollary of an electronic malfunction—faulty wiring in the cortex or central nervous system—and therefore as modern as Bell Labs. The child wasn't sick; he was simply disabled, physically and psychologically, and therefore incapable of meeting the demands of what had, by the beginning of the seventies, come to be regarded again as a perfectly acceptable classroom and curriculum. It was now the child who would be the target of remediation.

The research had been going on since the beginning of the century, and although it was spasmodic in the early years, and though it had sometimes bordered on unvarnished phrenology, it had, by the sixties, started to generate a considerable body of literature. As early as 1902 a physician named George F. Still reported a link between a "morbid defect of moral control" in children and such diseases as epilepsy, brain tumor and meningitis,[10] and by 1937, in a book called *Reading, Writing and Speech Problems in Children,* a neurologist named Samuel Torrey Orton associated various language problems (aphasias) in brain-damaged individuals with particular parts of the brain.[11] Word blindness (alexia) was caused by damage to the parietal lobe in the back of the skull, word deafness (auditory aphasia) by a problem in the temporal lobe down near the bottom, and so on. Orton hypothesized that the same "syndromes" in otherwise intelligent children indicated a similar brain dysfunction. Delays and defects in language development resulted from the failure of children to establish "unilateral brain superiority," the total dominance of one side of the brain, and of a "master hand." He preferred right-handedness to left, but said the total control of either would help cure problems like stuttering, clumsiness and poor handwriting. Orton was a pioneer —the pioneer—and his work contains in seminal form all the assumptions on which contemporary LD theory is founded: the medical diagnosis totally based on school behavior and academic performance; the assumption that a ninth grade boy with an above-average IQ and above-average achievement in reading but with only fifth grade achievement in spelling suffers from a pathological syndrome; the idea that academic achievement in reading, writing, spelling and arithmetic should synchronize, and that performance in no single area should fall behind the others; and an unbounded faith in the power of IQ tests to assess innate intellectual capacity.

Orton reminded his readers that his learning-disabled subjects had no reason other than cerebral dysfunction to fail academically, for they were "children of superior intelligence . . . from educated families and good schools."[12] Quite properly, Orton is venerated in the movement as the founding father.

Three years before Orton's book appeared, a team of researchers, writing in the *New England Journal of Medicine*, began to make the connection between classroom behavior problems and neurological disabilities. In an article called "Organic Drivenness: A Brain-Stem Syndrome and Experience," they pointed out that a deviant behavioral syndrome involving hyperkinesis, distractibility, short attention span, impulsivity and poor coordination which often appeared as a sequel to encephalitis could also be observed in people with no known brain damage or illness. They called the syndrome "organic drivenness"—the first of the forty-odd names that were to be attached to such behavior—and concluded that it was medically determined by a dysfunction of the central nervous system.[13]

A great deal of the early research in the field was done with organically damaged individuals or with other institutionalized patients suffering from medically demonstrable conditions; since some similar forms of behavior could sometimes be observed in other individuals (who showed no signs of organic damage), similar syndromes were inferred by analogy. In 1947, for example, Alfred A. Strauss, director of a school for brain-injured children, reported that such children (most of them "mental defectives" with severe signs of pathology) exhibited a distinctive behavior—centering on hyperactivity—which could be traced to injuries or diseases during the perinatal period, the months immediately preceding and following birth.[14] In 1955, Strauss, collaborating with Newell C. Kephart, expanded that concept to include "so-called 'normal' brain-injured children" whose behavior and learning problems suggested a brain injury which could not be established: there was no history of perinatal illness, and no sign of organic damage. The diagnosis was based entirely on inferences drawn from behavior.[15]

If Strauss and Kephart made the leap, others would try to build bridges. In 1957, Maurice W. Laufer, a Providence psychiatrist, announced the discovery of a new syndrome: hyperkinetic impulse disorder.

> It has long been recognized and accepted [he wrote] that a persistent disturbance of behavior of a characteristic kind may be noted after severe head injury, epidemic encephalitis, and communicable disease encephalopathies, such as measles, in children. It has often been observed that a behavior pattern of a similar nature may be found in children who present no clear-cut history of any of the classical causes mentioned.
>
> This pattern will henceforth be referred to as *hyperkinetic impulse* disorder. In brief summary, hyperactivity is the most striking item. . . . There are also a short attention span and poor powers of concentration, which are particularly noticeable under school conditions. . . . The child is impulsive . . . irritable and explosive . . . [and manifests] low frustration tolerance. Poor school work is frequently quite prominent. The previously described behavioral items in themselves create a pattern which makes it very difficult for the child to participate in the work of a school room. In addition, there is often visual-motor difficulty which, combined with the other difficulties described above, makes for poor work in arithmetic and reading. In writing and reading, "reversals" are frequent and the handwriting is often crabbed and irregular.[16]

The sickness, in brief, was the inability to function in school.

Laufer's description of the "hyperkinetic impulse disorder" was the major break between the classic medical description of hyperkinesis and the vague set of ailments now attributed to millions of children. It made room for a whole series of school related symptoms not included in the medical literature, which describes the true hyperkinetic as a rare individual, perhaps one in 2,000, who seems to be driven by an inner whirlwind, not just in school, but constantly.[17] Unlike the children who now appear to be "hyperkinetic" only in the classroom (but not, for example, in front of the television set), the true hyperkinetic was always moving, climbing, and knocking over furniture, and in constant danger of injuring himself or others. Yet even the looseness of Laufer's definition did not permit the inclusion of all the childhood symptoms that annoyed teachers and parents: clumsiness, fidgetiness, awkwardness, poor speech, unreasonableness, or some inexplicable difficulty in reading, spelling or arithmetic. As a result, the definition was further extended, and new names were created to fit each form of social and academic nonconformity. In the process, the terms became vaguer and the possibility of finding a real connection with organic cerebral damage grew dimmer.

In what was to become a key document establishing the new disease and converting unacceptable behavior into a medical ailment, a team of national authorities headed by Sam D. Clements of the University of Arkansas Medical Center published a monograph in 1966 which purported to eliminate "professional disjunction and discord." The problem, they said, was "the general lack of knowledge, understanding and agreement in the broad area of minimal brain dysfunction among the clinicians who are accountable for the diagnosis and treatment of deviating children."[18] The team, supported by the National Institute of Neurological Diseases and Blindness of the Public Health Service, and by the Easter Seal Research Foundation, acknowledged, after two years of work, that from "the purist point of view" minimal brain dysfunction was "in most instances an unproven presumptive diagnosis." Having made that concession, however, the experts committed themselves to a "pragmatic" case, arguing that "we must accept certain categories of deviant behavior, developmental dyscrasias, learning disabilities, and visual-motor-perception irregularities as valid indices of brain dysfunctioning."

We cannot afford the luxury of waiting until causes can be unquestionably established by techniques yet to be developed. We cannot postpone managing as effectively and honestly as possible the large number of children who present chronic differences we feel are more related to organicity variables than others.[19]

Of the 38 terms which Clements and his task force identified as currently in use to describe the condition—"organic brain damage," "cerebral dys-synchronization syndrome," "dyslexia," "perceptual cripple," "learning disabilities"—they chose "minimal brain dysfunction" as the official new label. The "minimal" indicated the absence of extreme behavior, and "dysfunction" was used to get around the necessity of finding an organic problem. Henceforth, MBD would simply mean any form of behavior that adults found troublesome.

Children with "minimal brain dysfunction," Clements wrote, are those "of near average, average, or above average general intelligence with certain learning or behavioral disabilities ranging from mild to severe, which are associated with deviations of function of the central nervous system. These deviations may manifest themselves by various combinations of impairment in perception, conceptualization, language, memory, and control of attention, impulse, or motor function. . . . These aberrations may arise from genetic variations, biochemical irregularities, perinatal brain insults or other illnesses or injuries sustained during the years which are critical for the development and maturation of the central nervous system, or from unknown causes. . . . During the school years, a variety of learning disabilities is the most prominent manifestation of the condition which can be designated by this term."

To compound the confusion in this "clarification" of the problem, the monograph goes on to list 99 of the most prevalent "symptoms" of MBD. They include "spotty or patchy intellectual deficits"; "achievement low in some areas, high in others"; "poor spatial orientation"; "hyperkinesis," or its opposite "hypokinesis"; "high incidence of left, and mixed laterality and confused perception of laterality"; "general awkwardness"; "slowness in finishing work"; "reading disabilities"; "arithmetic disabilities"; "spelling disabilities"; "poor printing, writing, or drawing ability"; "easy fatigability"; "peer group relationships generally poor"; "thumbsucking, nail-biting, head-banging, and teeth-grinding in the young child"; "slow to toilet train"; "explosive"; "low tolerance for frustration"; "sleep abnormally light or deep"; "socially bold and aggressive"; "physically immature, or physical development normal or advanced for age"; "possibly antisocial behavior"; "very sensitive to others"; "better adjustment when playmates are limited to one or two"; "possibly negative and aggressive to authority"; "sweet and even-tempered, cooperative and friendly"; and "impaired ability to make decision, particularly from many choices."[20] The task force did concede that "the most striking omission throughout the literature was the lack of attempt at a definition of the terms used or the condition discussed," that in spite of all the terms and symptoms there was "a shortage of interpretative elucidation." The Clements definition, it was suggested later, was "merely a sophisticated statement of ignorance." Nonetheless, it not only became a staple in educational theory, but more important, the document legitimized the diagnosis of MBD and seemed to give teachers and physicians scientific authority to stigmatize any difficult or disruptive child with a new ailment, to prescribe drugs, or to recommend other means of treating this "syndrome." Clements and his colleagues at the University of Arkansas would go on to become favorites of the drug industry and producers of important drug company literature.

The true believers—and that included many teachers, parents and doctors—simply ignored the scientific and definitional problems.[21] The umbrella term had been created, and it suited the needs of an age looking for new "humane" forms of remediation and control. It was not simply that projects like Clements's lacked scientific (or even linguistic) validity, but that there was accumulating positive evidence that neither the symptoms nor the disease had any scientific foundation. There were studies which indicated that hyperactivity is a normal variant of temperament and not a neurological disorder; that there were as many children who read better than their IQs indicated—and were consequently "hyperlexic"—as there were who read below IQ expectations; that the behavioral deviations listed by Clements as symptoms of MBD could not be related to any single syndrome; that the classic belief in unilateral dominance (right-handedness or left-handedness) as a necessary base for neurological integrity could not be verified and that "consistent lateral preference is of minimal adaptive value"; and that reading ability, like musical talent or athletic skill, is a "normal physiological variant," relatively independent of general intellectual functioning.[22] By the early seventies, a number of scholars were prepared to agree with Francis M. Crinella, a research psychologist at California's Sonoma State Hospital, that "we just don't know much at all about the various types of children who are classified in these 'grab-bag' diagnoses, except that they are quite dissimilar from each other."[23] What was ordinarily described as hyperkinesis, said a clinical psychologist in a report at the 1974 meetings of the American Orthopsychiatric Association, "is often a social term which calls for a definition based on the acceptability of certain behavior in [a] specific situation."[24] It might be better, another researcher suggested, to call the disorder "dysactivity" rather than "hyperactivity" to indicate that the problem is not too much activity but, in the view of parents and teachers, the wrong kind.[25]

The growing bewilderment within the medical community was underscored by a comprehensive review of the research literature by L. Alan Stroufe and Mark A. Stewart published in *The New England Journal of Medicine* in 1973. The authors point out that although "the concept of 'minimal brain dysfunction' has now been widely accepted," the reasoning behind it was "circular—that is, authors have assumed that behaviors such as hyperactivity were signs of brain damage independent of neurologic indexes, and, therefore, that many behavior problem children had brain damage."[26] They note that a positive response to stimulant drugs has been used as a confirmation of brain damage, although normal children have shown the same response; that only a small minority of children who have the clusters of behaviors which get diagnosed as MBD seem to have brain damage; that neurological "soft signs" or irregular electroencephalograph results (two of the most respected methods of diagnosing MBD) have not proved to be good indicators; that no current neurological test or combination of tests can differentiate hyperactive or MBD children from control subjects; and that no unitary MBD syndrome, much less any group of subsyndromes, has been established. There simply is no such thing as MBD, said Roger D. Freeman, a child psychiatrist (now at the University of British Columbia). Every time the designation is used there is a chance that it will simply mask another ailment.[27] Despite such doubts, however, the career of MBD, hyperactivity and learning disabilities was firmly established, not only in the journals, but in thousands of educational programs and in the mind of the public. As early as 1971, William M. Cruickshank of the University of Michigan, a national authority in special education, had complained that the LD label was being applied to children who stuttered, teased the family cat, had night terrors, couldn't swim, masturbated, didn't like to go with girls, bit their nails, had poor eating habits, didn't keep their rooms neat, wouldn't take baths, or didn't brush their teeth:

> Teachers have questioned me about disrespectful children, children who will not listen to the adult, children who cry, children who hate, children who are sexually precocious, children who are aggressive—all in the belief that they are learning disability children. One parent asked me if the fact that his college student son wore long hair and, he "suspected," lived with a girl outside his dormitory was the result of a learning disability.[28]

Although Cruickshank was pleading for "less inclusive terms and more refined concepts" the terms have, if anything, grown more inclusive, the concepts vaguer and the speculation wilder. MBD was caused by delayed development, a chemical imbalance in the central nervous system, nutritional deficiencies, vitamin deficiencies, genetic anomalies, allergic reactions, children's television, Lysol and other household sprays, cigarette smoke, fluorescent lighting, or food additives; it was associated with certain physical anomalies and could therefore be identified by the shape of the head or the texture of the hair, and it could be cured with special diets, megavitamins or other nutritional strategies. By 1973, the National Education Association, the largest teacher organization in the country, issued a press release warning of a national outbreak of "school phobia," and in 1974 someone suggested in a journal article that truancy could be an allergy.[29] Every problem—at home, in school, in the community—was linked to MBD or LD.

I I I

They are nearly all middle class, suburban and college educated, good parents, good citizens, veterans of the League of Women Voters or the PTA or the AAUW, and they tell similar horror stories, stories of their misunderstood children, of teachers who threw up their hands in despair, of pediatricians who had no referrals or suggestions, and of doctors and psychologists who misconstrued and misdiagnosed, and who tended to treat most "learning disabilities" as emotional problems. "You felt like you were all alone," one of them said, "and no one could help. The educators made you feel like your child was a freak, and most of the medical people just didn't understand." In the late sixties, they began to find each other and started to organize, and by the mid-seventies they had formed hundreds of local and state organizations enrolling more than 45,000 members, most of which are now affiliated with the Association for

Children With Disabilities (ACLD), and which were picking up 5,000 new members a year.

Among the oldest and most active is CANHC, the California Association for Neurologically Handicapped Children, a group of some 4,000 parents, most of them mothers, who devote endless hours in spreading The Word: talking to the medical and educational communities about learning disabilities, donating books to libraries (and operating their own traveling library), sponsoring films, inservice training and conferences, and monitoring and supporting legislation affecting programs and funds for LD children. The scope of those interests is suggested by CANHC-GRAM, a monthly newsletter with helpful hints about education and child rearing, notes about the status of education bills and court cases, lists of books and articles to read, pamphlets, records and films to buy or borrow, descriptions of new diagnostic tests, board games for LD children, therapeutic day schools, evaluation and remediation centers and meetings to attend: one typical issue listed eleven LD meetings for the month, among them a "Symposium on Delinquency" and a workshop on "Sensory and Perceptual Dysfunctioning in Infants." The message is positive, saying "you can do it"—part Boy Scout, part Billy Sunday.

> Nine of ten CANHC parents went through misdiagnosis (said an officer of the organization). Things are getting better now. We can tell people where to go, and I'm almost envious of people who are going through diagnosis right now. But before now the doctors just hadn't heard about this, they hadn't been taught in medical school. It's not easy to diagnose. The signs aren't great, and there are more than 300 symptoms. Ten years ago almost everyone was told their children's problems were emotionally caused, and it was the mother's fault. As someone who thought she was doing a good job as a mother and had been a good elementary teacher, it was a real trauma to be told I had given my child an emotional block to learning.

At first, the stories are heartrending: the concerned mother defending her child against the bureaucratic intolerance of the school system; the insensitivity or ignorance of the diagnosticians; the feeling of helplessness against the authorities. The turning point in those stories comes when the parents find CANHC or a doctor "who knows LD or MBD," and then the hidden reason for school failure or behavioral eccentricities is revealed—a mysterious neurological handicap, a chemical imbalance, a quirky syndrome. It still means tough sledding all the way through college—and the child must make it through college—but now there is a reason and understanding professionals to help make the decision and show the way to proceed: medication, therapy, special courses or a special school, an LD tutor and all those helpful coping hints in the books and pamphlets. But there is also something else, a sigh of relief, guilt assuaged, a label to explain the anxiety: "Even though it wasn't true," one mother told us, "my being told that my child's problems were my fault—I had gone through all that guilt. That was the worst part. Once we knew we had this special problem, all the guilt was gone."

They speak as converts, but in bearing witness to their new faith, their voices betray a brittle anxiety which finds any kind of abnormality almost too much to bear. There is, for example, the suburban San Francisco mother and CANHC officer who explains that each of her three boys is learning disabled, and each in a different way. With the first, she said, her background as a teacher enabled her to pick up "good warning signs." "He scooted around, but never crawled right. He walked and talked late, and in kindergarten he wasn't learning to identify letters and numbers. I knew he wasn't progressing. After kindergarten I was lucky to get him into a special class. I didn't have any help in those days. I had to do it all by myself. He's succeeding now in his second year of college, but this child has an ulcer. You see, these children are very sensitive to stress." Two of her three boys, she said, have high IQs, "the kind who would get As in school, but will wind up with Bs if their problems aren't diagnosed." With the younger boys life has been easier because they have been under the care of a Southern California pediatrician named Leon Oettinger, Jr., who specializes in MBD, sits on the CANHC medical advisory board and believes in the widespread use of psychoactive drugs to modify behavior. On amphetamines, Oettinger said, the LD child "functions better as a child."[30]

For six years, the two younger boys have been on medication—most recently a combination of Ritalin, an amphetamine-type stimulant, and Mellaril, a tranquilizer. In their mother's estimation, "it has made a difference. If one forgets his pills for a day, I know it the second he comes through the door, and when we've changed medication or dosage, the teachers as a group reported that academic achievement went up. . . . We've been told that the fifteen-year-old will be on medication for the rest of his life; he'll always need it." Has she ever considered letting the boy try to get through a week or a month without drugs, or with a placebo? "No," she replies, "I do what the doctor tells me to do, and he's never suggested that." The clue to their problems, she suggests, may be hereditary. "I still haven't found a tranquilizer that doesn't put me on the ceiling, and that doesn't do the opposite of what it's supposed to do. There's something funny in my makeup."

In the hands of organizations like CANHC, the theories of the LD specialists, no matter how vague or undefined, harden into the tenets of orthodoxy. "I have no problems with labeling," said Nancy Ramos, the Palo Alto mother who serves as CANHC president. "By the time we got one, I was very glad for anything that told us where we were. When you don't have a reason it's pretty frustrating." She herself has had one son on drugs for eight years and has no qualms about it. "You can't compare the effects of medication on these children with its effects on other children. These children have a totally different body chemistry." People like Ramos have been active in school and community organizations most of their lives, and they show a healthy skepticism about the ways of schools and doctors uninitiated to the mysteries of LD, but they appear to be totally trusting of the professionals and methods within the circle of enlightenment, ready to suspend all disbelief, and ready to make alliances with the drug companies where necessary. They talk in sycophantic superlatives about doctors who understand LD and have done so much for their children. They listen appreciatively when psychiatrist Camilla Anderson, keynoting a symposium on learning disabilities, tells 1,500 suburban mothers and teachers that MBD causes everything from bad financial planning, violent crime and slums to unconventional sexual positions, and when she urges sterilization for all MBD victims, and they gratefully reprint Anderson's 164–item list of the most common irritating (or worrisome) habits of children—all of them identified as manifestations of MBD: "perseverative masturbation," "gullible," "new generation psychology," "need for structure," "bossy," "demanding," "bed wetting," "running away."[31] Ramos herself echoes the message: A good many LD children come from single parent homes, she says, "but it's not the broken marriages that cause LD, it's that the learning-disabled child broke up the marriage in the first place."

The various affiliates of ACLD have developed a symbiotic relationship with certain doctors and scientists. The literature of assurance is available at the meetings, the literature of doubt is not. Drug promoters like Oettinger—who also appear at legislative hearings as experts for the drug companies—chair symposia of "recognized authorities," and pharmaceutical houses like CIBA-Geigy and Abbott Laboratories help underwrite them, but physicians who warn that amphetamines are dangerous—that they may (among other things) cause liver damage or stunt growth—are rarely represented. What the members want to hear are assurances, as Oettinger has said, that concern about the long-range effects of drugs was created, apparently out of whole cloth, by "the lay press" and "by unwise and ill-informed comments by congressmen, columnists and others [with] an inability to comprehend their value."[32] CANHC, despite its active and growing membership, assigns no one to monitor the research literature on learning disabilities and pediatric psychopharmacology. "We leave that to the doctors," Ramos said. "They know what they're doing."

There are exceptions, even within the movement, people whose children or whose friends' children have been hurt by excessive medication or who, for other reasons, remain suspicious of the medical exorcists and their simple demonology. In 1973–1974, CANHC came close to impeaching Caroline Rodriguez, at the time the organization president, who had serious doubts about drugging practices, chafed at the narrow focus of the organization, and wanted to reform the entire school structure to accommodate genuine diversity. Her own son, she said, had become so stupefied on Dilantin, an anticonvulsant, that he fell down and broke his leg (he also suffers from liver damage apparently caused by another drug), and her neighbor's son began to have crying fits after he started taking Ritalin, the drug most frequently prescribed for hyperactive children. When the neighbor reported the effect to her pediatrician, he referred the boy to a psychiatrist for his emotional condition. "He simply refused to read the *Physician's Desk Reference*," which would have told him that crying fits are not an uncommon effect of the drug. "The doctors are convincing the mothers that the pills will work and will make the difference," Rodriguez said. "But pills and a special program only mask the real differences of these children, something the schools won't face up to. I see lots of kids on Ritalin, and I'd hate to call that improvement. The kid is a bag of bones, but as long as he behaves and shuts up, nothing else is important. A lot of CANHC people are hyperactive parents whose logic is faulty."

The learning disabilities movement is so closely associated with certain physicians, school practitioners and research groups that it is sometimes hard to determine which came first: was it the client or the doctor? In Arkansas, where Clements and his University of Arkansas associates are major promotors of the LD ideology, there are scores of local ACLD chapters (and thousands of children on drugs), while in neighboring Missouri, the organized movement is just getting under way; there are more than 40 CANHC chapters in California (where the organization is represented in the legislature by a volunteer lobbyist), and dozens of ACLD chapters in Texas, Oklahoma and Illinois, but only a handful in northern New England. As in similar organizations, there are signs that, as the organizations gain maturity, the professionals start taking over. At the 1974 international ACLD conference in Houston, for example, only 2 percent of the 5,500 participants were lay parents; the majority were school and social service personnel showing off their programs or looking for new ones to take home. There were demonstrations of ongoing screening methods, workshops in dyslexia and dyscalculia, reports on projects in Ochlochnee, Georgia, and Rapid City, South Dakota, sessions on the Gattegno techniques, discussions of precision teaching, classroom management modification, and the prevention of juvenile delinquency among LD children, and reports on cerebral allergy as a major cause of LD, on the use of biofeedback techniques to control hyperactivity, and—for the collectors of the esoteric—on the use of Ritalin in controlling hyperactive dogs.

ACLD has had phenomenal growth in suburbia but, not surprisingly, negligible success in attracting poor and minority group parents whose children generally have as much or more difficulty with school achievement and behavior. The LD label itself appears to function as an exclusionary mechanism: it assumes at least an average IQ and therefore precludes many poor children who do not perform well on standardized intelligence tests. It has already been noted that the minority child in a class for the educable mentally retarded bears striking similarities to the affluent child in an LD class. The classification "mentally retarded," however, carries a stigma not associated with LD, a label that seems to function as a way of dissociating middle-class children from blacks and other minorities. Parents who cannot tolerate one set of labels talk freely about their children's neurological dysfunctions and learning disabilities, and teachers, an equally middle-class group with middle-class attitudes, have indicated that they prefer the term "learning disabled" over five others with similar meanings. A report of a federal study on the labeling of children concluded:

> The term learning disability has appeal because it implies a specific neurological condition for which no one can be held particularly responsible, and yet it escapes the stigma of mental retardation. There is no implication of neglect, emotional disturbance, or improper training or education, nor does it imply a lack of motivation on the part of the child. For these cosmetic reasons, it is a rather nice term to have around. . . . Many critics of the term regard [it] as a middle-class nicety. Low socio-economic level children exhibiting the same behavior are likely to be labeled mentally retarded. In addition, critics assert, learning disabilities spring from a discrepancy between parental expectation, which is sometimes unrealistically high, and the performance of the child, which may be at his level of capacity.[33]

In the symbiosis between parents and professionals, everyone has something to gain: for the parent, the payoff comes in the alleviation of guilt and in the protection of social status and self-esteem; for the practitioner, it lies in the generation of new jobs, specialties and funds, and in the creation of a new mystique enhancing professional status. For both, it is a way to maintain belief in the dynamics of class success, the belief that white, affluent, well-mannered parents simply cannot produce offspring who can't behave or can't learn and are therefore no better than ghetto blacks.

I V

If the researchers sometimes admit bewilderment and the more sophisticated clinicians urge caution, their voices are rarely heard in those places where decisions are made about children. The pressure has simply been too great: "Before scientists have had a chance to systematically study and refine the issues," said a team of medical researchers at Harvard, "the field has become the domain of educators and the drug industry."[34]

It is nearly impossible to overestimate the role of the pharmaceutical houses in shaping medical and lay opinion about learning-disabled children. We are not talking here about their campaigns to convince practitioners and parents that medication—usually stimulant drugs—is the answer to problems in learning and behavior (which will be discussed later) but primarily about their part in creating the idea that any number of common childhood behavior quirks are medical problems in the first place. The promotion of drugs to cure learning disabilities and related syndromes—particularly MBD and hyperkinesis—is, quite obviously, related to the promotion of the ailments themselves; less obvious is the fact that most of the research dealing with "learning disordered" or "behavior problem" children has been drug research—experiments designed primarily to find out more about the effects of the drugs and not about the institutionalized children who became the subjects of the experiments. The leap that created "hyperkinetic impulse disorder" was drug related, a test to determine whether the medication that helped control erratic behavior in organically brain-damaged adults would produce similar effects on pediatric patients, many of whom had no history of organic illness. Since then, dozens of other experiments have been founded on the same dubious premise: that if the drug worked, or seemed to work, the subject must be suffering from the ailment for which the drug was administered. In many respects, the cure preceded the ailment. Until federal regulations were tightened (somewhat) in 1970, CIBA-Geigy promoted Ritalin—its league-leading drug for hyperactive children—for use with children who exhibited "functional behavior problems," a category so vague that no child need be excluded. Each weeknight of the year, the company had a salesman and a sympathetic doctor in some meeting of parents to talk up the ailment and its remedies.

Since 1972, the drug companies have been prohibited by federal regulations from promoting products like Ritalin directly among parents and teachers: Ritalin is regarded as a "dangerous drug" by the FDA and the Bureau of Narcotics and Dangerous Drugs. The regulations do not, however, prevent the firms from promoting the ailment or from defining it in the broadest possible terms, a process that is reinforced by the extensive set of relationships between the drug companies, certain doctors and research teams, and the lay movement. Many of the "authorities" in the field—Oettinger in Los Angeles, C. Keith Conners in Pittsburgh, John E. Peters at the University of Arkansas, among others—conduct research supported, in whole or in part, with funds from CIBA, Abbott or other pharmaceutical laboratories. It is also people like Oettinger, Conners and Peters who appear at the ACLD meetings and workshops and whose travel to those meetings is paid for by drug company grants to the sponsoring organization. "Whenever we need money," Oettinger said, "they'll give me some." There is no way to know how extensive those relationships are, or how much money is involved. When we spoke to him, Oettinger acknowledged that he had received several grants from CIBA for studies on Ritalin and was about to get another; simultaneously, CIBA was supporting work by the Arkansas group, by Conners, and by another team at Johns Hopkins, and Abbott was making similar grants for work with Cylert, another stimulant drug product for hyperactive children which had just been licensed by the FDA.

The message is simple: almost any troublesome behavior can be a sign of MBD. In a flier entitled "The MBD Child: A Guide for Parents," for example, CIBA raises the question "What is MBD?" and answers as follows:

> Minimal Brain Dysfunction (MBD) is the most common medical term for a group of learning and behavioral disorders that occurs in some children. MBD is never exactly the same in any two children, and the precise cause is not known—so MBD is difficult to pin down to a simple definition. . . . One current theory is that MBD children suffer a delay of brain maturation. This means that the brain, although fully formed and otherwise normal, is not yet ready to take over some of its important jobs. One such job is thought organization, which enables the child to concentrate, sustain interest, behave in an orderly way, be patient, and learn reading, writing and arithmetic. Muscular coordination may also be affected. However, not all these functions are lacking in every MBD child.[35]

The material distributed to doctors, though far more extensive, is no more specific. CIBA publishes a 96–page *Physician's Handbook: Screening for MBD,* complete with picture and word cards to use in screening patients, which is available to any physician.[36] Written by Sam Clements' colleagues at the University of Arkansas and published in September 1973, the *Handbook* begins with a full-page description of MBD as defined by Clements in 1966; nowhere in the text does it suggest any other interpretation or mention any of the subsequent research which questions or invalidates that definition. The publication points out that authorities in the field have said that a "team of child specialists"—a pediatric neurologist, a child psychiatrist, a clinical psychologist, an educational diagnostician, a language specialist and a social worker—was necessary for an accurate evaluation of a child believed to be suffering from MBD, but it goes on to say that "such evaluation teams rarely existed outside of a large medical complex and, even when available, could not possibly evaluate the large number of children referred." Now, it assures the doctor, with diagnostic procedures simplified and services and treatments concentrated, "family practitioners, pediatricians, psychiatrists . . . are in a strategic position to identify MBD children at an early age."[37] The key to the simplified diagnosis is a diagram composed of overlapping circles, a circle for "pure hyperkinetic type," a circle for "pure learning disability type" and, where they overlap, a shaded area for the "mixed types." The large area of overlap indicates that most children belong to the "mixed type . . . the largest segment of MBD." To accompany the circles, the *Handbook* provides three lists of symptoms including the familiar ones (short attention span, distractible, impulsive, hyperactive, dyslexia, dyscalculia, and all the rest), a set of tests of reading, language and mathematics abilities, a "neurological screen" and psychological tests. The publication never indicates, however, that its definitions and assumptions constitute something less than established dogma in the field, nor does it cite a single piece of journal literature in the field which questions those assumptions. (All references are to articles by the committed, most of them by Clements and his colleagues.) "The relationship of the terms MBD, SLD, hyperactivity, and dyslexia needs to be clarified," the *Handbook* explains. *"Minimal brain dysfunction* is the medical term for these children. Specific learning disability (SLD) or simply *learning disability* is the educational term." The object throughout is to simplify a complex and confused area to the point where anyone can diagnose anyone else, where almost anyone can qualify for the treatment, and where every doctor will be persuaded that there is indeed a pervasive ailment called MBD for which he must take responsibility.

Most educators no longer need persuasion. Since the end of the Great Society in 1968, "learning disabilities" has become a bonanza in an otherwise depressed and barren territory, a source of funds from state and federal agencies which have been cutting back in other areas of educational support, a fertile field for prospective or unemployed teachers "where you know there'll be a job," and a means of attracting students to schools of education facing diminishing enrollments. In the process it has become the foundation of a new and thriving industry of private schools, diagnostic centers, clinics, ranches, summer camps and remedial projects, and of the materials and literature which these employ to work their cures. Compared to education, the pharmaceutical industry is a model of restraint.

The new territory, uncontrolled and largely undefined, offers something for everybody, and all sorts of people are working it: advocates of basic education or moderate school reform, cultists of body and spirit, miracle workers, and, at the interstices between education and medicine, a small but growing number of operators creating even newer and more fanciful patterns of illness. It is a wide, all-encompassing spectrum:

In a suburb outside San Francisco, Dr. James Benvenuti, pediatrics consultant to the Contra Costa County Department of Education, proposes a prekindergarten screening program for "temperament" and neurological characteristics to identify hyperactive, "difficult to raise" and "shy" children. Group therapy is to be offered to the parents of children so identified, and letters sent to "private doctors indicating hyperactive and other findings at school. It will be suggested that medication be prescribed to assist in these student's school success. Access to county clinics and county auxiliary services with a medical follow-up shall be available to families who qualify for these county services." It is assumed, the proposal says, that "15–30 students will be identified as dysfunctional kindergarten students (14–28 percent) and will be targets of this . . . program in phase I." The proposal was killed, partly owing to the adamant objections of a suspicious first grade teacher. Nonetheless Benvenuti regularly takes children identified by the schools for their "unusual behavior or learning problems in class" and gives them "predelinquency screening" which, in his view, is synonymous with hyperkinesis. The basis for that screen is the Benvenuti Behavior Rating Scale and a chart of nine "hyperkinetic syndromes," among them "developmental hyperkinesis," "XYY chromosome disorder," "malignant hyperkinesis," and "pseudo-hyperkinesis (malingering)," an ailment that is contracted "after patient observes a hyperkinetic friend or relative get attention which the patient wants." Children diagnosed as hyperkinetic (predelinquent) are referred to private physicians or clinics, their diagnoses are given to teachers and other school personnel, and both children and parents are offered counseling and therapy. In Benvenuti's ideal model, everyone is a patient, teachers included, and everyone will participate in treatment. For the moment, however, it is the children who get the treatment —in his estimation 20 to 35 percent of them are hyperactive —and the teachers who are being taught how to administer it.[38]

In Denver, the Day Care Center sponsored by the Department of Psychiatry of the University of Colorado Medical Center offers "psychoeducation" for some 25 pupils in the intermediate grades who were referred by their schools as "borderline functioning academically and socially" and "marginally adaptive." The school is a training facility for the psychiatry department, the pupils receive intensive psychotherapy, and many of the techniques used suggest that the youngsters are emotionally disturbed. Nonetheless, according to Gaston Blum, the center's director, almost all the students "fit into a minimal brain dysfunction group, with a fair percentage hyperactive, disorganized and disoriented, and with different kinds of language problems," and the institution therefore receives federal and foundation funds to study learning disabilities. The environment is highly structured: a psychomedical team is on constant call, and the academic program includes a behavior modification scheme in which chips are awarded for work successfully completed. In a "reinforcement period," students use workbooks, flashcards and math games to develop skills; in the lunchroom they are required to sit at small, round tables monitored by teachers who enforce good manners and correct those who use bad words; and in the gymnasium, where they spend a great deal of time (for "psychomotor skill development"), they are required to move from station to station correcting body posture in three-way mirrors, repeating various movements and practicing coordination. ("Without these skills," a staff member explained knowingly, "a child can't socialize. As a child develops motor skills, his self-image improves.") Although the student-patients are described by the staff as extremely difficult, disordered youngsters, their behavior—at least within the school—is considerably more docile than that of most preadolescents in other schools; two-thirds of them are not on medication and it is therefore hard to ascribe the general tractability to the effects of drugs. There is none of the usual horseplay of the conventional school—it is not permitted—and the lunchtime off-color remarks of a thirteen-year-old boy can cause general consternation among the staff. In one incident we witnessed, a supervisor was visibly upset by the "bad language . . . words about intercourse" used by one of the boys. She had difficulty repeating the words, but finally, after being pressed, she managed to say them: "jerking off." Another teacher reported an instance of behavior that she regarded as "acting out" and "regression" in a "borderline girl." The student had put a sunflower seed in a teacher's glass of orange juice. "She is such a manipulator," the teacher said, and the staff agreed. For such careful monitoring of their children's behavior, parents pay $39.50 a day.

There are other points in the spectrum. For teachers in Essexville, Michigan, Lincoln, Illinois, Carroll County, Maryland, and Wayne, Nebraska, federally funded learning disabilities projects have provided an opportunity to tinker with the school curriculum, get additional personnel to work with "problem" children, and, under the aegis of the new LD terminology, try approaches as traditional as the three Rs. In Wayne, for example, the teachers decided that as many as 43 percent of their pupils had "specific language disabilities," organized something called Project Success, and instituted a structured program emphasizing phonics (letter sounds), drill, a "multisensory approach" to language teaching reminiscent of methods developed by Maria Montessori nearly a century ago (the child is supposed to "hear, say, and touch the letters, as well as see them") and a physical education program in which a high school wrestling coach was transformed into a part-time "motor-perception teacher."

For affluent children, parental concern with school or behavior problems can lead to any one of a proliferating number of public or private diagnostic centers, academies for neurological development, perceptual motor training schools, centers for educational therapy, psychoeducational centers for human development, summer camps for dyslexics, ranches for underachievers, or day and residential schools for the "bright but learning behavior problem student." (How many such places serve truly handicapped youngsters, and how many are only failing private schools or the domains of crackpots looking for a new market of desperate parents is hard to say; the market, in any case, is growing.) For other children assigned the LD label, it means placement in a special "learning disabilities" kindergarten as the first step of formal schooling, with the chances of returning to the mainstream dependent on the district. In one federally funded program conducted by twelve rural Illinois school systems, less than half of the pupils placed in LD kindergartens returned to a regular first grade the following year. In other systems, children identified as learning disabled in preschool screening programs are kept in regular classrooms but sent on an individual basis for tutoring in special LD centers.

In most school systems, the screens, labels and rhetoric are running far ahead of the remediation. Despite all the exotic talk about MBD and dyslexia, the organizational gearing up, the pseudo-scientific schemes for screening, and despite all the consultants, diagnostic referrals and educational decisions, the "cures" are the balance beam and the sandpaper letters, the flashcard drills and letter games, the jigsaw puzzles and somersaults. (And, of course, the drugs, about which more in Chapter III.) A typical program, *The Remediation of Learning Disabilities: A Handbook of Psychoeducational Resource Programs*[39] by Robert A. Valett, professor of education and director of an LD center in Fresno, California, promises special education teachers and remedial specialists a program to attack 53 separate disabilities for $12. The "Gross Motor Development Psychoeducational Resource Program Number 4," for example, which deals with "Walking," offers a "definition" ("the ability to walk erect in a coordinated fashion without support"), an "educational rationale" ("Walking is a neuromuscular act requiring balance and coordination. Children should be presented with opportunities to develop increasing skill in more difficult tasks."), and two full pages of simple drawings of a boy following a "marked path," carrying a bamboo pole across a narrow balance beam, doing a "ladder and beam walk," and walking blindfolded with feet on either side of a balance beam.

In school after school, the techniques reflect some combination of the methods proposed in the Valett program: balance beams, walking exercises, felt letters, games and puzzles. The most important influence in promoting those methods, Marianne Frostig, now a *grande dame* in the field, has advanced the idea that perceptual motor skills (e.g., hand-eye coordination) and reading ability are linked and that the way to remediate problems in the second is to improve ability in the first: the most commonly used remedial techniques are those employing Frostig materials and "principles." The research on those methods indicates, however, that there is no evidence for Frostig's conclusions. "Over a dozen research studies have been carried on to test the transfer of improvement in perceptual skills on the Frostig materials to learning to read," said a psychologist at Columbia who reviewed the results, "and the great majority . . . have shown no transfer."[40] Some of the methods used by LD specialists, he said, were based on sheer fantasy; none had any demonstrated validity. The kids learn to hop, jump and skip, and their coordination may improve; their ability to read does not.

V

It is impossible to estimate the full impact. In one sense, the scientists had simply given the schools new justification for doing the things they had been doing anyway; in another they had helped create a new and apparently permanent set of invidious labels for ordinary children; and in still another, they had provided a rationale for segregating children that teachers and school administrators wanted to remove from regular classrooms, thus permitting them to get around a growing number of court decisions limiting the schools' power to arbitrarily track or otherwise segregate children. No one can fully calculate their effects, for example, on a child labeled as learned disabled and placed in a special class who comes to believe in the designation, or the effect on the way other teachers and children will treat him. Yet the lack of validated remedies and the vagueness of the terms—when they mean anything at all—suggest that the ideology of LD may be far more significant than the specific practices being carried on in its name, however silly or dangerous some of them may be. We seem to need LD and MBD, require them not only as explanations for failure and as props to middle-class status—only black children are supposed to fail because they are stupid or because their parents are inadequate—but also as a means of control: getting the difficult children out of the classroom, tranquilizing the restless, treating the deviant. We will say more about those things later in this book; what we want to emphasize here is the use of the ideology itself. If one were to invent a means whereby the difficult children of socially respectable people—children who disrupt the routines of institutions and communities—were to be controlled without giving offense or generating political opposition, one could do no better than attribute to them an illness so new and so particular to one class of society that it carries no stigma, no innuendos of character and no denigration of ability, but which, at the same time, makes possible—indeed necessary—the controls and "treatment" that the system deems necessary. Such a disease would make it possible to maintain the legitimacy of the system without generating suspicion or resistance among those who appear to be its most obvious failures. The more meritocratic the educational system becomes, the more stringent the requirements of performance and behavior, the more likely that affluent children will be included among the deviants; the more narrow the criteria of success, the greater the pressure to create escapes, rationales or remedies for the privileged. If affluence and influence can be transmitted only through the mechanism of "good" schools and "good" colleges, then the children must themselves be "treated" to become acceptable candidates, and the price of the treatment—financial and psychological—becomes one of the means by which status is maintained.

One of the more striking things about the parents who attend those LD conferences and join organizations like CANHC or ACLD is the joylessness, bordering on desperation, of the tone in which they discuss their children and their lives. "You could watch in wonder," said a woman in Grosse Point, Michigan, "when the classroom clown and bad boy settles down [thanks to medication] and directs his energy and good mind toward learning. Even his parents like him and tolerate him long enough to do things with him." It may be difficult to make judgments about the lives and attitudes of otherwise rational people who believe that marriages are wrecked by learning-disabled children, but it seems clear that those children are judged by their success, even by their parents, and tolerated for their institutional conformity, and it is therefore hardly surprising that their parents seize on demons and look for exorcists to drive them out.

What that entails is a grim willingness—perhaps even a desire—to yield those children up to institutions and therapists who will teach them to believe that conformity is health and deviance is illness, train them to accept the notion that school success is a condition of self-esteem, and condition them to the idea that good behavior depends on therapy and medication. The suburban parents of the fifties told William H. Whyte, Jr., in 1956 that "they had to learn adjustment the hard way, without the benefit of an education anywhere near as contemporary, or socially conscious, as what the schools are now offering. If they have made their adjustments as successfully as they have, they wonder, how much more successfully may their children when they come of age?"¹ The parents of the learning-disabled children of the seventies *are* those children of the fifties, and LD seems to be one of the indications of how important that adjustment has become. It is the social system, of course, that establishes the definitions and conditions of adjustment, and the system's agents—school officials, policemen, judges and probation officers—who are beginning to find the ideology so useful.

THREE

The Smart Pill

Frank, an attractive but very thin sixth grader, sits quietly in an examination room of the Learning Disabilities Clinic at the Kaiser-Permanente Medical Center in Oakland, California. A clinic doctor checks Frank's cumulative record from the urban school he attends. Then he checks the boy's eye movements. Frank has a slight reading problem, a bit below grade level. But the main trouble, according to his mother and teachers, is that he has "trouble concentrating." He's not one to sit still, his mother says.

Still, he is doing better in school this year. He is on traffic patrol, an honor, and he has even done some independent projects. At home, his mother says, he's "kind of lazy" and can sit and watch TV forever. Frank explains that he doesn't like school, and that's why he won't sit still.

The doctor tells Frank: "It's not that you won't sit still. You *can't* sit still." "No," Frank insists, "I won't." "I don't believe you," the doctor says, and continues to question Frank, but the boy stubbornly holds his ground: "I won't because I don't want to."

Frank has been on Ritalin in every grade except the fourth, when the teacher said he was fine without it. He doesn't take it in summer, because he doesn't need it when he's not in school. "Do you know what the Ritalin does to him?" the doctor asks. The mother says no, she just knows he doesn't eat much when he's on it, that's why he's so thin. And the school says he's a little better on it. The doctor talks rapidly to the mother about hyperactive and hypoactive children, about low arousal, and sleep-deprived and seemingly lethargic children. Frank's mother nods as the words go by. "Keep him on Ritalin," the doctor concludes. "He seems to need it."

It is the first time he has seen the boy, and the visit took fifteen minutes.

John was referred by his teacher to the school psychologist "because he has difficulty adjusting to the full routine of the kindergarten program." The psychologist reported that he exhibited "short attention span and signs of emotional conflict. John was confused about the difference between what was real and fantasy."

John's mother is Japanese and his father was a black serviceman. They were married in Japan and moved to the United States shortly thereafter. The father was then almost immediately sent to Vietnam, and John's mother knew nothing about either the English language or American culture; she was afraid of America and left their home only to buy food. John himself showed a great deal of fear of his new surroundings, spoke very little English and was baffled and frightened when he arrived for his first day of kindergarten. The school psychologist's report, written four months after John started school, mentioned nothing of "hyperactivity."

Several months later a school nurse's report stated that John "tends to be hyperactive—i.e., can't sit still for any length of time." The nurse also reported that the parents were asked and refused to participate in therapy with John. John continued to perturb his teachers by asking "weird" questions, many of them about death. He felt, and said, that "nobody likes me." The nurse referred the boy to the school doctor, who recommended a psychometric evaluation. Said the doctor's report: "I am unable to decide with the physical and brief studies here whether he is retarded, has had little stimulus, or has 'hyperactivity.' I am not sure that he fulfills many of the hyperactivity syndrome requirements."

A month later the school psychologist, the teacher, the principal, the nurse and the doctor conferred and placed John on 20 milligrams of Ritalin a day. His behavior soon changed, according to his teacher; he stopped jumping around so much and could sit still for longer periods of time. Only his "weird" thoughts continued to disturb her. The teacher stated that John no longer required her constant attention and she was relieved to have him on the drug.

Shawn, a four-year-old, is brought to a suburban general practitioner by his mother, who has heard from several of her friends that the doctor is a strong advocate of Ritalin. Her complaint is that Shawn is overactive and mean, and can't get along with his playmates. Even Shawn's brother and sister think he's mean, she explained tearfully. In addition, the boy wants everything right away and can't seem to wait for rewards. She said she found it almost impossible to love this child.

Medical records showed a history of a normal delivery, and a physical examination of the child revealed nothing unusual from a neurological or organic standpoint. The doctor then prescribed 10 milligrams of Ritalin twice daily. The mother reported back that the child was easier to get along with, but now he wanted to "talk, talk, talk." The doctor then cut the dosage to 5 milligrams three times daily, and this "decreased some of his loquaciousness." The mother told the doctor she "was delighted. . . . I can love this child again."[1]

The Franks, Toms and Shawns are among an estimated 500,000 to 1,000,000 children, predominantly boys, who live on a regimen of psychoactive drugs: Ritalin (methylphenidate hydrochloride), Dexedrine (dextroamphetamine), Cylert (magnesium pemoline) and several others.[2] Most are between six and thirteen years of age, though a few are as young as two, and though an increasing number stay on the drugs through, and beyond, adolescence. Whatever their age, they are all targets of a relatively new phenomenon that regards chemical intervention as a legitimate solution to the classic problem of controlling and making acceptable the behavior of children who annoy teachers, upset classroom routines, or otherwise fail to conform to adult expectations. People who deplore the old modes of control—corporal punishment, chastisement, school suspension and expulsion—and have lost hope in less punitive solutions—special classes, tutoring, counseling—are often quick to embrace drug therapy. Despite the fact that stimulants—and particularly amphetamine-type drugs—have been recognized as the most dangerous and abused pharmaceuticals on the market and on the street, chemotherapy has become the "enlightened" answer to spanking.[3]

In theory it is a temporary remedy, something to help "manage" a child and permit him to sit still and concentrate until the normal processes of maturation or the obvious rewards of good behavior enable him to develop other forms of control; such management, according to the rationale, prevents or mitigates academic failure, social ostracism and the resulting cycle of emotional problems. Increasingly, however, there are indications that chemotherapy may become indefinite, that it masks the problems, and that it simply defers, perhaps forever, the more permanent remedies.[4] What is certain is that for roughly one of every ten children labeled "hyperactive" or "learning disabled," chemotherapy is the first line of "treatment," that their ranks have been growing at a phenomenal rate, and that for an increasing number, the temptation to extend medication indefinitely may be producing a new way of life. There is the story of Paul, reported with approval at a psychiatric meeting, who was making progress in school on a heavy diet of Ritalin. When the drug was discontinued, Paul began to have trouble on his highly competitive hockey team: "He just couldn't let himself go and really 'get in there the way dad and the coach tell me to.' It was decided to reinstitute Ritalin in a backup role so Paul would not worry about going out of control and hurting someone. He was given 10 milligrams one half-hour before each of the remaining practice sessions and in the morning and at noon during the weekend conference competition. . . . His proud parents called the next Monday to say he had scored two goals."[5] There is the testimony of the head of the School Nurse Division of the National Education Association who told a Congressional committee that five students in her high school were on Ritalin at their own discretion. "They were taken off the medication and they still came back to the 'springs inside,' the inability to control their behavior. So the doctor put it on a PRN, which means when necessary, so because they are senior high school students they come up to the health office and come to me and say 'I think I need my Ritalin now.' "[6] There are dozens of similar stories, stories of children and adolescents who have learned that the pill is the thing which enables them to get along, to be liked, to function. By the beginning of the seventies, the kids were learning new words to old schoolyard tunes: "I got my Rit-lin; you got your Dex. Slip us a pill; we won't be wrecks."

For most children, the road to medication begins at home or in the classroom. Some doctors talk about the mother "who roars into the office with her kid in one hand and a women's magazine article about these drugs in the other, saying 'I want you to slow my kid down before I go crazy.' " In other cases it is the pediatrician or the doctor in the clinic who, partly in response to pervasive drug company promotion, first suggests a drug trial. But in most instances, the initiative comes from the school. The teacher sends home a note (or calls a parent conference or refers the child to the school psychologist or counselor), to express her concern about a student's behavior or performance, suggesting that he is hyperactive or learning disabled, and recommending a visit to a neurologist or pediatrician who specializes in such ailments. Perhaps, the parents are told, a neurological workup would be helpful. Some parents resist, even to the point of changing schools or moving to another community, but most comply; the child, after all, is the school's hostage. What they are usually not told is that in many districts the preferred practitioners, those most frequently recommended, are physicians who are quick, rather than cautious, about writing prescriptions, and who are casual about monitoring the effects of the drugs on their patients. In one San Francisco suburb, for example, the school psychologist invariably recommends a pediatrician who already has 2,000 patients on Ritalin, Dexedrine and similar drugs or combinations of drugs (sometimes a stimulant and a tranquilizer) and who sees his function as "shaping the life styles of these children and their families." A nearby pediatrician who is skeptical about drug use gets no such referrals. His reports to the school that "this child is clearly within the normal limits of neurological maturation, and has no problems that are not within the purview of the school," were regarded as inadequate.

The process is reinforced by the drug companies. In an illustrated brochure distributed to physicians, CIBA Pharmaceutical Company, which makes Ritalin, informs the doctor to expect two waves of MBD children: "a wave in the fall," since "it may be only a matter of days or weeks before the school notifies the parents of the child's disruptive behavior," and a "wave in the winter," when the MBD child with specific learning problems "comes to the attention of school authorities, parents—and, thus, the physician—because performance has fallen below grade standards."[7] The message is picked up by schools, by individual teachers and even by the retail drug store. "Is Your Child Over Active?" asks the newspaper advertisement for Thompson's Pharmacy in Liberty, New York.

Often a small child with a seemingly large amount of
excess energy, who is very restless, aggressive and impulsive is simply described by loving parents as "all boy" or
"she's a little devil." However, it is possible that there is
an underlying cause that could have ill effects on social
development as he or she grows older. Call it to your
doctor's attention if you think your child is hyperactive.
The earlier the problem is identified, if there is a problem,
and helped the better the social adjustment that will be
made. There are certain drugs available for therapy that
can be of great help. You or your doctor can phone us.

In theory it is a decorous process—a helpful suggestion, a
hint from school to parent—but increasingly it is being reinforced and replaced by direct intimidation, by teachers or
counselors informing parents that the child is hyperactive
and that if he is not medicated, the school will have to keep
him back a grade, suspend him or transfer him to a special
class for the "emotionally handicapped," the "learning disabled" or some other category of benighted individuals. In
Little Rock, Arkansas, the Daniel Youngs were harassed so
much by the public schools that they moved to Indiana,
where their children had no further problems. "We received
almost daily notes from the children's teachers and calls
from the school. We were told our children had completely
quit trying and were failing every subject. We knew what
they were trying to accomplish by this because we knew
parents in the neighborhood that submitted . . . because they
couldn't take the pressure. Believe me, it wasn't a pretty sight
to see little children's personalities changed with the use of
drugs. The pressure kept building. My son (who was then
eight years old) was not allowed to have recess with the other
children because it was too stimulating. The final blow came
when my son came home crying hysterically. After I calmed
him down I found out the problem. He had been put in a
cardboard box for two weeks. I went down to the school in
a rage. The box was gone. . . . They did not deny that the
cardboard box had been used for him. He was easily dis-

tracted. I was told this way he could learn without distractions. . . . Near the end of the school year I received the final
and decisive call from the school principal [who said] that
the school officials were very seriously considering taking it
out of our hands. When I found out how they hoped to
accomplish this, I was panic-stricken. . . . The school officials
were contemplating using our children in a trial court case
to see if children could be put [on medication] without the
parents' consent." In Providence, the mother of David Wat-
son had a similar experience. From a report in the *Providence
Journal*:

> David's mother, Mrs. Verne Watson, said she had felt
> forced by school officials into drugging her child and it has
> become "one big nightmare."
>
> She said she had been constantly harassed by the school
> about her child's behavior and got a note from the school
> nurse which stated simply: "Your child is hyperactive. He
> doesn't sit still in school. Please see a physician."
>
> Mrs. Watson said she tried to fight keeping her son on
> the drugs after she saw the "side effects" the pills were
> having on David, but when she told school officials she
> could no longer keep up the therapy she was told that
> David might have to be expelled.
>
> She added: "David would complain he didn't like the
> feel of his body when he took the pills. It took his appetite
> away and he would cry a lot. His dreams got so bad he
> couldn't even talk about them. He would get up in the
> night and walk the floor for hours. His body would shake
> and quiver something terrible."
>
> Mrs. Watson said physicians kept increasing the dosage
> of Dexedrine until it reached 40 milligrams a day.
>
> "His body began to tremble so much he couldn't hold
> certain notes during his trumpet lessons and he would
> plead: 'Could I just not take the pills on the day of my
> lessons?' "
>
> Finally, she said, her son collapsed before school . . . and
> told her, "I just can't take them anymore. They're tortur-
> ing me." She said she called the school that day and told

officials "David is not coming." Family court action has been initiated against her because of David's truancy, she said.[8]

Despite such stories—and there are many more—many parents and the vast majority of teachers have become true believers: between 88 and 96 percent of teachers believe they can diagnose a hyperkinetic child and three-fourths feel that they have an obligation to recommend that a doctor be informed of the problem. One team of researchers also found that "an appreciable number of teachers recommend contact with a physician, and mention the possibility of Ritalin." Despite that expression of certainty, however—and despite the fact that the overwhelming majority of teachers claimed they knew what Ritalin is used for—their knowledge of its properties and effects was abysmal. They "had little specific and accurate information" about the drug; and although those with the most experience with Ritalin-medicated children were the most enthusiastic about its use, they were as ignorant of its effects as teachers without personal experience.[9] And so the notes keep coming, and the faith in drugs continues to grow. Their use, said one school superintendent "is almost a necessity with certain types of children. Without them no educational process could take place at all." In the future, it was predicted, teachers will be trained in medicine and pharmacy so they can administer drugs which effect classroom behavior. "Stimulant and other drugs are now a fact of life in the management of hyperactive children in schools."[10]

I I

There is nothing new in the statement that Americans are great believers in the proposition that drugs can heal all ills and solve most problems.[11] The national faith has always rested on the creation of a "new man," a creature free from the tragedy and frailties which plagued the Old World; inevitably that produced a belief that any disease or malfunction could and should be cured, and that anything substantially short of physical (and social) perfection was not altogether American. The development of a relatively sophisticated medical technology and the growth of a gigantic cosmetics industry converted the faith into compulsion: halitosis and hyperkinesis are both manifestations of antisocial tendencies. The compulsion, in turn, generated a view of man as something not quite human, a mechanistic organism subject to constant technological manipulation, something that could almost always be repaired, adjusted and improved. Adults might be beyond help, but the young—the new models— could be tuned and modified indefinitely. Drugs, not surprisingly, became significant elements in the process.

The compulsion goes a long way to explain the promiscuous prescription of drugs. Yet the significance of psychoactive medication for "hyperactive" or "learning disabled" children is almost impossible to understand without some comprehension of the peculiar research—sometimes sloppy, sometimes distorted, and nearly always misinterpreted—that is invoked to validate its use. For more than a decade, the accumulating studies have been cited by drug companies, physicians, government agencies and others to prove what they do not prove, to reassure the doubtful and to reinforce a growing myth about pills, happy children and productive classrooms. In most instances it is difficult to know where science ends and promotion begins. The national faith in perfection and the compulsion to create it override the deficiencies of research and medicine and conceal the increasingly significant political power that the search for perfection threatens to produce.

The pioneer was a physician in Providence, Rhode Island, named Charles Bradley who, in 1937, reported that daily doses of Benzedrine, an amphetamine, had caused a "spectacular change in behavior" in thirty patients in an institution for children with neurological and behavior disorders.[12]

The youngsters, five to fourteen years old and with normal intelligence, ranged from those with "specific educational disabilities, with secondarily disturbed school behavior, to the retiring schizoid child on the one hand and the aggressive, egocentric epileptic child on the other." During a week of experimental Benzedrine therapy, fourteen of the children showed "a great increase in school material" and "a definite 'drive' to accomplish as much as possible during the school period, and often to spend extra time completing additional work. Speed of comprehension and accuracy of performance were increased in most cases." In addition, a number of the children became "distinctly more subdued," "more placid and easygoing."

Bradley's "study" was hardly systematic. He had no control group, no objective standards by which to measure behavior changes, and his subjects were a mixed group of severely disturbed youngsters whose problems could have stemmed from any number of causes. But his initial findings —the combination of improved school performance and subdued behavior—convinced him he was on to something. The findings also gave rise to the theory of the "paradoxical effect"—that amphetamine-type drugs which stimulated adults tended to subdue the behavior of certain children. Bradley subsequently found that the effects of the drugs might not be as paradoxical as he had once assumed; in one study almost a fifth of the medicated children became not more subdued but more stimulated in their behavior—more alert, energetic, interested and aggressive.[13] Despite those observations, however, subsequent research (in the words of a recent review of the literature) "proceeded largely on the assumption that amphetamines did indeed produce a paradoxical calming effect on children, and subsequent developments in the use of amphetamines on children have been very much influenced by this assumption."[14]

For more than a decade, Bradley's work was almost forgotten; through the fifties and into the early sixties attempts to cure disturbed, institutionalized children were low on the list of social priorities, and no one had ever heard of "learn-

ing disabilities" or of "hyperkinesis" in a general school
setting. The most promising psychoactive drugs, in any case,
seemed to be the tranquilizers, and their use derived from
institutional desires to maintain order and to keep children
still without physical restraint. In 1963, however, a group of
researchers at the Johns Hopkins University, having found
that tranquilizers were no better than placebos in managing
troubled children—usually a mixed group described as "neurotic," "hyperkinetic," "defective" and "antisocial"—
turned to the stimulants and began to report what they regarded as positive results.[15] The subjects were institutionalized disturbed and delinquent children, the object was to
make them calm and cooperative, and the drugs prescribed
were dextroamphetamine (Dexedrine) and Ritalin, an amphetamine-type agent that had been used in adults to control
mild depression and senile behavior.

It was the beginning of an era. The Hopkins study not only
fanned interest in the pediatric use of stimulants, but also led
to the research partnership that has, for more than a decade,
produced its most publicized and influential results. The
partners were Leon Eisenberg, a psychiatrist, who was one
of the authors of the 1963 report, and C. Keith Conners, a
clinical psychologist. Working with the support of a series of
lavish NIMH grants—now amounting to well over $1 million
—first at Hopkins and later at Harvard and at the Massachusetts General Hospital in Boston, Conners and Eisenberg
became not only the leaders in pediatric psychopharmacology research, but also the country's most influential
proponents of the use of stimulants for hyperactive children.
Every step of that work was supported by NIMH (and occasionally by the drug companies), and the agency's enthusiasm, verging on ecstasy, became so great that NIMH sometimes became their partner in promotion. In 1973, for
example, Ronald S. Lipman, head of the Clinical Studies
Section at NIMH, wrote an article in the agency's *Psychopharmacology Bulletin* which declared that the use of stimulant
drugs with children

gained scientific credence [through] the more sophisticated methodology employed by the Hopkins investigators. The extensive publications of this group, spanning more than a decade of research experience, have firmly established the short-term efficacy of the stimulant medications in reducing hyperactivity, distractibility, and impulsiveness. The stimulants were also effective in enhancing performance on a number of cognitive-motor tasks including the Porteus Maze, paired-associate learning, and various subtests of the Wechsler Intelligence Scale for Children (WISC) and the Wide Range Achievement Test.[16]

Lipman's enthusiasm echoed the words of another HEW official, Thomas C. Points, Deputy Assistant Secretary for Health and Science Affairs, who had told a Congressional committee in 1970 that there was a fairly common hyperkinetic syndrome that "lends itself to safe and effective drug treatment"; that "clinical reports and the extensive literature of controlled studies indicate a highly favorable clinical response"; that Ritalin and Dexedrine particularly are "safe and clinically effective in a very high percentage of hyperkinetic children"; and that there is "no evidence to suggest any feeling of euphoria and no evidence to suggest that these drugs are addicting in children." The drugs, he said, improve behavior and learning, without dulling the child or decreasing "his activity level in appropriate situations. . . . Rather these drugs enable the child to sit still and attend in those situations, such as in the classroom, where this behavior is both appropriate and, indeed, necessary if the child is to profit from the educational experience and not become a school dropout." He estimated negative side effects at a reassuringly low 12 to 14 percent, and insisted—under questioning—that the drugs not only modified behavior but "increased . . . learning capacities . . . arithmetic improves, and so forth."[17]

The basis of that enthusiasm was an accumulation of studies purporting to demonstrate scientifically that stimulant drugs are safe and effective in "treating" or "managing" learning-disabled children. The studies were consistently plagued, however, by extraneous factors, by problems of definition, by the so-called placebo effect (a Hawthorne effect in which children "treated" with a placebo of inert pills appear to improve), by lack of long-term followups, and by little demonstrable improvement in academic performance.[18] The studies showed that the drugs made custodians and teachers happy; but they were unable to define a syndrome or measure its cure. By 1967 Conners and Eisenberg began to use schoolchildren rather than institutionalized patients for their experiments, and in a report on the use of Dexedrine on "learning-disabled" children concluded that though the drug had no effect on "intellectual ability" it had produced "significant improvement in teacher ratings of behavior." The difficulty was that there was no clear definition of "learning problems" and no criterion, other than teacher complaints—any complaint—for who was admitted to the study. The complaints included: "Quite talkative, speaks to students in a loud voice during class , , , Short attention span. Below average in all academic areas. No behavior problem, though. . . . Academically dull. Shows good artistic potential and wants to convert most subject matter to art. During a lesson in arithmetic, he may take out paper and begin to draw. . . . Values are placed on clothing. Is an extremist, lacks interest in school. Shows overt behavior when asked to do any work in school. . . . Very playful, a clown, hums and sings. . . . Giggles for no reason. . . . Very unconcerned about passing or failing. . . . Boisterous. . . . Excitable. . . . Talkative but shy. . . . Restless. . . . Has poor work habits. . . . Frequently daydreams. . . . Anxious. . . . Sucks her fingers and uses bathroom frequently. . . . Does not respond readily to constructive suggestions."[19] What the children did have in common was race and social class: they were all poor blacks attending the fifth and sixth grades in two Baltimore ghetto schools. The teachers reported that the students taking Dexedrine improved in "classroom behavior, attitude toward authority, and group participation." There was less jiving, less hustle. The investigators reported "some euphoria combined with faster reflexes, endurance, and tolerance of fatigue," which, in turn, honed down the rawer edges— sulkiness, stubbornness, oversensitivity and hostility. No questions were raised about the desirability of such behavior, about whether docility made for better learning, about the relationship of social background to classroom behavior, or about the attitudes of the teachers themselves. Nonetheless, the Baltimore study has become a model for subsequent research and one of the most important pieces of evidence validating the use of stimulants. Conners and Eisenberg had found a way to make life in an inner-city classroom more bearable.

The accumulation of positive reports from Conners and Eisenberg prompted NIMH and the drug companies to support more research in the field, and stimulated a flood of scientific reports and popular magazine articles, an orgy of conferences, many of them also funded by the pharmaceutical houses and a rapid increase in the use of the drugs. In pharmacology, Eisenberg once said, "the certainty with which convictions are held tends to vary inversely with the depth of the knowledge on which they are based." Yet if the studies of the late sixties and early seventies demonstrated anything, it was precisely that combination of certainty and ignorance. Most of them, said Roger D. Freeman, a psychiatrist who reviewed the literature, "suffer from multiple sources of invalidity. On the strictly scientific level, there is little evidence that any drug is effective in enhancing learning. . . . Many drugs impair learning."[20] The common belief, despite Bradley's later findings, and despite similar observations in clinical practice and in other experiments, was that the drugs had that "paradoxical effect" on hyperkinetic children.[21] Because of peculiar organic or chemical characteristics in the neurology of hyperkinetic children (which no one understood), the drugs would not produce the euphoric, stimulating effects that they produced in adults, and there was, therefore, no danger of creating drug dependence, psychotic episodes or hallucinations.[22] That thesis, carried another step, brought some researchers and most practitioners to the tautological and politically satisfactory conclusion that the drugs themselves could be used to diagnose hyperkinesis or MBD: if a child responded appropriately to the drug, he had such an ailment; if he did not, then he was not afflicted. The drug, said one pediatrician, "normalizes these children," and, as a consequence, "the child functions better as a child."[23] Such reasoning obviated a whole set of political and social difficulties which might otherwise have stood in the way of the drugging process. It would be unthinkable to give amphetamines and amphetamine-type medications to children who acted out too much in school or at home—to feed them speed just to keep them docile—but it was quite another thing to treat a medical syndrome, a specific dysfunction, and to use drugs from whose pernicious effects the patient was supposed to be immune. The disease, the medical "entity" called MBD, was, as often as not, a creature of the drug, a diagnosis determined by the treatment. By 1970, 200,000 to 300,000 American children were on psychoactive medication, and as their numbers grew, so did public awareness of the new ailment.

What no one pointed out was that the research on which those prescriptions were based had never been limited to children diagnosed as hyperkinetic (by whatever definition) but had almost invariably included a broad spectrum of individuals who created problems for their elders; from the beginning, moreover, the prime object had been not cure but control. By the early seventies, however, many of those subjects had been retroactively relabeled to suit the political and social needs of the times; *ex post facto,* the mixed bag of behavior problems became uniformly hyperkinetic. In 1973, for example, Eisenberg published an article in *Hospital Practice* on the value of stimulants for hyperkinetic children. The article, widely circulated among learning disabilities groups and physicians, assures the reader that the drugs are effective for children meticulously diagnosed as hyperactive but not "in children with disorders other than hyperactivity." The effects on them, he warned, are unknown. To make his case, he described his own 1967 study with those humming, finger-sucking Baltimore children. In six years even those who had once been simply "school behavior problems"—including some described as "shy," "withdrawn" and "very quiet"— became hyperactive.[24]

The problems are further compounded by confusion about how the drugs work on children and uncertainty about their effects.[25] In spite of the belief that hyperkinetic or MBD children respond in a special way, the only study that has included "normal" children showed that they responded in exactly the same way as those said to be hyperactive.[26] (In his *Hospital Practice* article of 1973, Eisenberg was still talking about the paradoxical effect, though as early as 1966 his colleague Conners was denouncing it as an "artifact of observation."[27]) Some researchers think that hyperactive children are overaroused and that amphetamines reduce arousal; others believe the opposite.[28] One study found that Ritalin significantly reduced the measured activity level of antisocial, hyperactive boys while placebo had no effect;[29] in a second both Ritalin and placebo reduced motor activity;[30] and in a third motor activity was actually increased by Ritalin.[31]

None of the findings may mean much. Of the 756 reports on the psychotropic medication of children published between 1937 and March 1971, only a handful reflected controlled studies using the direct measurement of behavior to indicate drug effects; in more than half of those studies, no significant difference was found between drug and placebo effect. When psychological testing was the criterion, the percentage of studies which showed no effect was even higher. It was only in the studies where subjective "clinical impressions" were used as a criterion that significant effects were reported.[32] "The literature," according to a comprehensive review in the *New England Journal of Medicine,* "shows striking parallels between the effects of stimulant drugs on normal adults and on problem children." Reaction times are decreased, and performance "in simple arithmetic problems and other tasks requiring attentiveness (e.g., typing) are enhanced." What that meant was that drugs improve performance on "repetitive, routinized tasks that require sustained attention. Reasoning, problem solving and learning do not seem to be affected in adults or children."[33]

If it is hard to understand the efficacy of the drugs, it is even harder to get a clear picture of their side effects. The most commonly reported include loss of appetite, serious weight loss, insomnia, depression, headaches, stomachaches, bed wetting, irritability and dizziness (many of which afflict large proportions of those who take such drugs) but an increasing number of reports also indicate severe psychological effects.[34] It was common knowledge that in adults even small doses of amphetamines can produce a "model psychosis" hard to distinguish from schizophrenia. Because of the "paradoxical effect" children were supposed to be immune to such reactions. They were not.[35] In one case an eight-year-old boy who was taking 5 milligrams of dextroamphetamine twice daily for "disruptive classroom behavior" and who first showed "an immediate improvement" on medication grew paranoid, complaining that people he could not see were throwing snowballs at him from behind, touching his thighs and genitals during the night, and spying on him. He also heard voices that he could mimic. For a short period, he was taken off the drug and the hallucinations stopped, but after the school sent him home because of his hyperactivity, the medication was resumed, the dosage was increased, and the hallucinations started again. Eventually he appeared to have outlasted them and he "did well during his last four months at school and passed."[36] In other instances, children taking amphetamines were described as "overtly psychotic."

There have been similar reports about Ritalin, which is usually described as smoother and safer than Dexedrine and which has, as a result, become the favored of the pediatric psychostimulants. In one case, a six-year-old girl on Ritalin first became cranky and plaintive, then cooperative and relaxed, but after a week she started to show "grossly bizarre" behavior, hiding in a closet and cowering in a corner, becoming apathetic and mute, "almost like a vegetable," then babbling incoherently, staring into space, and contorting her body. In another case, a ten-year-old boy started screaming in his sleep on the second day of a Ritalin regime, then became more irritable, more hyperactive and physically abusive to younger children, saying that he "felt like he wanted to tear everything apart." He saw animals marching around a whirlpool; food assumed a strange taste and his mouth went dry. Later he became weak and depressed. In a third case, a fifteen-year-old girl who had been taking Ritalin for six years for hyperactivity tripled her usual dosage during a weekend camping trip in order "to relax." For two days she had visual hallucinations, with logs and shadows becoming bears and people. She was sure that some boys had placed a smelly substance on her neck.[37] Among other reports of "unusual side effects" was the case of a two-year-old boy who screamed for several hours after being given 10 milligrams of Ritalin, and the onset of psychosis in a six-year-old boy who had been "well adjusted except for hyperactivity," and who began to exhibit bizarre behavior, with visual and tactile hallucinations, that included seeing and feeling "worms all over him."[38]

There are growing indications that the drugs may have even more fundamental long-term effects, particularly on growth and in creating psychological drug dependence. In 1972, Daniel Safer of the Johns Hopkins University Medical School reported that relatively high doses of Dexedrine or Ritalin taken over a period of months may permanently impair weight gain and growth in stature, that even after a child came off medication he might not regain the weight and height losses suffered during "treatment."[39] Equally important were reports that for most children the drugs provide only maintenance and not "treatment," and that they therefore create long-term dependency. The only available studies in which drug-treated children were followed into adolescense "suggest that the outlook for children treated primarily with drugs is relatively poor. In their teens, these children were still having trouble in their families, often behaving antisocially and presenting academic and behavioral problems in school. The last result is particularly disappointing since drug treatments have generally been aimed specifically at helping problem children do better in school."[40] For Mark Stewart, a child psychiatrist at the University of Iowa, those observations were reinforced by extensive personal experience in studying and treating hyperactive children as they approach adolescence:

> They come off the drugs at fourteen or so, [he said in an interview] and suddenly they're big, strong people who've never had to spend any time building any controls in learning how to cope with their own daily stress. Then the parents, who have forgotten what the child's real personality was like without the mask of the drug, panic and say "Help me, I don't know what to do with him. He's taller than I am and he has the self-discipline of a six year old." At that point the parent sees the only solution as going back to the drug. They can only deal with the medicated child; that's the seductiveness of successful drug treatment —that it temporarily solves the problem without asking the people involved to do anything.[41]

Stewart's alternative to the drugs is to train and guide parents, individually and in groups, in the job of coping with a difficult child, of doing the "parenting" that will enable the child to behave in a way that will lead to self-confidence and self-acceptance. "The problems of raising hyperactive children are like those with other children," he said, "only more so. Raising a child is a difficult job; raising a hyperactive child is more difficult. There's no magic solution, but there are practical approaches and help available."[42]

> Physicians and parents commonly assume [said Sroufe and Stewart] that a hyperactive child who is "success-

fully" treated with stimulant drugs over a period of months or years will acquire good habits because of the reinforcements he is given for his good behavior while on the drug. The followup studies . . . do not seem to support this idea. . . . Another common assumption about the use of drugs is that they will "help the child do better in school." Successfully treated children do more of their assigned work in class, but one may question whether this is a truly important goal; doing assigned work is not the same as learning. . . . It is often argued that drugs may break up a vicious circle of unhappiness, but negative consequences for the child's self-concept may be equally important. The child can conclude that he is not responsible for his behavior: "I can't help being bad today. I haven't had my pill." The child comes to believe not in the soundness of his own brain and body, not in his growing ability to learn and to control his behavior, but in "my magic pills that make me into a good boy and make everybody like me."[43]

Sroufe and Stewart's doubts about the long-range efficacy of the drugs were confirmed by the first long-term study of the effects of Ritalin on hyperactive children, published in the January 25, 1975, issue of the *Canadian Medical Association Journal.* The study, conducted by a research team headed by Dr. Gabrielle Weiss of the Montreal Children's Hospital and funded by CIBA, found no improvement among youngsters receiving the drug in comparison with those taking no medication. The children, who had been treated with Ritalin for three to five years (an average of fifty-one months), did no better than a carefully matched drug-free group on a range of measures of academic performance, emotional development or delinquency. Weiss and her colleagues also confirmed Safer's findings that children who had taken Ritalin, even in moderate doses and with "drug holidays," failed to grow at expected rates.

Concurrently, Dr. Herbert E. Rie, professor of pediatrics and psychology at Ohio State University, had found in the first two years of his long-term study that Ritalin has no positive effects on the scholastic achievement of children diagnosed as hyperactive. At first, teacher ratings indicate an improvement, Rie told us, because "the kids slow down dramatically and are out of people's hair, but when objective testing is done, they're not performing one bit better. In fact, what we're observing on this round of measurement is that the youngsters on drugs are far less responsive and enthusiastic, and are far more apathetic, humorless and zombie-like. It's there and you can see it and measure it, and we don't know why it hasn't been picked up before."

I I I

By 1974, CIBA's Ritalin had become virtually synonymous with pediatric stimulants. In the previous six years, while the prescription of such drugs had been growing at a rate approaching 50 percent a year, tripling between 1970 and 1974, Ritalin's share of the market, currently estimated at $30 million annually, grew from about 50 percent to something over 80 percent. That success is all the more striking in view of the fact that 100 tablets (of 20 milligrams each) cost anywhere between $9.90 and $16 at the pharmacy ($12.50 is a typical price) and that a comparable prescription of Dexedrine, whose action is similar, costs $5. At the heart of that success lies an aggressive promotion and sales campaign pushing not only the drug but the ailments it is supposed to mitigate, if not to cure, a brilliant blend of social mythology about bright happy classrooms with bright happy children and carefully selected citations from medical literature which, on closer inspection, totally fail to support the conclusions that the advertising suggests. One ad, for example— ubiquitous in the more popular medical journals—shows an elementary school classroom in which all the desks are neatly aligned and all the students attentive except for one blurred child, near whom the teacher stands. "Help the MBD child achieve his full potential," says the copy. "Here is a child who seems to get very little out of school. He can't sit still. Doesn't take directions well. He's easily frustrated, excitable, often aggressive. And he's got a short attention span. . . . He is a victim of Minimal Brain Dysfunction, a diagnosable entity that generally responds well to treatment programs. And Ritalin can be an important part. . . ." The small print points out, among other caveats, that Ritalin is only adjunctive therapy to other remedial measures, but the essential point of the ad is seductively clear: the kid who is antsy at school can benefit from Ritalin. The advertisements are reinforced by manuals and pamphlets addressed to physicians, among them the 95–page screening handbook discussed in Chapter II, and a booklet called "Minimal Brain Dysfunction: Guidelines to Diagnosis/Guidelines to Treatment" (with photos of a blond youngster one couldn't resist helping) which urges that "the MBD child should be treated now" and warns that "drug therapy can make the difference between keeping the MBD child in his normal class and having him placed elsewhere." The booklet points to "clinical results with Ritalin over a decade of experience as an aid to management of Minimal Brain Dysfunction."[44]

To support its bright promises about the drug's effectiveness, the physician's booklet cites three examples of validating research. The first is an uncontrolled study by an Argentinian physician who reported "marked improvement" in 40 percent of his subjects (based on teacher and parent reports and direct clinical observation).[45] The actual report, published in 1962, warns about possible skewing of drug effects —"some of the parents," said the physician, "were not providing us with a truly objective opinion of what was happening to their child"—and that, in turn "could color the final results of a study." (Those qualifications, of course, are not mentioned in the CIBA booklet.) The second is an unpublished paper that compared the effects of Ritalin, phenobarbital and placebo on *ten* children. (Ritalin won, but research has consistently shown that phenobarbital makes children more jumpy.[46]) The third is a 1969 report on the effects of

Ritalin in a CIBA-funded double-blind study involving forty children for "approximately six weeks."⁴⁷ The study found that Ritalin was better than placebo in improving attention span, as the CIBA booklet notes, although not in improving verbal ability. The booklet mentions "a strong placebo effect," not adding that, depending on the measurement, anywhere from 37 to 67 percent of the children on placebo also showed significant improvement, which, as the authors themselves pointed out, "makes it more difficult for improved behavior to appear as a function of the drug treatment."

Through the late sixties and early seventies, the CIBA literature was backed by a direct sales campaign in which company representatives were urged, in the words of one CIBA executive, to become "more effective pushers." The objectives were teacher training institutes, juvenile probation officers, PTA meetings and whatever other community groups might be hospitable, "Your ingenuity in the promotion of Ritalin," the executive said in his 1971 territorial sales report, "is becoming more apparent."⁴⁸

The CIBA representative in Paducah, Ky., reports having a community of approximately 10,000 that has established a screening program of preschool children to identify as early as possible those children most likely to have learning disabilities. . . . [The salesman in Kansas City reminds his co-workers that there are] a few people whom we frequently overlook when making presentations and contacts on functional behavior problems in children. Two in particular are the juvenile court officers and probation officers. The juvenile court system comes in contact with children of all ages but their primary value . . . would be to discuss Functional Behavior Problems with teachers and school officials. . . . Juvenile bureaus connected with local police are prime targets; even though they are in contact with older children they can spread the word. . . . [The salesman in South Bend, Ind.] reports that at an inservice meeting of medical education personnel . . . a physician brought two hyperactive children to use in a demonstration on the basic symptoms of Functional Behavior Problems. That's getting involvement, folks.

The most common approach was to send out salesmen, often accompanied by doctors, to community meetings; some, equipped with a film, appeared at a different gathering every night, five nights a week. An article published in 1971 described one such evening:[49]

Here in Dublin, an obscure San Francisco suburb, babysitters are doing big business. Moms in curlers and dads in sneakers have driven over to Fredrickson Elementary School for a PTA meeting in the multipurpose room. Just as official business is ending, a white Continental swings into the school driveway and zips past the parked station wagons. The car brakes by a side door and out pops the featured speaker. A solicitous janitor hurries out into the rain and helps Daniel Martin, M.D., remove a videotape unit from the trunk and lug it inside.

Once on stage, Dr. Martin launches into his controversial subject. Mothers and fathers, he asks, is your child overactive? Does he have trouble sitting still? Is he aggressive, greedy, impatient and cruel to animals? Does he do poorly in school and throw a lot of temper tantrums? Do you sometimes find yourself suppressing the urge to kill the little monster? If so, don't despair. Help is available, and it's called Ritalin—"R-I-T-A-L-I-N."

You want proof. OK. Douse the lights and let's look at this videotape featuring Kevin and his mother.

While his mom tells us Kevin is a cretin, her son does a freak-out for the camera. He jumps up and down, plays with balloons, mimics mom, screams shrilly and tries to light matches. Off-camera, Dr. Martin asks if Kevin has had his Ritalin today. Mom says no, so the doctor gives him 20 milligrams. A few minutes later the boy comes back on the screen, now every inch the model child. "How do you feel, Kevin?" asks Dr. Martin. Kevin says everything is beautiful.

The Dublin parents are suitably impressed, just as parents have been in San Francisco, Los Angeles, Oakland, Fremont, Castro Valley and dozens of other California communities where Dr. Martin has shown his tape. . . . [Dr. Martin] claims [Ritalin] can do everything from halting bed-wetting to making A students out of failures. "We gave it to one terrible little boy," he says, "and a few minutes later the child was actually taking the garbage out for his mother. She almost flipped out."

. . . "The diagnosis can best be made by the parent or teacher," says Dr. Martin. "Why, my wife was even able to diagnose one of these kids simply on the basis of what his mother said on the golf course. At my office, it's easy to spot these kids when they come in and try to light a bonfire."

Addressing the Dublin PTA, Dr. Martin urged parents to watch for nine danger signals in their children that might suggest a need for medication. These were: hyperactivity, low frustration tolerance, aggressiveness, impulsiveness, reliance on companionship, inability to postpone gratification, poor school performance, poor peer relationships and overt hostility.

. . . "Now I want you to understand we aren't curing these kids; we're just keeping them under control. It's just like we don't cure diabetics with insulin. Usually we'll start your 3- or 4-year old with five milligrams three times a day, then up it to 15 milligrams three times a day by the time they are 8 or 9. We suggest giving it at 8 A.M., noon and 4 P.M. The drug does cut down the appetite a bit and can cause a little insomnia—that's why we don't like to give it after 4 P.M. Each pill should last for four hours; if it doesn't last that long, then we up the dose.

"The funny thing about this drug is that when it wears off, it's just like jumping off a cliff. I had one kid who took it at 7:30 A.M., and it wore off in the middle of English class at 11:30 A.M. She was flunking the class, and so we increased the dose and she passed easily. We can go as high as 100 to 140 milligrams a day if we have to, and that's a pretty big slug for a little kid. Of course we have to be careful of an overdose—too much medication makes them a vegetable."

CIBA's more blatant promotional activities and the concomitant spread in the use of stimulant drugs on children have generated a series of reactions from government agencies. In 1970 the U.S. Food and Drug Administration ordered the pharmaceutical companies to stop using "functional behavior disorder" as an indicated syndrome for the drugs—the substitute was "minimal brain dysfunction," which would later also be dropped; in 1971, CIBA was told to stop promoting Ritalin directly to the public (there would be no more pushers at the PTA); and in 1972 Ritalin was put on the government's schedule for "hard narcotics," which imposes greater restrictions in labeling and marketing. (FDA had discovered, among other things, that Ritalin was being dissolved and shot up by junkies to stretch their heroin highs or to add a kick to their Methadone.) In the meantime, a Congressional committee headed by Representative Cornelius Gallagher of New Jersey conducted hearings on the use of pediatric stimulants in the course of which HEW officials stoutly defended the safety and effectiveness of the drugs and cited Conners as a model scientist who guarded against bias and conducted "objective" studies.[50] The hearings nonetheless prompted HEW's Office of Child Development to establish a "blue ribbon panel" to consider the matter and to "inform educators that perhaps it is as much of a problem of the kind of schoolroom children have to adjust to" as it was a problem of faulty neurology. Five months later, the 15–member panel, headed by Daniel X. Freedman, a psychopharmacologist and chairman of the Psychiatry Department at the University of Chicago, issued a report so even-handed in its generalizations that it was possible to quote it in support of any position. The panel had done no independent investigation of practices in doctors' offices and schools around the country, relying entirely on existing studies and information. Its strongest statement was a recommendation that pharmaceutical companies promote stimulants ethically and only through medical channels.[51] The report, said two researchers who reviewed it, "managed to arrive at two fundamentally opposite sets of findings, neither of which contained anything that was not already known." In a subsequent interview Freedman said he was concerned about "the pill pushers in the jungles of America" but what was really required was more complete information on "patient management." Physicians, he said, had to be trusted to make their own decisions.

It was all too little too late. Despite the imposition of the FDA restrictions, the sale of Ritalin continued to climb. Placing the drug on the hard-narcotics schedule meant, among other things, that prescriptions could no longer be refilled; each new purchase required a new prescription. As a consequence, many physicians began to write larger prescriptions and the company began to market the pills not only in batches of one hundred, but also in containers of five hundred and one thousand (more than a two-year supply for most children). Nor did the restrictions stop the literature circulated to doctors, the pamphlets on MBD distributed to parents, or the endless succession of meetings and conferences for physicians sponsored by the drug companies. In Sweden, public health authorities had banned the use of Ritalin altogether; it was regarded as too dangerous and too easy to abuse. But by 1974, Ritalin had become a household word in America.

IV

Late in 1974, a drug named Cylert became the latest and potentially the most important entry into the arsenal of psychostimulants. Abbott Laboratories, which makes it, describes Cylert (magnesium pemoline) as "a mild central nervous system stimulant . . . structurally dissimilar from the amphetamines, but [with] certain similar pharmacologic properties." In 1968 the company tried to get approval of the FDA to market Cylert as an antidepressant but failed. In 1969, Abbott tried again, this time labeling it as medication for MBD, and by late 1971 it had submitted the results of two studies purporting to demonstrate its safety and effectiveness. What followed provides some indication of how the small world of physicians, university scientists, pharmaceutical company executives and FDA officials operates in validating the drugs used on children.[52] The two studies were similar. Both had been designed by Keith Conners, and both were partly funded by Abbott. One was conducted at 21 clinics in different parts of the country, the other by Conners and his colleagues at Massachusetts General Hospital. (Eisenberg was listed as "principal investigator" in the Cylert study, but he never became a major participant.) Both studies concluded that Cylert produced "improvement" bordering on the phenomenal. Teachers, parents and psychologists who rated the Cylert-treated children before and after medication reported better behavior, increased ability to pay attention, and higher test scores. Children "treated" with a placebo also "improved" (as they almost always do in such tests) but not nearly as much as those on Cylert. The studies also concluded that the drug produced few significant negative side effects—"no hematologic, liver, kidney or cardiovascular effects," Conners wrote, "of consequence." Since the drug had poor solubility, moreover, it would be hard to shoot up. Cylert, it appeared, was on its way.[53]

Then an unexpected hitch developed. A fastidious FDA medical officer named Carol S. Kennedy began to turn up discrepancies in the studies. Among the documents Abbott submitted were reports by Conners—one just published in *Pediatrics,* the other about to be published in *Psychopharmacologia*—which stated, among other things, that the children tested did not have "severe neurotic, psychotic or neurologic symptoms, or history of family psychopathology sufficient to account for the current behavioral symptoms," that they were between six and twelve years old, and that the study, which spanned eight weeks (with a followup in the twelfth week, four weeks after medication was discontinued), included "medical evaluation on days 14, 28, 42 and 56 at which time weight, pulse, and blood pressure were recorded." Going through the raw data on which the reports were based, Kennedy found that no medical examinations were conducted on days 14 and 42; that 21 of the 84 children studied had "medical conditions which were inadequately investigated or which made them inappropriate for inclusion in the study"; that physical examination forms for four patients were signed prior to the date on which the examinations were conducted; that in a number of instances dosage appeared to have been changed by someone other than a physician; that six of the children tested were under six years of age; that many psychological report forms were undated; that in a number of instances school reports from teachers were not obtained for several weeks after the conclusion of the study, or not obtained at all; that although the Conners design for the study provided that all subjects have IQ scores above 80, several were below 80 on at least two scales, and one was below 80 on three; and that for 31 of the 84 children studied there were indications of "psychopathology in child/ family or environmental factors" significant enough to require their exclusion from the project.[54]

> The submitted study [Kennedy reported] is considered unacceptable by scientific standards operant within the past decade. The submitted study is of extremely poor quality, and published material contains obvious, gross distortion of the actual data. Nevertheless, this published material will no doubt be used for future reference by the Scientific Community. . . . This reviewer is compelled to consider any prior reference material as unacceptable without accompanying raw data for review and evaluation by FDA professional staff. . . . The study contained gross deficiencies with respect to both safety and efficacy.

Compared to the 21–clinic project, however, the Conners study appeared to be a model of scientific precision. Even before Abbott submitted the multiclinic results to FDA, the company's medical monitors had discarded 40 percent of the cases as unacceptable for procedural reasons; after FDA review, Carol Kennedy attacked the remainder as suffering from "gross deviations from the protocol," among them the inclusion of children with signs of "gross psychopathology, gross environmental factors, congenital heart disease, . . . significant hearing loss, visual loss" and other departures from a study design which required the exclusion of subjects whose behavior or learning problems could be attributed to physical, emotional or social factors. (Among them were children with alcoholic fathers, fathers in prison and mothers who had recently been deserted; children who had been in a succession of foster homes; and children who were regularly beaten by parents.[56]) Kennedy also found cases where the person recording clinical side effects—supposedly a medically trained professional looking for weight loss, liver damage or other medical conditions—was comically unfamiliar with common practice: side effects recorded included "starting to learn," "careless," "cooperative," "cleaned room first time," "fine things" and "super." In addition, she found scores of cases for which clinical report forms were missing or undated, at least one where medical tests indicated that the child was an epileptic whose health, in Kennedy's opinion, could have been jeopardized by the drug, and at least one where the investigator discovered that the child had been flushing his pills down the toilet. (There was no way to know how many others were not discovered; some were supposed to take nine a day.) She also informed her FDA superiors that the "hyperkinetic index" by which children were rated "consists of ten items which are totally nonspecific and could include almost every type of child" ("excitable, impulsive," "is not learning," "restless, in the 'squirmy' sense," "childish and immature"). Equally important, she raised serious questions about whether the safety of the drug—particularly as it affected blood and liver—had been demonstrated, and she cited separate reviews by an FDA pharmacologist and two staff chemists raising additional questions about possible drug dependency. The Cylert application, she concluded, was "nonapprovable," and by June 6, 1972, she had drafted a letter to notify the company. "This medical officer," she would say later, "cannot condone such [research] practices, and it is the obligation of the FDA to assure that future studies with investigational drugs used in children meet scientific standards and avoid unnecessary hazards to the patient populations."[56]

Two weeks after the draft was written—the letter had not been officially transmitted to the company—Abbott submitted a reply. In 1970, said the firm, Abbott had been informed that its study design was "excellent." "Because of the history of close cooperation . . . we were taken by complete surprise by the reversal of position on FDA's part." The company declared that it was prepared to submit "additional drug dependence studies, consolidation of the information on liver enzyme findings [and] data on heights and ophthalmologic examinations in patients receiving [Cylert] over prolonged periods of time." The reply was buttressed by letters from eight authorities, among them Conners, Eisenberg and several Abbott consultants endorsing the design of one or both studies. "There are no more objective procedures," wrote Donald F. Klein, a member of the Psychiatry Department at Long Island Jewish–Hillside Medical Center in Glen Oaks, New York, and another prolific experimenter in pediatric psychopharmacology. Klein, it happened, was simultaneously a consultant in neuropharmacology to the FDA, a member of the Clinical Psychopharmacology Research Review Committee at the National Institute of Mental Health, and a paid consultant to Abbott. The most interesting endorsement, however, came from Abbott consultant Harry C. Shirkey, chairman of the pediatrics department at Tulane University Medical School. "Continuing long-term evaluation will be best after [Cylert's] release," he said, "since the drug would be denied for use in the meantime. Its effects on growth and development, its effect on puberty and sexual development . . . will be better understood with wider use."[57]

By July, the pressure was on. The company, according to an FDA rumor, had invested some $4 million in the Cylert project, and it wasn't about to lose it. "I was never told to change my findings," Kennedy said later. "It was just a matter of having to justify them over and over again. They kept saying 'we hope you're going to play the game.' " In the face of the pressure—and partly in response to Kennedy's suggestion—FDA appointed an outside committee to rereview the Cylert data and to draw guidelines for future studies in pediatric psychopharmacology: Gerald Solomons, a professor of pediatrics at the University of Iowa and director of the University's Child Development Clinic; Eric Denhoff, a pediatric neurologist in Providence who was once Solomons' research colleague; and Roger D. Freeman, a child psychiatrist at the University of British Columbia. All three had extensive experience in the use of stimulant drugs in children—at least one, Denhoff, was nationally known as an advocate of such medication—and all knew Conners and respected his work. In reviewing the raw data, however, they had come to agree with Kennedy's conclusions, and they arrived in Washington with slides summarizing what they regarded as the deficiencies in the individual cases. They had also prepared a report which concluded that "the drug lacks substantial evidence of safety and efficacy and cannot be approved because of the overwhelming deficiencies in the studies. . . . It is strongly advised that the data in these studies relating to clinical safety and efficacy be considered unacceptable in any future submission."[58] They were, in effect, telling the FDA to tell Abbott to start all over.

In September 1972 they met with officials of the FDA and with representatives of the company. The Abbott delegation included Klein, Conners and Paul Wender, who was then a half-time employee of the National Institute of Mental Health, three researchers who had participated in the multiclinic study, and three senior officials of the company. Conners acknowledged some discrepancies; they appeared, he said, in "a preliminary report" and would be corrected in subsequent documents. "You can lock yourself into a meaningless procedure at the beginning of a study . . . but it may be in the course of the study you decide that some aspect of this is totally infeasible." What he had reported about the medical examinations was what he had first intended to do, not what he did. Conners also said that some of the missing case reports had been submitted to Abbott which, he suggested, had neglected to send them to FDA. Such oversights, however, did not affect the final results; those "by any standard are clearcut."[59]

Conners and Abbott subsequently submitted detailed rebuttals to the Solomons committee review. Both acknowledged certain errors and omissions "clerical error by the physician . . . administrative errors . . . dating error . . . omission of psychometric testing materials . . . improperly coded . . . preliminary report"—but both stoutly defended the results. In the case of the multiclinic project, said Abbott, "the protocol required that the investigator make a judgment that the degree of family psychopathology was not sufficient to account for the child's behavior problem." In the case of his own project, said Conners, the study design was revised to eliminate medical tests at days 14 and 42—"the paper was in error"; followup physical examinations were done, though they "were not recorded until recording forms were supplied by the drug company"; a physician directed all changes of medication; and the five-year-old children tested in the study would not be included in the final analysis.[60]

On November 21, despite the rebuttals, the Cylert application was formally rejected, but by early February FDA began to reconsider. "There is considerable uncertainty," said Elmer Gardner, then head of FDA's Neuropharmacology Division, "as to whether the conclusions of the clinical studies described in our nonapprovable letter could be sustained if challenged in a court hearing." The report of the Solomons group had been written "in an openly antagonistic tone" and Gardner wanted "a completely fresh look at this application."[61] There was "no saber rattling pressure," an FDA official said later, "but we were aware that Abbott had some thought of some legal protest." By March, without precedent, a new outside review committee had been appointed, and by summer Carol Kennedy, who had worked on Cylert for more than a year, found herself studying soft contact lenses. "That crazy lady," said a member of the Conners team. "They finally got rid of her."

The fresh look, lasting eighteen months, is still shrouded in mystery. The new committee, headed by Daniel X. Freedman, the University of Chicago psychiatrist who headed HEW's "blue ribbon" panel in 1971, reported that "there is some evidence, though not conclusive evidence, that Cylert is effective over a period of eight weeks." The committee defended the Conners study ("no evidence . . . of negligence"), chastised the "sharp adversary tone" of the Solomons report, and dismissed the multiclinic study: its execution, said the committee, "renders it uninterpretable as a controlled study."[62] (A year later, five individual Abbott officials would publish the results as a scientific paper in the *Journal of Learning Disabilities.*[63]) Despite that qualified blessing, however, the Freedman panel recommended "longer term controlled studies . . . before marketing approval of this drug." A member of the committee said later that they regarded the Conners study as "above average" for the field; the average study, he explained, was "abysmal."

With the submission of the Freedman report in March 1973, the fog thickened. The committee never met again— Freedman was sick of the whole FDA routine—but three of its members continued as an "ad hoc panel" to FDA's Neuropharmacology Advisory Committee. They were delegated to make a "site visit" to Conners' establishment and to review the "longer term controlled studies" and other supplemental data submitted by Abbott.

According to FDA records, that data included information on "a total of 511 individual patients [who] had received Cylert including 314 who received long-term treatment for an average period of about one year."[64] Conners said he had given Abbott information on sixteen or eighteen long-term followups, and one physician-reviewer (all of whom are pledged to secrecy by FDA) said Abbott had submitted data from studies other than those reviewed by Kennedy. But the bulk of the cases, perhaps as many as 200 of the 314, came from the unanimously rejected multiclinic study. Its rejection, the physician-reviewer explained, went primarily to the issue of efficacy. On the issue of safety, the medical people who couldn't tell a drug side effect from a kid who "cleaned room first time" were apparently considered reliable.

In the spring of 1974, FDA held a series of meetings with its Neuropharmacology Advisory Committee, the "ad hoc panel," and other consultants to review the Cylert case. The chairman of the committee was Gerald Klerman of the Department of Psychiatry at Massachusetts General Hospital, where the Conners study was done and where Eisenberg was chief psychiatrist; its members included Jerome Levine, head of the Psychopharmacology Branch at NIMH, which (with Abbott) financed the study; and the consultants included Abbott consultant Donald Klein (who said he left the room whenever Cylert was discussed, though the minutes of the meeting do not show that). Both Klein and Robert L. Sprague, one of the three members of the Cylert ad hoc panel, had attended an Abbott conference in Key Biscayne, Florida, in March 1972 on the general use of drugs in treating MBD and on Cylert in particular. The conference included most of the twenty-one multiclinic Cylert investigators, a number of other drug researchers and two government officials (whose expenses were paid by the government). Sprague, who heads the Children's Research Center at the University of Illinois, said such meetings are "a common type of thing. . . . Some areas are so specialized that there are only a few people in the country who are knowledgeable, and they all know each other." In this particular case, he said, "Abbott didn't even pay all of my bill." No pressure, he said, was ever applied. What companies like Abbott and CIBA got out of such meetings was some expertise and, in some cases, a series of papers that they could publish under their aegis. Many people, moreover, consulted for more than one firm; for the companies to object would be self-defeating since there were so few knowledgeable people to go around.[65]

It is not clear what Sprague and his colleagues reported, what the Advisory Committee discussed or what the data showed. One reviewer said Abbott had submitted enough data to indicate "reasonable safety," particularly on the question of effects which may not show up until puberty, and Conners said his followup produced nothing to change his original conclusion that Cylert produced "no hematologic, liver, kidney or cardiovascular effects of consequence." A number of children, he said, showed temporary weight loss or suffered a few nights of sleeplessness, but nearly all got over it. But at least one consulting physician who attended the discussions of the Advisory Committee wasn't persuaded. The Conners statement, she said later, "is simply inadequate. One case is enough to raise concern, and the studies were poorly designed to allay such concern." It was her impression that "all these people were paid drug company consultants in harmony with the general attitude of the FDA. They all go through this pretense that all people who do research are honorable." The burden was not on FDA to show potential danger but on the company to prove safety. That, she believed, had not been done.

In the end, they hedged, tossing the matter back to the FDA staff, which would make the final decision anyway. The ad hoc panel made a strong recommendation that approval be contingent on a systematic Abbott followup of efficacy and safety after Cylert went on the market, a sort of provisional license subject to further review. Few of them were enthusiastic about the studies but, as one of them said, "there's been a rapid change in what's acceptable" and there was no point in penalizing the researchers or the company for operating by the standards of the time when the studies were done. Diagnosing and treating children with learning disabilities or suffering from hyperkinesis, they agreed, was a complex business, and designing adequate studies was more complicated still. Yet not one of them suggested that perhaps the whole business was unnecessary, that in most cases all the "ailments" they were trying to treat were nothing more than behavior that some adult didn't like. "Knowledgeable people" in the field were not necessarily wedded to Abbott, but their field was Abbott's field, and Abbott's racket was their racket.

In late August 1974, the FDA notified Abbott that, subject to the usual formalities of drug classification and labeling, the application was "approvable." By that time Carol Kennedy had left FDA and Keith Conners was moving from Massachusetts General to the University of Pittsburgh where, he said, there was a better job. It was a good thing, he explained, because Massachusetts had passed a law regulating drug experiments with children which made his research "impossible." There were "all kinds of insane people running around" who were paranoid about the sort of work he was trying to do.

V

In the final analysis, all the controversies about efficacy, safety and side effects, though highly significant, tend to be misleading. They turn attention from social and political considerations to individual medical questions and therefore conceal the most fundamental issue. From a political and social perspective, the most dangerous psychoactive drug is precisely the one that is medically the safest and psychologically the most effective; preparations that produce psychotic hallucinations in certain patients or that impair growth in weight or stature are to some extent self-limiting. The most popular line of resistance against the prescription of amphetamine-type drugs is the argument that similar drugs are among the most abused in America, that while the government is throwing people in jail for using speed, other governmental institutions are pushing it on schoolchildren. But what of the drug which, in fact or belief, has few negative medical side effects but which nonetheless makes the patient-student-prisoner-citizen more docile and manageable? The question of dependency on such a drug quickly turns from a medical into a political question whose very definition involves not merely the psychological state of the patient but also the social and political impositions of the society and its institutions. The belief in "my magic pills that make me into a good boy" is, after all, a political as well as a personal statement in which institutional benevolence and the need for personal accommodation are taken for granted. In such a situation the search for medical evidence of dependency may be quite futile; in some sense, indeed, "dependency" may afflict even those who have never taken a drug but who are nonetheless forced to accommodate to standards which become legitimate and normative through drug management of those who challenge or threaten them. A few years ago, a writer named Charles Witter asked, rhetorically, "Are we putting the Dachau inside the pill and the pill inside the kid?" But as in all such questions of liberty, this one has implications for every member of the population, not merely those who are chemically incarcerated. The subtlety of the process in itself helps create the necessary effect: e.g., "I do not need magic pills to make me a good boy." It is the ideology of drugging, the idea that people can and should be chemically managed, that represents the most pervasive imposition on personal liberty and the most dangerous extension of authority. The seductive counterargument that a certain drug isn't hurting a certain child—that, indeed, it has made him "happier" and more successful—and that one should not sacrifice his well-being to some political abstraction, is itself a disguised political argument in defense of the standards that determine his "happiness" and success. The argument seems to prove that while the child may not become dependent on the drug, those who recommend and defend it already are.

*   *   *

Early in 1975, the FDA decided that MBD lacked sufficient medical foundation to be associated with the prescription of drugs. Henceforth "minimal brain dysfunction"
would be too vague to be used as the "disease" for which a
drug could be indicated. The symptoms on the package labels for Dexedrine, Ritalin and Cylert would be the forms of
behavior which once constituted the separate elements of the
MBD definition: short attention span, hyperactivity, impulsivity. It appeared to be an admission that unacceptable
behavior by itself was sufficient reason to feed a child a
psychoactive drug, that no organic illness need even be suggested. The decision went a long way toward legitimizing any
number of studies which never managed to define or diagnose hyperkinesis or MBD with precision (since they were
undefinable) but which were nonetheless "validated" by
teacher or parent reports of improved behavior. Judged by
such standards, the drugs clearly worked for a certain percentage of children: there was no shortage of positive reports,
and there would be no shortage of people suggesting or demanding medication, and no shortage of doctors or clinics
ready to prescribe. The objections about the lack of a defin-
able syndrome had been removed and, in the process, the last
pretense of medical "treatment" eliminated. The drugs were
placed openly, officially and legally into the realm of behavior control.

FOUR

Screening for Deviance
and Other Diseases

The Doyle School of Bucks County, Pennsylvania, passes
easily as a model for the most contemporary in suburban
glass-and-brick education, with its pastel-painted interior
walls, its "resource centers," its bright displays, and its shiny
blond All-American children working at their equally shiny
and blond janitor-polished tables. Doyle is the kind of place
where mothers drop their children on the way to the tennis
club, where neither the furniture nor the students are
screwed down and where the movement of children from one
activity to another generates a steady hum in classrooms and
corridors. It is also the sort of place where the principal, a
burly, crew-cut ex-Marine-type named Donald R. McClintock, wanders frequently through the corridors greeting children by name and asking them how they are getting along.
The Doyle School and many of the other schools in the
county are marching cheerfully into the twenty-first century,
taking their teachers and pupils with them.

Beneath the facade of modernity, there is substance, a
program of "teaching strategies" based on "diagnostic edu-

cational grouping" (DEG) of all children into three categories—"oedipally conflicted," "developmentally arrested" and "ego disturbed,"—lately abbreviated to OC, DA and ED, or just plain groups I, II and III.[1] The groups are selected on the basis of a twelve-item questionnaire which each teacher completes annually about each pupil in her class:

01. Much of the time child appears
    1. Shy
    2. Immature
    3. Strange
    4. None of these

02. In general the child makes me feel
    1. Happy with him
    2. Angry or frustrated with him
    3. Sorry and a little frightened for him
    4. None of these

03. When the child talks his expression is
    1. Easily understood
    2. Immature
    3. Difficult to follow
    4. None of these

04. Child requires
    1. An average amount of attention
    2. More individual attention than usual
    3. Too much individual attention
    4. None of these

05. The child often appears
    1. Involved successfully or trying hard
    2. Restless
    3. Often in his own world
    4. None of these

06. With other children, the child is
    1. Liked or creates no problem
    2. Often in conflict
    3. Set apart
    4. None of these

07. Much of the time the child's behavior is
    1. Pleasant and likeable
    2. Stubborn and defiant
    3. Clingingly dependent
    4. None of these

08. Muscle coordination is
    1. Adequate
    2. A little uneven
    3. Poor
    4. None of these

09. Emotional growth and development is
    1. Forward and progressive
    2. Standing still
    3. Slipping backward
    4. None of these

10. Human figure drawings are
    1. Age adequate
    2. Immature
    3. Strange
    4. None of these

11. Success in school work
    1. Usual
    2. Erratic
    3. Infrequent
    4. None of these

12. Parents are
    1. Interested and concerned
    2. Defensive and overconcerned
    3. Disinterested or limited
    4. None of these

The questionnaires are fed into a computer which scores them and prints out lists of the children "in terms of their diagnostic group" for each classroom teacher, gymnasium teacher, school counselor and administrator. (They can also be hand-scored in a matter of minutes: Group I requires nine or more #1 responses; Group III requires five or more #3 responses, and Group II is everything else.) Typically, 60 to 70 percent of the pupils will be classed as Group I "oedipaliy conflicted" ("the healthiest stage of personality development"), 25 percent as Group II "developmentally arrested" ("an immature stage of personality development") and 5 percent as Group III "ego disturbed" ("the most troubled forms of personality disturbance").

In a mimeographed book, the teachers are provided with "teaching strategies for each group" which suggest, in summary, that Group I children do not require "repetitive drill of materials that they obviously know" and that "individual and joint projects usually produce positive results"; that Group II children do require drill and repetition, that they should be assigned structured tasks "that will end in success," and that they should not be required to do too much; and that Group III children are likely to have limited academic success, that their work "should initially be completely teacher directed," and that anything likely to end in failure should be scrupulously avoided. Although Group III children are automatically referred for psychological counseling, teachers are told that they "should not be ignored or rejected as an impossible task of teaching." The teachers are also told to arrange seating in such a way as to place children from Groups II and III near the teacher (they "need frequent physical, verbal, eye and voice contact with the teacher") or to surround them with Group I children, "who have much better control of themselves." Most emphatically, however, the teachers are urged to know which child belongs in which category, and not to expect too much from the developmentally arrested or the ego disturbed. What the teachers do in the classroom is hardly distinguishable from most other classes in other schools, but here, at least, they will have "scientific" explanations for the problems some children seem to have with learning or behavior. They have the kids screwed down in their heads.

McClintock wanders the corridors. "By the time the kids are through kindergarten," he says, "we've had them screened with the Gesell, done the DEG, the Metropolitans, the Detroit or the ITPA, and done maybe a followup on the Gesell." Like millions of their peers, they have, in other words, been screened, tested and assessed by a battery of instruments purporting to measure motor, social and personal development (the Gesell), linguistic development, visual and auditory "decoding" processes (the ITPA), intelligence, emotional stability and a spectrum of other factors. But in Bucks County, the most important criterion is the DEG itself. "We have all the science we need," said Joseph S. Tezza, the system's coordinator to Special Pupil Services, "but we avoid white-coatism; we try to put it all into teacher's language. The idea was to collect as much information as we could about how children grow—how, how, how—and then put it in a form that the teacher could handle." The teacher, said Tezza, "really uses this in her head"; it is a way not only of sensitizing her to the needs of her pupils but also of keeping track of those teachers who tend to give too many pupils low ratings on the questionnaire. They are all scoring one another, and the printouts—with pupils' names, diagnoses and other data—circulate around the school. It is only the parents and the children who are never informed that their schools have taken over Freud, translated him into pedagogics, and used the result to classify and label their clients. The DEG diagnosis will follow the child into high school, and perhaps beyond.

DEG was first developed in Bucks County in the late sixties by a team headed by Dr. William Stennis, a psychiatrist who was then practicing in the area and who served as a consultant to the schools. At its base there is a peculiar mix of elementary Freudian theory, folklore and social bias: homilies about bed wetting, "school phobia" ("a child's reluctance to come to school"), "personal hygiene," the role of parents, and "normal" development of sexual identity (e.g., girls play with dolls and become "mother's helper"). Teachers are told that "educationally" children "seem to thrive best when sexual roles are carefully assigned" and when the teacher "fosters competition with their peers," that Group I children usually come from happy, stable homes, and that most behavior problems come from Group II. Although Tezza said the school system is playing down the psychoanalytic language, it survives in a discussion of "general principles of child development" which is given every teacher as part of the "strategies" manual. In that document they learn, among other things, about the oral stage, the anal stage, the oedipal stage, the latency stage, and the characteristics of adolescence. It is vintage Freud.

Stennis regards DEG as an all-purpose screen for "children who are vulnerable to possible failure in life." He is convinced of the scientific soundness of the method, despite the fact that it has never been tested with any control groups, lacks longitudinal validation, employs totally subjective criteria, and offers only the vaguest of prescriptions and "strategies" to deal with the categories established. He is quite sensitive to the dangers of labeling, and has himself warned against it, and that is why he believes that any system must have "progressive or regressive linearity built into its design," giving each child the chance to move from one category to another. The fact that these categories are determined by the statements of one teacher, sanctified by computer processing and then returned to the same teacher as a scientific conclusion does not seem to trouble him. The important thing is to screen and diagnose early; society has only a few years—at most until a child reaches puberty—to deal with his problems. Thereafter the turmoil of adolescence makes intervention too difficult.

I I

The screens and tests proliferate: tests of cognition, intelligence, emotional development, hearing, vision, speech, language, gross and fine motor skills, tests to be used by pediatricians and psychiatrists, tests for teachers, tests for parents, tests in classrooms, gymnasiums and clinics, the Denver Developmental Screening Test, the Gesell Infant Scales, the Stanford-Binet, the Wechsler Preschool and Primary Scale of Intelligence, the Illinois Test of Psycholinguistic Abilities (ITPA), the Frostig Test of Visual Perception, the Peabody Picture Vocabulary Test, the Southern California Perceptual Motor Tests, the Bailey Infant Scales of Mental and Motor Development, the Development Screening Inventory for Infants, the Catell Infant Intelligence Scale, the Classroom Screening Instrument for Tentative Identification of Children With Individual Learning Disabilities, and scores of others, all of them advertised for use on infants and young children.[2] Very few American children begin school without exposure to some combination of these tests, and many are now being systematically screened by schools, state health departments, community clinics or private physicians by the time they are four. For an increasing number (and for nearly all those who are being screened with the support of public funds), the results of these screens—medical, dental and psychological—are being stored in centralized data banks maintained by the states or by local public health agencies.[3]

The pressure has been building since 1967 when Congress amended the Social Security Act to require states to provide screening, diagnostic services, and appropriate treatment to all children eligible for Medicaid. The screening is to include batteries of examinations for medical and dental problems, assessments of development and physical growth, immunization, and tests for politically fashionable conditions such as lead poisoning and sickle cell trait. The federal guidelines also require the maintenance of individual health care records for each child; those records will be available to the U.S. Department of Health, Education and Welfare "to evaluate the costs and effects of this program."[4]

Pursuant to the legislation, the states have been instituting screening programs designed to meet (and sometimes to exceed) the federal regulations. In the spring of 1974, to give an example of what is becoming a national program, the state of Illinois began to operate Medichek, a state-wide screening program conducted through local physicians and clinics which, it is hoped, will eventually serve all of the 560,000 Medicaid-eligible children in the state. (All, needless to say, are from low-income families.) Medichek includes "periodic assessment of health status, immunizations, anticipatory guidance and counseling, and screening tests for vision, hearing, intellectual development and for specific diseases where indicated."[5] The screens and services will also cover major behavioral and psychological problems for all clients from the time of birth. (The state hopes that each newborn can be assigned a social security number to simplify record maintenance. They will be numbered before they are named.) Like all other data, behavioral and psychological elements will be entered on the child's individual record and stored in a central computer maintained by the Illinois Department of Public Health. The computer will be used to follow up on individual cases, even when they move from place to place and from clinic to clinic. Meanwhile, a similar, though more comprehensive, program is being established in California. Where Medichek is entirely voluntary, however, the state of California will require "that each child, upon enrollment in the first grade, present satisfactory evidence . . . that he has received specified health screening and evaluation services within the prior two years, unless the child's parents or guardian has given written notice . . . that they do not want their child to receive such services."[6] All children under six are covered, the rich as well as the poor. Each county must provide, as a minimum, screening that includes "a health development history; an assessment of physical growth; a developmental assessment; an inspection for obvious physical defects; ear, nose, mouth and throat inspection, including inspection of teeth and gums; screening tests for vision, hearing, cardiac abnormalities, anemia, tuberculosis, diabetes . . . ; an assessment of nutritional status" and tests, where appropriate, for sickle cell trait, lead poisoning and other conditions. The results of these tests will be recorded in individual case histories for each child. Although some states have been slow to develop plans, all are likely to comply with the federal guidelines by 1975 or 1976. In the summer of 1974, Congress put teeth into the regulations with a bill that will withhold certain funds from any state that does not offer comprehensive screening and treatment to eligible children.[7] Operating alongside the medical screens is a proliferating and often redundant set of state programs which mandate the periodic screening of all public school children. Their ostensible purpose is to identify every conceivable sort of educational "handicap" and to place children in appropriate programs. By early 1975, more than 30 states, under pressure from the federal government (which has threatened to make funds for the handicapped contingent on screening), had passed laws requiring local school districts to conduct such tests. In most they cover not only the familiar categories ("learning disabled," MBD, "emotionally handicapped," "visually handicapped") but also include scales rating children for "impulse control," "intellectuality," "withdrawal" and "social behavior." The specific applications and consequences of those tests vary from state to state, but the objectives are similar. There is money for special education, for the handicapped and for other categories of disability (real or imagined): the more clients a system can create for such programs, the more special funds it can claim from state and federal agencies. The financial incentives are reinforced by institutional pressures within the schools themselves—demands from teachers that they be rid of difficult children, requests for extra help, the covert effects of racism and social bias, and the pressure of a series of federal court decisions making it far more difficult to arbitrarily expel or suspend children. No one knows how many children have been assigned to special classes as a result of those screens or how many have been properly placed. What is certain is that since the end of the sixties, the number of special education programs, including LD classes, has mushroomed, that available funds have tripled, and that, given the vagueness of the proliferating categories and the lack of effective techniques for remediation, there is no conceivable way that most of the screens can lead to proper placements. In Washington, court-ordered testing of "special" track children revealed that two-thirds had been mislabeled and misplaced and should have been in regular classes. Similar results have been reported in Philadelphia, San Francisco and other cities. Most of the victims of those misplacements have been children of minority groups, but many are not. Some have been returned to regular programs as a result of new tests, but for most, segregation in special programs tends to be a self-validating, one-way process from which there is no return. Once the placement is made, and once the label is attached, both are usually permanent.

The children, all four-year-olds, are meeting school for the first time. The place is a gymnasium in Muncie, Indiana, but it could as easily be suburban Cleveland, rural Illinois, Boise, Colorado Springs or New Orleans. The mothers turn the children over to a squad of clinicians and paraprofessional aides who will lead them through a labyrinth of screening stations, a bazaar of scales, instruments and exercises which will occupy more than three hours of each child's time. Forms are filled, notes taken, folders stuffed, tests administered: VMI, Frostig, ITPA, WISC, WRAT, Bender, Hooper, tests to uncover dyslexia, dyscalculia, aphasia, distractibility, mixed dominance, dyspractic movement, developmental lag, CNS damage, MBD. The mothers, in the meantime, are going through another set of questions, relating family social and medical histories to counselors, nurses, teachers and learning clinicians. At what age did the child walk? When was he weaned? Any particular problems during pregnancy or birth? Is the child aggressive or irritable? Are there discipline problems in the home? Does the child have problems falling asleep? Are there eating problems, bed-wetting problems, problems making friends, speech problems, problems of sucking, chewing or picking? It is all recorded, scored and

filed—a set of clues interpreted by varying standards—and
it will all become part of the record, may lead to additional
diagnoses, and will be used (presumably) to understand the
child, to place him in school, to arrange suitable instruction
or "remediation," and, where the screeners deem necessary,
to refer the child for pediatric, psychiatric or neurological
treatment.

Occasionally the screens catch a serious problem in a distinct medical area—a subtle defect in hearing or vision, for
example—and if the child is fortunate he will get the appropriate treatment, the right teacher, the perfect program. It is
equally likely, however, that he will get little or nothing, or
worse than nothing, a set of ambiguous labels, vaguely medical, vaguely pedagogical, which point to no remedial disease
but which will nonetheless get him assigned to a class for
children with learning disabilities, or a program for "exceptional children" from which he will never return, or to a
teacher who will use the label to "understand" the child's
inability to learn the things she is supposed to teach him, or
to a segregated cubicle within the regular class—a box to
prevent the child from seeing other children, and therefore
to "protect" him from distractions. Does he show mixed
dominance (i.e., does he sometimes favor the left hand, or the
left foot, and sometimes the right)? Did his mother report a
difficult birth, or was he underweight when he was born? Is
he shy, attention seeking, jealous, clumsy, hypersensitive,
hyperactive, temperamental, overaggressive, twitchy, jerky,
compulsive or easily distractible, or does he twist his hair
with his fingers, play constantly with his genitals, chew his
nails or wet his bed? Does he have trouble drawing certain
shapes or piling nine blocks or assembling a puzzle? All these
things are signs of trouble—serious, casual or negligible depending on interpretation, test construction, program and
current fashion—but in certain combinations they are almost
sure to lead to the conclusion that the child is emotionally
disturbed, learning disabled, antisocial, or all three. The
child showing mixed dominance and high verbal ability will

probably be placed in a class for normal children; the child showing mixed dominance without such verbal ability is headed for segregation with the learning disabled. He will rarely have a chance to prove himself in an ordinary kindergarten, and his chances of returning to a regular program are probably about fifty-fifty. Because the same characteristics which lead to the conclusion that a child is mentally retarded in one school will produce assessments of "learning disabled" in another, the screens and tests are defended as a way of preventing the stigma of an inaccurate assessment of "retarded." In practice, however, the label "learning disabled" often leads to the same thing: placement in a special class.[8]

In theory, screening and diagnosis are distinct, and the clinicians warn that the first should not be confused with the second. "Screening tests," said the developer of one major instrument, "are not intended to make diagnoses nor are they intended as substitutes for complete health appraisals; instead they are intended as a method of surveying a large population of asymptomatic individuals in order to identify those individuals who have high probability of harboring the particular disease under study."[9] (Among the more popular analogies is one which compares screening to the sorting of oranges: "The extraordinarily large . . . oranges can then be subjected to careful analysis—diagnosis—in terms of the causes and prevention of their oversizeness, assuming that they are undesirable for marketing, packaging and other reasons."[10]) Despite such caveats, however, it is usually the screen and not the individual diagnosis, if any, which produces the label, the school placement and the corresponding assumption of scientific accuracy. The burden therefore falls on the accuracy and validity of the test, the interpretation of the clinician, and the categories established by the system for "marketing, packaging, and other reasons." In Muncie every child is defined as learning disabled, each individual, presumably, has some problem; in Bucks County, the pseudo-psychoanalytic categories divide the population into three unequal parts ranging from more or less normal to seriously disturbed. But in most systems the children are divided between the "normal" and the "exceptional," meaning those with problems; the "exceptional" group is then further subdivided according to the categories, programs, budgets and theories of the particular system, and according to the categories which the tests themselves purport to define.

The growing number of systematic preschool programs represent only a fraction of the cognitive, behavioral and psychological screening of children proliferating through schools, clinics, prisons and hospitals, and account for no more than a small part of a commercial market loaded with tests and instruments for counselors, teachers, parents or anyone else, trained or untrained, who cares to buy and use them. Most of the tests involve some combination of exercises for the child being screened (hops, skips, jumps; figures to draw, puzzles to assemble, words to spell or copy) and a list of check-off items dealing with the subject's ordinary behavior. (Is he shy or withdrawn? Average, moderate, severe. Does he transpose sounds in words, say "nabana" instead of "banana"? Is his handwriting poor in comparison to that of his peers? Does he cry easily or for no apparent reason? Does he show excessive affection toward peers or adults in the school? Does he hold his book too close?) It is impossible to describe or assess even a portion of them, although each is advertised on the basis of statistical "validation" with groups of various sizes, and often comes with varying degrees of endorsement from the leaders in the disabilities area. As often as not, however, the validation rests on a tautological demonstration that the test agrees with the classroom assessments of teachers, or that it is consistent with other tests, or that it is more or less accurate in predicting future performance on a similar test.

One of the most successful and reputable instruments developed in the past decade is the Individual Learning Disabilities Classroom Screening Instrument (ILDCSI), which is selling so fast, not only in the United States but also in Australia, that the publishers claim that they have a hard time keeping up with the demand.[11] ILDCSI is designed for classroom teachers to examine children for "high risk or multiple learning disabilities," "auditory perception disability," "motor development," "social emotional involvement" and a number of similar categories. The manual accompanying the screen recommends general forms of remediation for children scoring above a certain level and suggests psychological or medical intervention for those at the top of the scale.[12] ILDCSI was first developed in 1967 by a team under John H. Meier, an educational psychologist and ex-seminarian who was then on the staff of the Rocky Mountain Educational Laboratory and who subsequently became director of the John F. Kennedy Child Development Center at the University of Colorado Medical School. The test, however, was never validated in any study using controls or in any longitudinal followup, raising at least the possibility that the screen will identify almost anyone as learning disabled, socially or emotionally disturbed or otherwise handicapped and that it will miss children not identified by teachers as having problems (perhaps because they are not causing trouble in class). Equally revealing is the fact that although the test was developed and tried on second grade children, it has since been adapted by Marian T. Giles of the University of Northern Colorado, a former colleague of Meier, for three different levels covering the entire spectrum of elementary and secondary schooling: preschool and kindergarten; grades one through three; and grades four through twelve (i.e., children anywhere from nine to eighteen years of age). The validation for the preschool test was based on one sampling of 23 children in one school; the validation for the "adolescent level" screen was based on a study of 10 children selected from two classes taught by the same teacher. There were no controls, and the teachers who selected the children as disabled were also the ones who filled out the screening instrument for the children they selected.[13] The published manuals sold with the screen point out that more research is required;

they also quote Meier's statistically dubious finding that 95 percent of the children identified as learning disabled in the original study were diagnosed for "organic brain syndrome." Despite those deficiencies, the tests are thriving on the commercial market, they are being advertised in educational journals, and they are being used on thousands of children. In a special issue of the *Psychopharmacology Bulletin,* published by the National Institute of Mental Health in 1973, C. Keith Conners, the drug expert, cited the Meier screen as "the best of its kind known to this writer." A validity study, he said, "showed that *the screening produced no false positives and very few false negatives.* "[14] (Italics in the original.) In fact, there was no such validity study. Meier readily conceded in an interview that the validation was weak, that there were "a lot of contaminants" in the research, that there was no longitudinal followup (and therefore no way to know whether there were false positives) and no controls in "the classical sense." The screen, Meier said, was founded on hypotheses about the relationship of motor-perceptual skills to reading ability which have since been discredited. Despite those shortcomings, ILDCSI is regarded as a model of validation. Most of the tests on the market have little or none.

One would imagine that the shortcomings of the screens used on children would be mitigated by the subsequent diagnosis of individual disabilities identified by the test. In the majority of cases, however, there is no separate diagnosis, no followup, and, with the exception of psychoactive medication, no medical treatment. The screen itself is used to place the child in school and determine his "needs." The decision is managerial, not therapeutic. Equally significant: even in those instances where a child identified as "learning disabled" or hyperactive or socially maladjusted is subjected to further diagnosis and "treatment," the diagnosis, founded on the same premises as the screen, may simply compound the problem. One can treat poor vision or hearing, or infection or malnutrition, but how does one cure a child who can't get along with his teacher?

The model diagnosis of a learning-disabled child, reported with great pride by Eric Denhoff, one of the leaders in the field, and by Lester Tarnopol, the author of a commonly used text, concerns an attractive and highly intelligent child named Roy whose only flaw seemed to be his inability to read as his second grade teacher thought he should.[15] Roy was seven at the beginning of the case study, eleven at the end. In the interim, squadrons of doctors, psychologists, learning experts and various kinds of specialists subjected Roy to four years of tests and examinations; they placed him in special classes, subjected him to high doses of psychoactive drugs (a daily 40 milligrams of Ritalin), sent him to summer school camp, gave him two years of psychotherapy, counseled his parents, and then concluded:

> The future of this boy is still questionable in spite of the hopes held out by a faculty of earnest, well-meaning professionals running a full-time school. Hopefully their offer to accept this boy will help solve the problem, but we are not in a position to guess the future.

Nowhere in the extended report of the case is there any assessment of the boy's teachers or his schools; there is considerable speculation, however, about "organicity," "hyperkinetic syndrome," "a multiplicity of problems in the learning process," "visual-perceptual, visual-motor, and auditory difficulties," as well as a number of other conditions, among them the observation that (after two years of treatment) "at home he is a problem; he seems to be stubborn and asserts a lot of independence." As the prime illustration of that independence, "his mother cited . . . the time that he had refused to go to catechism."

What the diagnoses and interventions seemed to accomplish was a marked reduction in Roy's tested ability, including what the authors call "a remarkable drop in verbal ability" and which they describe as "a classic example of what happens to the child with an untreated perceptual-motor disorder." His verbal IQ score had dropped from 129 to 97, his overall IQ from 138 to 117. (This is not to say that those scores are reliable or revealing, but since the initial IQ test results were among the elements that supported the conclusion that Roy's intelligence exceeded his class performance, and that consequently confirmed the "disabled" designation, they indicate that either the premise or the conclusion was shaky.) The authors explain that "we have frequently observed a massive drop in verbal IQ in children who do not learn to read," an observation that leads to any number of questions never raised in Roy's diagnosis and treatment. The authors go on to attribute their failures in the case to the fact "that we were not originally sufficiently influenced by the organic aspects of the case, particularly because of the psychologist's psychodynamic orientation and the benign report of our visual-perceptual expert."[16] They had been misled by their own specialists, and in the process they had reduced Roy from what appeared to be an unusually bright boy to an ordinary problem.

Beneath the circular logic of "validation" and medical mythmaking lies an unquestioning acceptance of the criteria of the institutions on whose behalf the selections are made. The common assumption that teachers are reliable predictors of classroom performance, including the ability of the individual child to learn, may well be correct; it is the same teacher, after all, or his colleagues, who will do the teaching, give out the grades, determine promotions and assess behavior.[17] Yet the assessments often seem to say more about the tolerance and attitudes of teachers than they do about the disease of the child. The following is from the official record for Steven, a boy enrolled in a suburban California school. The comments are complete and unedited:[18]

> *Kindergarten teacher:* Steven is rather immature. Has social problems—keeping hands to himself, following rules and considering feelings of peers. Has some difficulty with work activities. Needs much repetition of directions. Eager to do activities. Likes singing, finger play, etc. Likes to talk.

First grade teacher: Steven has continued to find classroom discipline a bit of a struggle. Steven appears quite energetic and must always be "thumping" or "wiggling," even when he is involved in an engrossing problem. Steven enjoys being with the other students and delights in sharing orally. Steven earnestly tries to capture all that is around. When Steven learns to channel his energy he will be a social leader.

Second grade teacher: This child has caused me a lot of concern. *Very hyperactive and immature.* I recommend a medical exam at the end of the year. Perhaps he needs something to calm him down.

Third grade teacher: Still hyperactive, noisy and *nosey.* Mother *refuses* to have any drugs administered He is always into someone else's projects, cannot leave others *alone,* but he is a good sharp student.

Fourth grade teacher: Steve is a very active boy. I have him seated by himself and this helps. His hyperactivity reflects in his work. (Too fast and inaccurate.) He is a capable boy and intelligent. Seems to have tapered down towards the end of the school year. Not malicious or mean.

Fifth grade teacher: Still very active and talkative—Comes to teacher with all problems—He can do good work when he tries.

However valid the assessments, once they are translated into medical or pseudo-medical judgments, the results evaporate into a fog of jargon and speculation. One recent survey of classroom teachers showed that 88 percent were confident that they could identify the hyperactive children in their classrooms; in a related study, however, examinations of 100 children deemed sufficiently hyperactive by teachers and school counselors to be referred to a clinic showed that the doctors could agree on only 13 percent as being hyperactive. And in a study conducted at the University of Maryland School of Medicine, a sample of 92 children of average intelligence who had reading difficulties in school (in the judgment of their teachers) and who were examined for hard medical problems "failed to reveal any statistical relationship to suggest a diagnostic pattern." Treatment recommendations emanating from the evaluation "were primarily educational, emphasizing that reading problems are pedagogical problems with the medical evaluation playing a minimal part in their diagnosis and treatment."[19]

I I I

The tests legitimize the categories, and the categories the tests. Both rest on definitions and judgments, particularly where they are concerned with behavior, socialization, learning disabilities, emotional disturbance or "soft" signs of neurological dysfunction, which are so arbitrary that they generate doubt even among those who are professionally committed to be sympathetic. In one survey, for example, a team of educational psychologists at the University of North Carolina concluded that there are "serious defects in the instruments used for early identification and perhaps in the conceptual rationale, providing shaky foundations for such instruments. Much more professional attention needs to be applied to the measurement problems which often seem, at present, to be brushed aside in the hurry to answer practical, clinical questions."[20]

> The enthusiasm which generated these tests has not carried over to the technical development of the instruments. It has been pointed out . . . that none of the popular tests that purport to measure perceptual motor abilities and are currently widely disseminated among special educators meets appropriate standards for evaluation devices. . . .
> We do not know how many overreferrals . . . we may find when we move from clinical testing to broad screening efforts.

In more than half the cases in which the screen identifies a problem—even the kind of problem susceptible to a distinct medical remedy—no effective services are provided. In the hard medical areas it is expensive, and in the "soft" categories which define no specific medical condition it is usually impossible and often unnecessary.[21] A number of studies suggest, moreover, that screening usually identifies problems which had already been obvious, and that in those instances where serious medical deficiencies have been found (as in the dental screens provided to Head Start children), it is usually more efficient and cheaper to offer diagnosis and treatment without prior screening.[22] Although the advocates of screening, backed by the growing involvement of the federal government, are promoting the development of appropriate services, their chances of success—for medical and economic reasons—are, at best, minimal. In the meantime, however, the proliferation of screens will have the ironic effect of giving children labels for which society has no cure and of placing them in segregated dead-end programs from which there is no return. The labels are permanent, and when the screening deals with emotional or behavioral areas, the "disease" is more likely to be social than medical.

Despite that "thicket of problems"—or perhaps because of it—the search continues, producing ever more elaborate devices, computers, brain wave machines and other electronic paraphernalia designed to tap the heads of children without the crude detour of a paper test. There is, for example, the Sensation Cognition Computer developed by E. Roy John of the Brain Research Laboratory at New York Medical College which purports to monitor cortical activity. The machine, according to an announcement in the newsletter of the California Association for Neurologically Handicapped Children, "presents visual and auditory stimuli to the brain and analyzes and prints out brain activity. The system is said to be expected to detect, very early, signs of minimal brain dysfunction." And there is Dr. John Ertl's Neural Efficiency Analyzer, a little black box with a screen designed to detect learning disabilities. The machine is connected to a child's head with a set of electrodes to measure, in Dr. Ertl's words, "the rate of speed with which the brain processes information, or responds to a stimulus, and it measures the synchronization between the two halves of the brain. In normal people—those without brain damage or learning disorders—the left side of the brain is well synchronized with the right side of the brain. . . . The Analyzer can detect the difference between both sides, and if it is greater than a certain value, we can be pretty sure that there is something wrong." Dr. Ertl, former director of the Center for Cybernetics Study at the University of Ottawa, conceded that the machine hadn't caught on; in one study funded by the Ford Foundation, the machine failed dismally, but Dr. Ertl said the data in that study were incompetently collected and that, in any case, the machine was now being used differently. An official of the California State Board of Education said the device still lacked empirical validation, but he acknowledged that the Analyzer had potential. "We do know there is a relationship between minimal brain dysfunction and learning disabilities."[23] As long as there are people talking about that "relationship," the Johns and the Ertls will keep trying. The ideal, says John Meier, is preconception screening to keep certain people from having children at all, or to provide massive intervention where the tests of parents indicate a good chance that they will have an infant at risk. No one, however, has yet answered the question posed by Robert E. Cooke, the chief of pediatrics at the Johns Hopkins University Hospital: "What are the implications over the long haul for a child with a mild imperfection in a society which doesn't tolerate imperfections? If you decide not to feed the abnormal child, where do you stop? How 'abnormal' should an individual be before you knock him off?"[24]

*   *   *

The prime function of all screening devices is mystification, a ritual conferring legitimacy on institutional decisions. Where there is pressure from minorities for decent medical treatment, the screen is a relatively cheap yet sufficiently broad and elaborate facade of social concern; it proves that something is being done. Where there is need to justify the practices of institutional management—or the biases of teachers, or the failures of instruction, or the demands of social control—the screen provides a sufficiently elaborate ritual to legitimize existing practices without offending parents or voters. A teacher filling out a form designed by a "scientist" and processed by a computer appears far more objective than the same teacher without form or computer deciding on her own that Steve or Roy is learning disabled, developmentally arrested, ego disturbed or hyperkinetic. A learning clinician with a folder of charts, a stack of printouts and a wall of certificates from Colorado State and Abilene Christian possesses a mystery not accessible to ordinary mortals. Giving the parent a copy of a similar test simply makes him a collaborator in the mystification process: no seller of screening instruments tells the customer that his wares are junk.

Inherent in the ritual are conflicting pressures for economy and efficiency on the one hand and for a maximum degree of mystification on the other. The computer lends itself admirably to both functions: that the process is usually a good illustration of the old GIGO principle (garbage in, garbage out) does not eliminate altogether the machine's oracular powers. (The ultimate in economy is a suggestion from the Research and Development Center for Teacher Education at the University of Texas that peer-rating techniques can be used to identify learning-disabled children; a child identified by his classmates as one who "does not worry," said the scholars at the Center, should be tested for hyperactivity and learning disabilities.) Nor is it surprising that the enterprise is ridden with jargon, undefined terms, statistical gibberish and circular logic. Orwell noted years ago that the corruption of language has certain political uses, but that jargon also serves the processes of mystification and reinforces the status of the "professionals" who invent and possess it. If one analyzes that language—the journal articles, the speeches the content of the screens themselves—one can get a fairly clear idea of how screening legitimizes in pseudo-medical terms a particular set of social norms, and how the enterprise, as it becomes increasingly universal, converts the behavioral requirements of schools and other social institutions into a set of scientific imperatives: the ability to sit still; follow directions; accept adult authority; play amiably with other children; pay attention; write, read, print, draw, hop and jump on schedule. As the tests proliferate, those requirements—however similar they had always been from one place to another—are elevated from the context of individual practice and personal preference, and from the context of character and good behavior, to the rarified regions of a universal medical "science." That science simultaneously disregards unmeasurable or ineffable individual characteristics—musical talent, for example—and, at the same time, hardens others into medical versions of the slots that the institution has created. This is not to argue about the virtues of the institutional requirements themselves or to debate the presumption that a child should (or should not) be able to sit still or draw circles or solve puzzles at a certain age; it is only to question the medical inferences which follow the behavior and the underlying ideology of scientific normality which sustains them. The very fact that the need for such behavior is culturally determined and (in nearly all cases) subjectively measured—that the behavior, in other words, is debatable—while the conclusions drawn from it purport to be precise and scientific, illustrates the uses of screening in mystification and the uses of mystification in control. The screen teaches, and screening educates. It appears almost inevitable that the foremost lesson of that education is to condition the subject to screening and the legitimacy of its purpose and to instill the idea that he will be tested, measured and examined not only in the overt tasks required by the institution, but in arcane areas which concern his inner being and which he is expected not to understand. He learns, in other words, that the system routinely requires him to betray himself, and that the conclusions drawn from that betrayal will be used to manage him. Always, of course, for his own good.

FIVE

In the Matter
of Predelinquents

The pastel-green offices of the Social Service Bureau are located on the second floor of the city police station, one story above the squad room, and two above the basement pistol practice range. Occasionally a police officer passes down an adjacent corridor on the way to a storeroom, though otherwise the presence of the police is felt in less tangible though perhaps more significant ways.

The city is Wheaton, Illinois, a middle-class Chicago suburb of 31,000 people once designated by *Look* as an "All-America City," but it could as easily be Bell Gardens, California, or Providence or San Antonio or any one of hundreds of other communities which in the past decade began to operate programs for children and adolescents identified as delinquents, "predelinquents" or potential delinquents, or designated in some other manner as requiring social readjustment. Few of their clients have ever been before a juvenile court, and fewer still have been found guilty of a criminal offense. Some were arrested for shoplifting, joyriding or other minor crimes; many have committed no act more serious than running away from home, smoking marijuana or violating a local curfew. Most of them have been enrolled arbitrarily by police officers, school officials or social workers without trial or recourse to any of the formalities of due process.

Joyce Bauer, a recent high school graduate of 17, was taken to the police station by her mother and accused of being a runaway. A week before, she had left home without permission, had gone to stay with family friends in Milwaukee, and had returned voluntarily. Her mother was concerned because she believed that Joyce had had "marital relations" with her boy friend. The police officer who handled the case wanted the social workers at the Bureau to determine whether she was pregnant. Joyce was sent to the project office for counseling.

Ken Wilson, also 17, was found with a friend in a local parking lot and arrested for smoking marijuana. Ken was a high school track star, a leader in church youth groups, and an Eagle Scout. The officer who handled the case was angry because Ken was said to have told one of his friends that he intended to continue using marijuana, but to make certain that he would not get caught again.

Marsha Alexander, the 15-year-old daughter of a dentist, was picked up by police at 4:30 in the morning; she had been riding around town with three older friends. Since Marsha had once been reported by her parents as a runaway, she already had a police record. Like the others, she was sent to the Bureau for counseling.[1]

The rationale for most of the delinquency programs established in the past decade, usually with federal support, is "diversion," or, more generally, "prevention and treatment." They are sometimes associated with local school systems, but even when they are not they operate with the same ideology as the LD programs in the schools. Increasingly, moreover, both the schools and the delinquency projects associate delinquency with learning disabilities, hyperactivity and a variety of common neurological "dysfunctions." The tracks, in other words, run parallel, and often they are identical. The predelinquency projects function on what is by now the banal assumption that the formal processes of the juvenile justice system—courts, probation, detention—tend to be stigmatizing and ineffective in preventing further delinquent acts, that often, indeed, they have precisely the opposite effect, that the majority of adult criminals are graduates of the juvenile justice system, that the system provides little or no "treatment," and that a child labeled delinquent by the authorities is more likely to behave as if he were. There is general agreement that juvenile justice procedures are themselves arbitrary and discriminatory, that absorption into the system depends as much on social status, race and attitude as it does on the act committed, and that a third of the boys and half of the girls in state and local detention facilities have no record of any criminal act and were sent there as "neglected" or "dependent" or for so-called status offenses, acts which, like truancy or running away from home, are "crimes" only if they are committed by children. (In 1972, for example, there were some 350,000 juvenile arrests reported in California. Of these, 52.7 percent were for "delinquent tendencies" or "predelinquency" and another 18 percent were for "minor" delinquent acts.)[2] Although juvenile courts were themselves established early in the twentieth century to divert children from the adult criminal justice system and to provide "protection" and "supervision" without the criminal process, its stigmas and sanctions, the courts have come under heavy attack for their propensity to treat juveniles as criminals without affording them the due process protections of a formal trial. Court records are full of instances where minors have been sentenced, ostensibly for their own good, to indefinite terms for committing acts (such as shoplifting) that would merit no more than 30 or 60 days if they were committed by an adult.

> Juvenile court proceedings [wrote Edwin M. Lemert, who is generally regarded as the authority in the field of diversion] originally were held to be civil in nature, confiden-

tial, and to be concluded without creation of a record. Events proved them to be punitive, correctional and stigmatizing in effect if not intent. . . . The location of juvenile courts within the regular system of courts, their close relations with police departments, use of jails for detention, and dispositions depriving children of their freedom all sustained the punitive and stigmatizing features of these courts.[3]

In the traditional juvenile court proceeding, procedural rights generally gave way to the ideology of "custody," "protection" and "treatment." In 1967, however, the Supreme Court ruled, in the case of *In re Gault,* that even in juvenile court, minors were entitled to counsel, to adversary proceedings (right to confrontation and cross-examination) and to the privilege against self-incrimination.[4] "Under our Constitution," wrote Justice Abe Fortas, "the condition of being a boy does not justify a kangaroo court." As a consequence, it became more difficult for juvenile authorities to counsel, "treat" or otherwise manage those who were regarded as delinquents or potential delinquents (or simply as problems for the schools or other authorities), and, at the same time, more attractive to develop other institutions and procedures to deal with cases that might not stand the new tests imposed by the Supreme Court. The accumulated criticism of the failures of the juvenile justice system and the *Gault* decision thus coincided to stimulate the search for successful programs of diversion. As the principle of *parens patriae,* the court as father and protector, was driven out of the judicial institutions, it found a new home in diversion.

The new projects are ostensibly designed and rationalized as diversion from the juvenile justice system, but since they are usually part of the system, as branches of police or probation departments, and as their most intimate collaborators, the distinction is often impossible to establish. Their boards and supervisory staffs are heavy with cops and probation officers, and their objectives are often indistinguishable from those of the institutions which create and support them. "The Social Service Bureau," says the Wheaton brochure, "is the social/emotional evaluation and treatment division of the Wheaton Police Department." In the typical case, the juvenile client is first given a "diagnostic assessment" consisting of interviews and the completion of a questionnaire which covers, among other things, the client's family history, income and education; his medical and psychiatric history; his attitude toward the "offense" that brought him in contact with the police or the Bureau; and such items as: "Do you take drugs?", "Are you often emotionally upset in any way?" and "Have you ever attempted or expressed a desire to kill yourself or anyone else?" The client and his parents are assured of confidentiality, although they are also told that a "summary" of the social worker's assessment will be forwarded to the police; in a number of instances, moreover, the parents are asked to sign a blanket form authorizing the Bureau to "release any and all information now or hereafter acquired." James Collier, the bearded director of the Bureau, explains that the diagnosis is "largely an attitudinal thing. We believe in sound assessment before we decide on a treatment plan. We may find in the assessment that the problem is not with the primary client but, say, with the parents; we then try to get the parents to come in for marital counseling. Or the treatment plan could be a conservative form of psychotherapy, or behavior modification, or it could be task-oriented. We'll try anything that's likely to work." Part of the diagnosis may also include an examination of the client's psychiatric records, and the treatment may include "changing the kid's attitude about us. We'll work on an unmotivated client for a while to get him motivated." He concedes that in some instances there is overt coercion: the juvenile officer informs the client that if he doesn't enroll in the program his case will be taken to the juvenile court. Participation is made a condition of "station adjustment," a sort of informal police probation which requires the juvenile to "avoid association with persons of poor reputation and habits," "obey the reasonable rules and directions of your parents and juvenile officers," and adhere to curfew hours.

In most instances, the therapy which follows the initial interviews and assessment consists primarily of counseling, either individually or in groups, generally over a period of two or three months: "helping the parents to communicate directly with each other . . . attempting to strengthen Ronald so he could better cope with the home situation . . . helping Jim to understand the consequences of his acting-out behavior." In the case of Ken, the marijuana-smoking Eagle Scout, the worker observed that a "good respectful relationship had developed" between herself and her client. "His strength of self," she noted, "and his home and physical and mental ability have helped him to see peer conformity as not so important," and she closed the case. In other cases, diagnosis and counseling are followed by referrals to juvenile court or to community psychiatric facilities. "We've established good relations with the intake officers," Collier said. "We can get the waiting lists by-passed; we can get a kid in right away." The Bureau does not recommend drugging or other forms of chemotherapy, but it does make referrals to family physicians or county medical facilities. Behind those referrals is the authority of the cop.

> Of significance to the treatment relationship [said a report on the Wheaton project] is the fact that the offender has to first deal with the police officer about his behavior. Being in a position of authority, the officer comes face to face with any denial or provocativeness that the law violator may present. A confrontation is made with those individuals who do not want to recognize their behavior or do anything about it. . . . This initial confrontation by the officer can lessen the amount of resistance that the social worker must deal with later.
>
> We have found that the police officer can be instrumental in not only getting the client to come in for help but be a motivator for his staying in treatment.[5]

The Wheaton Bureau prides itself on a close working relationship with police and other community agencies: "The social worker has the responsibility to help the citizen better understand himself in order to function more acceptably in society. He does this by providing a corrective interpersonal relationship through the use of social work skills. . . . The policeman provides the pressure and the initial motivation for change, being representative of the community. Each needs the other. Only by working together and cooperatively can both be successful in doing the job we are meant to do, and in doing it well."[6] The Bureau literature contains extensive sections on confidentiality, the varying responsibilities of cops and social workers and the general rights of clients. In practice, however, both privacy and other client rights are regarded as indefinite and negotiable: "Use discretion in what you tell an investigator," the social workers are told. "Psychological data is usually not important and should not be given. At the same time, have an open mind and evaluate each question as he asks it." (One of us was given virtually unlimited access to client files.) What the Bureau is most proud of is, in fact, that collaborative relationship between social workers and cops which places the authority of the law squarely behind an indefinite extension of the social service system into the private lives of children and their families.

I I

The concept of "early intervention" spread rapidly in the late sixties and early seventies. Stimulated by rising national concern about juvenile crime, the growing application of medical analogies to crime prevention and the changing priorities of the federal government, police, probation departments, school systems and other community agencies went heavily into the business of early identification, diagnosis, diversion and treatment. While funds for the Office of Economic Opportunity and Model Cities were being curtailed, substantial amounts were becoming available for crime and delinquency. By 1974, the Law Enforcement Assistance Administration (LEAA) was disbursing funds at a rate approaching $1 billion a year. Smaller amounts were also available through the Youth Development and Delinquency Prevention Administration of HEW and from the National Institute of Mental Health through its Center for the Study of Crime and Delinquency. While a major percentage of those federal funds went to purchase police hardware, an estimated 20 percent flowed into juvenile delinquency diversion programs, educational experiments, screening projects and various forms of diagnostic and treatment centers.

Many of the resulting projects offer nothing more than vocational or family counseling, mini-bike clubs and athletic programs; others promise intensive therapy, send police "counselors" into the schools and operate ambitious programs of behavior modification in public school classrooms. Many require some form of police "contact" for enrollment; others take referrals directly from schools, parents and other sources, and a few have conducted their own screening programs to find children with "maladaptive tendencies" or "delinquent tendencies" before those children have committed any act that could even remotely be regarded as anti social.

Early in 1973, the city school system of Baltimore began to develop tests which it intended to administer to most city school children to identify "maladaptive tendencies" and "potential delinquents." The tests, which included standard psychological inventories, evaluations by teachers and special screens developed by school psychologists (all with LEAA funding), were to be followed up, in the words of one school official, "by some kind of educational program and therapy aimed at prevention." By December 1973, the tests had been given to a sample of 4,500 children, most of them in ghetto schools, all without their parents' knowledge or consent. At that point word leaked to the local newspapers; both the papers and the Maryland chapter of the American Civil Liberties Union mounted a campaign against the program, and it was officially abandoned.

In Orange County, California, first and second grade children identified by their teachers as potential delinquents were enrolled in a program called VISA (Volunteers to Influence Student Achievement) and assigned to adult big-brother counselors in the community. Parents were told that their children were having difficulty in school, but the fact that the program was specifically designed for "predelinquents" and that it was funded by the California Council on Criminal Justice (CCCJ), the state agency which dispenses LEAA funds, was never made clear. The files of CCCJ in Sacramento contain a sample list of VISA clients, complete with name, school and the teacher assessment which placed them in the program: "Academic problems . . . mildly disruptive . . . poor peer relationships . . . absent father . . . general behavior problem . . . emotional problem . . . broken home." Officials of the County Probation Department, which was running the program, denied that it was designed as a "predelinquency" project. The program's own literature, including the grant application to CCCJ, emphasizes, however, that it "combines the efforts of the Probation Department, schools, police, and concerned citizens in identifying, matching and staffing students whose school performance indicates probable future delinquent activities." Although it was established primarily for children between the ages of nine and twelve, an investigator from the California Legislature told a reporter that at least one child had been enrolled "on the second day of kindergarten." The program was funded through the end of 1974; state officials were not certain whether it would be refunded thereafter.

In Montgomery County, Pennsylvania, the three county school systems (Lower Merion, Norristown and Wissahickon) initiated CPI ("Critical Period of Intervention") to "identify children who may be susceptible to drug abuse." The project included "diagnostic testing" comprising questions about religion and intimate relationships between the pupils and their parents, among them items about whether one or both parents "tell me how much they love me." Students were also asked to identify other children in their classes who made "odd or unusual remarks," gave inappropriate answers to questions or had a tendency to quarrel with others. In the fall of 1972, the parent of a child in one of the schools filed suit to stop the tests, and in October 1973, a federal court ruled in the parent's favor. "The ultimate use of this information," the Court said, "is the most serious problem. . . . How many children would be labeled as potential drug abusers who in actuality are not, and would be subjected to the problem of therapy sessions conducted by inexperienced individuals? . . . There is too much chance that the wrong people for the wrong reasons will be singled out and counseled in the wrong manner."[7]

Ever since the late sixties, the federal government has regarded the establishment of youth service bureaus as the most significant local step in diverting youngsters from the juvenile justice system and in preventing juvenile crime. In 1967, the President's Commission on Law Enforcement and Administration of Justice recommended that "a great deal of juvenile misbehavior should be dealt with through alternatives to adjudication, in accordance with an explicit policy to divert juvenile offenders away from formal adjudication and to nonjudicial institutions for guidance and other services."[8] By the early seventies both LEAA and HEW (through its Youth Development and Delinquency Prevention Administration) were committing a major portion of their delinquency prevention funds to the "youth services system" which, by 1973, was proclaimed by YDDPA as "perhaps the best way we now have to cope with the problem."[9] The bureaus, which were to link police, courts and probation departments with other community institutions, were originally conceived primarily as referral and placement centers, institutions which would match clients with the appropriate social services. In recent years, however, the bureaus have taken on substantive functions of their own, partly because no appropriate services were locally available, and partly through what appear to be the inevitable processes of institutional self-aggrandizement.

Since the distinctions between diversion, prevention and early identification were never made clear (just as there is no clarity in the meaning of delinquency itself), the rationale of "diversion" often tends to cover a search for clients whose brushes with the law, if any, are so marginal that they would simply be ignored if the program did not exist. In Alameda County, California (which includes Oakland), a delinquency prevention project sent workers to find and counsel the brothers and sisters of kids who had been identified as delinquents on the theory that in some instances "acting out is functional within the family system," and in Bell Gardens, a Los Angeles suburb, Police Chief Ferice B. Childers defended the assignment of police "counselors" to schools with the statement that "to be effective, a juvenile delinquency program must be conducted so that it will reach all young people, those without apparent problems, those youths who need help prior to being apprehended, and those who have come to the agency because of delinquent behavior."[10] Under the social work principle of "outreach," no crime need be committed before the solicitous hand of the law is extended with offers of help.

Pursuant to their indefinite mandate, the bureaus have ventured willy-nilly into family therapy, probation work, education, athletic programs and, in some instances, into activities that constitute direct extensions of police detective work. "The youth counselors," said Chief Childers, "must work with police detectives, and yet they must be independent of each other. A young person must have confidence in the youth counselor so that he will feel free to talk about any problems. The information obtained must be given a classification of 'confidential,' subject, however, to inspection by the Commission as an investigative body or the Youth Services Commander in the Police Department."[11]

Because the funding process is decentralized and locally administered—through block grants to state agencies which in turn disburse the funds to the projects—there are no hard national data on the number of programs, the size of their clientele or the scope of their activities: LEAA simply does not know where its money is going or how it is spent. The best estimate is that there are perhaps 1,200 projects spending $100 million a year to reach between 200,000 and 400,000 kids.[12] In 1973, Indiana spent 22 percent of its block grant funds (totaling $12 million) on juvenile delinquency projects; Ohio allocated nearly half (or $24 million); California about 15 percent of $46 million.[13] The typical project employs perhaps six full-time staff members as well as a number of paraprofessionals and deals with an estimated 200 or 300 juveniles a year.[14] Although most express modest objectives and nearly all seem to modify their goals once they begin to operate, a sample of three California grant applications, all funded by the state, gives some indication of what the more ambitious are dreaming about:

> Orange County: Individual, group and family therapy, behavior modification techniques and programs, guidance techniques and procedures, parent/foster parent effectiveness training, management of neurologically related behavior disorders by pediatric/neurological methods (including chemotherapy) and related techniques. . . .[15]

> Santa Clara County: The Sheriff's Department . . . has one of the better followup programs to keep in contact with the troubled youth and their families in order to explore treatment plan results or offer further suggestions. . . . The Sheriff's Department Juvenile Bureau also has an impressive data collection system and record system on each of their cases which aids in their followup program and research program.

> City of Chula Vista: Eight plainclothes agents will be assigned (to the school districts). Each agent so assigned will be responsible for investigation of all delinquents or potentially delinquent incidents occurring in his assigned area and will coordinate his activities with those of the school in his district. He will provide consultant services to the school in matters of criminal justice procedures. The police agents will provide preliminary counseling of

predelinquents and early delinquents to identify individual problems. . . . The youth will see the police agent as both an enforcement officer and as a friend or resource person concerned with youth problems.

The Bureaus employ a peculiar mix of seduction and coercion. The style tends to be mod squad: hip detectives, black social workers, girls in jeans and granny glasses, bearded graduate students and an occasional crew-cut YMCA type, all of them surrounded by stray copies of *Rolling Stone,* a couple of funky posters and the ubiquitous coffee pot. They tend to be directive in their counseling ("Your obvious goal," says the long-haired graduate student, "is to change them."), but the directiveness may be concealed under mountains of chit-chat and buddyship. "You tell the kid this is not a continuation of interrogation and it's not punishment; you tell him it's his obligation to be here, but it's not his obligation to talk to me. Sometimes you take a kid out to shoot some baskets, or down the street for a hamburger. I try to get the kid to see counseling as a sort of umbrella that'll keep the shit from falling on him. . . . I don't advocate game playing. I'm trying to get him to face reality, to build independence. I want these kids to be able to assert themselves for what they want."

Their attractiveness is undeniable, and the attractiveness in turn makes the process creditable: Phil Good, a former Youth Authority Corrections Officer who heads the counselors at the Bell Gardens Youth Services Bureau, worries about "playing God . . . enjoying your own benevolence too much, all the shit that's coming out of my mouth, and ripping the kid off"; or Detective Bob Byal, mustached and mod-suited, who goes into junior high school classrooms as a teacher and counselor trying to persuade the kids that he's not a narc and wondering whether "any other cop understands what I'm talking about"; or Dee Cox, black social worker, riding the streets at night in a patrol car, monitoring (and obviously enjoying) the police radio traffic, half cop, half counselor. They are not quite certain, any of them, who they are working for or exactly what they are supposed to achieve, and some are genuinely worried that they constitute a pacification squad designed to maintain order by messing around with children's heads. They concede that when it comes to the crunch they support and represent social institutions and not their juvenile clients. Beneath the worry about roles and purpose is the muscle of the law:

> We the undersigned understand that the person designated as JUVENILE below has been contacted by the Bell Gardens Police Department in a criminal matter. We further understand that the Police Department has the authority to file a petition request on the juvenile, the parents, or both as a result of the matter in question, thereby bringing criminal charges against either or both in this matter.
>
> In lieu of bringing such charges against the undersigned, the Police Department has elected to allow the undersigned to avail themselves of the Youth Services Center.
>
> In consideration of the forbearance of the Police Department to file formal charges against the juvenile as a delinquent or the parents as unfit parents or both, the undersigned do hereby covenant, warrant, and agree as follows:
>
> 1. To attend and actively participate in counseling sessions with a Youth Services Center Counselor.
> 2. To attend such sessions for a period of at least four weeks, two sessions per week, one hour per session.
> 3. To be on time for each scheduled session.
> 4. To attend and actively participate in any further counseling sessions, of whatever nature, as the Manager of the Youth Services Center directs.
>
> We the undersigned further understand that any failure on our part or any of us to abide by this contract in full will result in termination of the services of the Youth Services Center and that any future contracts by the Police Department will result in formal charges being brought against the juvenile, the parents, or both as prescribed by law.[16]

The contract assumes that the individual is guilty of the act which brought him into the program. The authorities may or may not inform him of his rights against self-incrimination and his right to a formal trial. The vast majority of those enrolled in diversion programs, however, have never been represented by counsel and have never received a clear explanation—no such explanation being possible—of the function of the project and its counselors: Whom do they represent, and just how is the child supposed to regard them? What resources does he have to challenge or resist? (There sit the frightened mother, holding a younger child, the angry, embarrassed father, the cop and the counselor, talking problems and offering help and shuffling papers: arrest records, school records, interview forms, personal history forms, a whole network of dossiers and records accessible to cops, teachers, counselors and, more likely than not, future employers and military recruiters, all representing vast power to control and all of them spelling trouble of some incomprehensible dimension.) There is no certainty that the child would necessarily receive better treatment by insisting on his rights: of those who do appear in court, however, those represented by private attorneys (as opposed to court appointed legal defenders) are more likely to be acquitted or to receive light sentences. There is evidence, moreover, that the majority of the kids enrolled in diversion programs would not be sent to juvenile court even if the programs did not exist, that they constitute, in effect, an entirely new clientele. Although some projects report that they have reduced referrals to juvenile courts or probation departments by as much as 20 percent, others, through their "outreach" programs, have substantially increased the social case load. In Placer County, California, for example, a project run by the probation department actively solicits referrals from schools, police and other community agencies; as a consequence of the program, the number of cases formally processed by the juvenile court declined but the number of predelinquent referrals to the probation department increased from 362 in 1971–1972 to 555 in 1972–1973.

Officials of many of the projects concede that since the majority of their cases are truants, self-referrals or "first offenders" accused by police of minor crimes or status offenses, many, if not most, would be "counseled and released" if there were no program.[17] (In Wheaton, the family court judge who handles juvenile cases has a reputation for leniency. For most of its cases, therefore, the Social Service Bureau represents the most intensive possible form of intervention, not the most limited. "We handle the tough cases," Collier said, the cases the cops can't handle themselves or unload on other institutions.) The most recent surveys, including a state wide study in Illinois, indicate that more than half the adolescents in the national population have committed acts (including shoplifting or other petty theft) which fit the legal definition of delinquency—43 percent have driven a car without a license; 22 percent ran away from home at least once; 10 percent have gone joyriding in a car "that was stolen for the ride."[18] Less than half of them have ever been arrested. The Illinois study indicated, moreover, that contrary to expectations drawn from official police or court records (which are based on arrests), girls commit almost as many delinquent acts as boys, whites as blacks, rich as poor:

> Youngsters from advantaged backgrounds violate the law; youngsters from poor families do the same. Although there is little difference in actual delinquent behavior, we know from official statistics that economically deprived youngsters—both white and minority group adolescents —run a much higher risk of being arrested for their delinquencies, appearing in court, and spending time in a correctional institution.[19]

Such conclusions reinforce familiar data about official discrimination in the handling of crime and delinquency. In juvenile cases, the chances of discrimination are further enlarged by a tradition and mandate that encourage the court to give social background, home environment and general attitude consideration at least equal to (if not greater than) the consideration given to the seriousness of the act itself. In cases where disposition depends entirely on the judgment of a police officer or a social worker, latitude is almost unlimited.

The projects accumulate mountains of statistics to demonstrate their effectiveness: number of juveniles "contacted" or arrested, number processed through the program, number referred to juvenile court, recidivism rates, truancy rates, crime rates. A self-study conducted by the California Council on Criminal Justice late in 1973 concluded that "overall these projects have been a positive factor in diverting juveniles from the criminal justice system."[20] That conclusion was immediately qualified, however, by the observation that the connection between the projects and reduction of delinquency, if any, was coincidental. More serious questions were raised in a draft of a confidential study produced by an independent firm of systems analysts which concluded that despite the accumulation of figures, adequate research data, precise definitions and reliable controls were almost totally nonexistent, and that delinquency is too often a reflection of "cultural intolerance of diversity and variability."[21]

> What is at issue here is the right to no treatment. It is an issue which must be resolved by those responsible for setting guidelines for diversion. From initial project evidence it is clear that many youth, who would otherwise have been counseled and released, are being diverted into some kind of program. Proponents argue that this is not a problem as diversion is voluntary. Yet is a referral to a youth service bureau voluntary where the alternative is being processed as a juvenile offender with an omnipresent threat of a reformatory in the background?

The critics argue that diversion programs deprive juveniles of "the right to get lost," that they represent "a proliferation of control agents." The essence of the process, said James Robison, a California criminologist who has consulted for LEAA, "is to shame the kid out of his behavior. These projects get cases that the cop doesn't want to deal with, and turn them over to someone who grooves on them. The cop at least has his idea of fairness, but the social worker feels that fairness is an irrelevant consideration; the social worker corrupts the cop. The thing is divided up gang-style so that no one is fully accountable; they can fuck over the kid both as victim and as offender. If the cop says something to a kid it might hurt, but if a mental health worker says the same thing it's much more insidious. They ought to put guns and badges on the social workers so the kids at least will know who they're dealing with." The criticism focuses on "over-reliance" on diversion and therefore concealment "of the fact that for much of what is now labeled as deviance, the problem is not how to treat it but how to absorb and tolerate it, or even encourage it. Not all deviant behavior requires treatment, whether in or out of the criminal justice system, yet the mere presence of a functioning mechanism of community services, with none of the obvious drawbacks of the penal system, is likely to result in the 'treatment' of many more individuals by official agencies."[22]

III

Ronald Filippi, M.D., is an associate professor and chief of child psychiatry at Albany (New York) Medical College. Clyde L. Rousey, Ph.D., is a speech pathologist and audiologist at the Menninger Foundation in Topeka, Kansas. In 1971, Filippi and Rousey completed a study of speech deviation among children and announced in a learned journal that they had found a new way "of detecting children prone to violence." This new way was based on the way a child pronounced the word "bird."[23]

> It is based on hypotheses, first advanced by Rousey, that speech sounds are related to character structure and personality dynamics. We screened two hundred and thirty-nine children, mostly from low income families, for the

capacity to articulate sounds, as well as for a variety of psychological and social indices. We found that children who exhibited a particular sound abnormality (the variant of the mid-central vowel *r* where the vowel *r* in *bird* is pronounced as *burrd*) are indeed distinguished by violent-destructive behavior, independently reported. They also differ markedly in their family structure and their interpersonal milieu, when contrasted with a completely "normal sounding" group. The procedure has unique advantages as a diagnostic tool in community mental health and merits further application with different populations.

Filippi and Rousey pointed out that certain abnormalities of speech "are significantly related to specific personality traits and dynamics." A child who cannot control his violence is also the child who cannot control his speech. "Where not yet manifest in behavior," they pointed out, "the potential for violence of such 'positive carriers' can be inferred from psychological tests." The speech test, they said, is fast and easy to use; it "can be administered by any person able to read and operate a tape recorder," something they regarded as "a prerequisite in these days of need for large-scale mental health screenings."

Peter S. Venezia, Ph.D., is associate director of the Research Center of the National Council on Crime and Delinquency in Davis, California. In January 1971, three months before the Filippi-Rousey study appeared, Dr. Venezia published an article in the *Journal of Research in Crime and Delinquency* in which he proposed the use of the "school environment" as the focal point for "prevention intervention" in juvenile delinquency:[24]

> It is there that comprehensive and relatively objective information about each child is readily available. . . . This information can be collected systematically and without intruding on the child or his family. There is evidence, too, that this information can be applied to the assessment of which children are in the preliminary stages of adjustment

difficulties. Preventive intervention, then, could be predicated upon a child's current needs, rather than upon a prediction of future behavior. There would be no need to label and treat a child as delinquency-prone or predelinquent even though, pragmatically, effective assistance with current difficulties might significantly reduce future maladaptive behavior—including delinquency.

Dr. Venezia observed that "there is considerable evidence that classroom teachers are uniquely capable of predicting the behavior of their pupils." Except for some preliminary work in England, however, "there has been no attempt to develop a systematic predictive approach that capitalizes upon this skill "[25] By following up on the possibilities, he thought, "the need . . . for a practical, acceptable, and efficient means of screening large numbers of young children" might be met.

Fred W. Vondracek, Ph.D., is associate professor of human development at the Pennsylvania State University, and head of a project called CARES (Computer Assisted Regional Evaluation System). Since 1971, Dr. Vondracek and his colleagues at the Pennsylvania State College of Human Development have been perfecting and implementing a computerized method of diagnosing juvenile delinquents for local probation departments and recommending appropriate treatment. Three county probation agencies (Lycoming County, Centre County and Huntington County) were using the system in 1974, but Vondracek is confident that the system, developed with LEAA funds, was ready for application not only by other probation departments but by schools. As CARES now operates, probation officers investigating juvenile cases feed interview data (by way of remote terminals) into the Pennsylvania State computer and receive back a case summary and a "syndrome analysis" based on a data bank collection of psychological and neurological problems "occurring with some frequency in a typical juvenile population." Among the syndromes programmed into the computer are "the passive-aggressive syndrome, passive-dependent syndrome, schizoid syndrome, compulsive syndrome, hypomaniac syndrome, aggressive syndrome, primary sociopath syndrome, and minimal brain dysfunction syndrome." On request, the computer also prints out a list of agencies where remedial services for the particular case can be obtained, thereby assisting (according to Vondracek's literature) the clinically untrained probation officer in deciding whether the child in question should be sent to a juvenile detention home or whether he can be "treated" in the community.[26] Among other things, CARES provides "standardized" and "objective" assessments based on comprehensive data covering "all significant aspects of [the youth's] development, physical, intellective, emotional, educational, social, etc." The input system includes an offense code applicable to every conceivable type of case: "Burglary," "Flag, Desecration of," "Flag, Insults to National or Commonwealth," "Forgery," "Library Property (Retention After Notice to Return)," "Murder and Manslaughter," "Robbery," "Rubbish, Scattering," "Sexual Intercourse," "Truancy," "Rape," "Running Away," "Ungovernable Behavior" and some sixty others. The input questionnaire also includes extensive items on "youth's cooperation with probation department," the worker's impression of the youth's emotional stability and an inventory of 116 true-false items, to be completed by the client, with such attitudinal questions as "you can't trust people," "my home life is bad" and "my own welfare comes first."

> Complex data collection and data analysis procedures utilized by highly trained professional personnel [Vondracek wrote] are combined with high speed data processing equipment as an inexpensive way to assist juvenile courts and probation departments to reach sophisticated decisions without the necessity for engaging expensive, highly-trained professional people to help them.

Filippi and Rousey, Venezia and Vondracek are part of a growing squadron of screeners and diagnosticians working the delinquency field. Its ranks include physicians and biologists at the Johns Hopkins University, the University of Wisconsin and the Educational Testing Service who, with support from the National Institute of Mental Health, are engaged in studies on the relationship of chromosome abnormalities to violent behavior. There are also the physicians at the University of California in Los Angeles who are trying to relate minimal brain dysfunction to violence, a psychologist at the University of Rhode Island who is certain that there exists a causal connection between learning disabilities and juvenile delinquency, and a psychologist at Hamline University in St. Paul who concluded that "the Cooperative English Test will enhance the prediction of delinquency for girls."[27] Their approaches, hypotheses and rationales vary, but they are sharers in the common faith that there exists a trait, a virus, a gene, an ailment or a "cluster" of traits, genes and ailments which, with varying degrees of success, can be discovered and treated. Nearly all of them are scientists or physicians with impeccable credentials, access to journals and federal funds and the attention of the more "progressive" cops, courts and corrections officials. Nearly all will argue that early detection, prevention and diversion are more humane and less stigmatizing than the formal procedures of the juvenile justice system, and that they are themselves civil libertarians working against the invidiousness of labeling (even as they invent new labels), and all talk about the search for economy and efficiency, something that "can be administered by any person able to read and operate a tape recorder." According to the common faith—and despite all the equally learned arguments about its vagueness—there is something called delinquency, or deviance, or a propensity toward violence. That something is taken from the varying judgment of cops, courts, teachers, parents and village boards—e.g., "she flies to pieces easily, tears up things, and kicks and screams"[28] as a definition of violence—and made part of the scientific analysis.

The attempt to develop scientific instruments to predict and diagnose, and thereby prevent, social deviance and delinquency has an extended history reaching into the dim recesses of memory. Among its more notable modern examples are the so-called Kvaraceus Delinquency Proneness Scale (KD scale), an inventory designed to measure degrees of emotional adjustment, the Minnesota Multiphasic Personality Inventory, the Cambridge-Somerville (Massachusetts) Youth Study conducted between 1937 and 1956[29] and the prediction scales developed by Sheldon and Eleanor Glueck of Harvard in the period between 1935 and 1950.[30] Under the system developed by the Gluecks, the child was to be rated on several scales which included personality traits (extroversion, stubbornness, "adventurousness"), psychological test factors, "character structure" ("social assertiveness," "defiance," "suspiciousness") and "social factors" ("discipline of boy by father," "supervision of boy by mother," "affection of father for boy," "cohesiveness of family").[31] A boy subject to "overstrict or erratic" discipline by his father, "unsuitable" supervision by his mother, "indifferent or hostile" feelings from his father, and to life in a family rated as uncohesive was marked for trouble, "whether or not he has yet overtly manifested any antisocial behavior."

In the past twenty years, such attempts at prediction have suffered what now appears to be a predictable fate. In an ambitious test of the Gluecks' system, the New York City Youth Board found that members of the treatment group selected by the rating scales were no less likely to become delinquent than members of a similarly selected control group; more important, of the 67 boys rated as likely to become delinquent in 1952, 50 had not become delinquent seven years later. It was not surprising, moreover, that since the study was conducted in a high-delinquency neighborhood, the social workers had difficulty agreeing on the ratings that went into the scales, particularly in homes without a father. In the Cambridge-Somerville study, where ratings were based on the selections of policemen and teachers (and subsequent assessments by professional "raters") the results were equally dubious: of 305 boys categorized as likely to become delinquent in 1937–1938, 191 (63 percent) did not become delinquents by 1956. As in the Youth Board Study in New York, treatment (consisting of "intensive" social work) produced negative results: the treatment group produced a greater percentage of delinquents than the control group.[32]

The common faith, however, survived the failures of its classic tests. It pervades university research projects, local diversion programs and the policies of the federal government. At the same time, however, styles and fashions of implementation have changed. The Gluecks believed, in accord with their times, that the family constituted the locus of assessment and intervention; their successors are more likely to be interested in learning disabilities, hyperkinesis, MBD and genetics. Character traits like "stubbornness" and "suspiciousness" are out, along with family cohesiveness and "discipline of boy by father," all quaint relics of another age. Chromosome abnormalities and neurological malfunctions are in. While LEAA and YDDPA were channeling their funds into diversion programs, the Center for Studies of Crime and Delinquency of the National Institute of Mental Health was supporting research projects in managing the behavior of "oppositional children" (defined as "failure to comply with explicit and implicit adult requirements"), studies on "Perinatal Brain Damage and Later Anti-Social Behavior" and at least three separate projects on the relation of the so-called XYY syndrome in males to violence.[33] (Females usually have an XX chromosome pattern; most males are XY. It is the Y gene that determines whether an individual will be male; there has been speculation, largely unconfirmed, that, in the words of Ashley Montague, "the addition of another Y . . . represents a double dose of those potencies that may under certain conditions facilitate the development of aggressive behavior."[34])

In one of those chromosome studies, researchers at the Johns Hopkins University subjected 7,000 boys from black ghetto homes in Baltimore to blood tests without telling either the boys or their parents why the tests were being conducted or how the results were to be used. The boys were enrolled in a free community medical program at Hopkins where blood samples were routinely taken to test for anemic conditions; the researchers, headed by Dr. Digamber Borgoankar, and supported by a $300,000 grant from NIMH, simply used the same samples for the XYY tests. At the same time, they also tested some 7,000 boys in various state institutions—delinquents and neglected children—again without informed consent. Early in 1970, Diane Bauer, then a reporter for the *Washington Daily News,* discovered the project and published a series of articles which reported, among other things, that the results of the tests on the institutionalized boys were to be turned over to state correctional authorities.[35] The articles produced threats of a Congressional investigation, a suit in state courts demanding that the tests be stopped, and a flurry of attacks from civil liberties groups. In response, Hopkins temporarily suspended the project, drew up a consent form and resumed the tests. The form, which promised confidentiality, said nothing about the fact that the state had no confidentiality law for doctors and that, in the opinion of Maryland's director of juvenile services, the results could still be made available to the courts "for whatever use they can make of them." The form pointed out that the project was designed to find out whether certain boys have "a tendency to violate the law" but it said nothing about XYY or violence. Four years later, in an interview, Saleem Shah, the director of the NIMH Center for Studies of Crime and Delinquency, insisted that the Maryland authorities were never given individual data from the Hopkins research; they received only "aggregate information" on the XYY factor.

The search for a genetic test to predict aggressive behavior or antisocial tendencies represents perhaps the ultimate in the passion to identify potential delinquents. Montague, among others, has suggested that it might be desirable "to type chromosomally all infants at birth or shortly after

... to institute the proper preventive and other measures at an early age." So far the proportion of XYY males in the general population is unknown, and not even the staunchest believers in the "syndrome" argue that such an abnormality is a certain indication of future violence. At most, they suggest, there may be a statistical difference. Since the XYY abnormality was first reported in 1961, however, a vast mythology has become associated with the pattern. It depicts XYY males as tall, mentally dull and prone to dangerously aggressive behavior. (Mass murderer Richard Speck was said to have been an XYY male, a belief which later turned out to be false.) Fifteen years of study have demonstrated that XYY males tend to be taller than average; they have proved nothing about dullness or violence.[36] Shah argues that he has never been "enthusiastic" about early screening, that his agency helped squash the Hutschnecker proposal and that the XYY prevalence studies supported by the Center are simply designed to check out the speculation about the syndrome. The studies, he said, are helping to prove that "there is no real difference" between the proportion of XYY males in the prison population and the general population. What he was much more interested in, he said, was "those youngsters who are getting into difficulty in school . . . youngsters who have academic and behavioral problems. These youngsters are very vulnerable to later labeling as delinquents."

Shah's care in hedging his expressions of interest in the genetics of delinquency and crime does not extend to his colleague David Rosenthal, chief of the psychology laboratory at NIMH. In December 1972, Rosenthal appeared at the annual meeting of the American Association for the Advancement of Science to deliver a paper called "Heredity in Criminality" in which he concluded that while no single gene could account for all criminality, "we can conclude that hereditary factors play a role in psychopathy and criminality." Criminals, he said, "tend to be predominately [sic] mesomorphic," they show a higher incidence of EEG abnormalities than the population at large, and they are often "psychotic or near psychotic," all characteristics he believed often to have a genetic origin. Rosenthal also declared that "chromosomal aneuploidy may . . . contribute toward a propensity to crime," that "some investigators believe that a number of hyperactive children eventually become criminals, and some evidence suggests that the hyperkinetic syndrome is inherited" and that "many criminals have a low IQ [which] is well known to have a high heritability." Rosenthal conceded that "we need a great deal more research" to determine whether the genetic factors "can be substantiated beyond doubt." With increased knowledge, he said, it might be possible to provide "hereditarily disposed individuals" with the kind of environment "in which criminal behavior is neither gratifying nor desirable . . . and in which provocative factors are kept to a minimum." Lombroso had said it all in 1876.

In the meantime, the chromosome studies continue. No one, needless to say, knows of any method to immunize an individual against the effect of his genes, assuming such an effect existed, and no one has yet tried to create the proper environment for "hereditarily disposed individuals." There had been a proposal from the Center for the Study and Reduction of Violence at the University of California in Los Angeles that would have included development of "behavioral indicators, profiles, scales, biological correlates, and social and environmental indicators of life-threatening behavior [which] will be structured into transportable models for use by teachers, clergy, social workers, counselors, psychologists, physicians, penologists, etc." But that part of the proposal was dropped in response to attacks by civil libertarians even before LEAA, to which UCLA had applied for funding, decided that the Center was too hot politically. (The attack on the Violence Center, particularly by the Children's Defense Fund, was one of the major reasons for LEAA's announcement in 1974 that it would no longer fund programs in behavior modification.[37]) In the meantime, the only possible remedy, as suggested by scientists at the University of

Colorado, is "genetic counseling." In plain language, that means abortion.

IV

The most seductive in the new generation of delinquency theories, and the one most likely to have extensive impact, derives from the association of delinquency with learning disabilities and/or MBD. "A hyperactive child," said a California psychiatrist, "is a predelinquent." Stated more tentatively, the argument says that while not all learning-disabled children are future delinquents, nearly all delinquents are learning disabled. It has become a common refrain in the diversion projects, in the literature on learning disabilities and among some judges and probation officers.[38] In some respects, of course, the argument is as old as the belief that school failure put a child on the road to crime. But where the old folklore was tied up with character and hard work, the contemporary version purports to be based on purely medical considerations: clusters of chemical imbalances, quirky hormones, problems in "visual motor integration" and faulty neurological wiring beyond the control of the individual. Even if the kid wanted to do it, he couldn't; he needs to be treated, not to be chastised. Delinquency is thereby separated from stigmas of character, inferences about parental inadequacy and innuendos of race, class or economic bias. It's nobody's fault.

The most prolific practitioners in the new territory, and certainly the most unequivocal, are Allen Berman, assistant professor of psychology at the University of Rhode Island and director of the Neuropsychology Laboratory for the Rhode Island Training Schools, and Chester D. Poremba, chief psychologist at the Denver Children's Hospital, who also served for many years as chief psychologist for the Denver Children's Court. Berman and Poremba have been making the rounds of conferences on learning disabilities to spread the word that, as Berman said, "delinquents are disabled." Berman came to that conclusion after four years of work (under an LEAA grant) with inmates at the Rhode Island Training School for Boys: "Seventy percent of the youngsters being imprisoned in the training school had measurable disabilities significant enough to warrant professional attention. . . . These figures certainly don't portend that every disabled child who doesn't get treated will become delinquent. Nevertheless, after carefully reviewing the case histories of these youngsters, I feel that our project has demonstrated that failure to recognize significant disabilities early in a child's school career sets into motion a devastating series of events that, for a large number of unfortunates, ends up [in] a reformatory or a juvenile court."[39] Poremba, after a study of 444 students in a Colorado juvenile placement center, concluded that 90.4 percent had learning disabilities "with an average of 2.3 learning disabilities per student."[40] On his list, the disabilities include problems of visual or auditory acuity, neurological problems or any other difficulty "that has to be corrected before the child can continue learning meaningfully." After an appearance as speaker and workshop moderator at the 1974 International Conference of the Association for Children with Learning Disabilities, Poremba declared that similar studies have shown that Oklahoma has a linkage of 85 percent between disabilities and youth crime, and that comparable figures in Minnesota are "in the upper 80s."

Poremba is convinced that most existing programs of delinquency rehabilitation should be abandoned because they focus on the same activities which produced the failures in the first place. "Truancy," he says, "is the kindergarten of crime." The solution is not more formal schooling but some alternative, gardening for example, that will permit the child to feel successful. In his anti-institutional sentiments, Poremba runs against the grain of the conventional wisdom —"if the school can't teach, bomb it"—and he sometimes manages to sound like the educational radicals of the sixties,

John Holt, Paul Goodman and Edgar Friedenberg. He is not
an advocate of ordinary remediation, not a pusher of balance
beams, drill and rote learning. Yet his observations nonetheless reinforce those who, like Berman, see the problem in
essentially medical terms and who see the earliest possible
intervention as the only solution. "There are 604,800 learning disabilities or combinations of disabilities. . . . We're
finding kids with disabilities faster than we're training teachers to handle them. Many teachers don't know beans about
disabilities." In Colorado, he estimated, between 18 and 28
percent of the kids are learning disabled. "These kids go to
school every day, and failure leading to their loser self-image
is reinforced by academic failure. The whole school system
says we are here to provide you with an education so you can
succeed, and then it promptly fails them."

The argument can go in two apparently separate directions, suggesting on the one hand the segregation of learning-
disabled children into special programs where they can "succeed," or pointing, on the other, to some form of "treatment"
to eliminate or cure the problem. Either way, the social
response is essentially the same. Despite Poremba's anti-
institutional rhetoric, public institutions almost inevitably
offer institutional solutions. The gardening and the call to
"bomb it" disappear, and the special classes for emotionally
disturbed or learning-disabled children, the tests, drill and
special exercises, reassert themselves (along with prescriptions for psychoactive drugs, programs of behavior modification, family therapy and all the rest). When a reporter asked
officials of the Denver school system about Poremba's
findings, they immediately began to talk about the system's
classes for handicapped children, its special crash courses for
teachers and the various diagnostic procedures they employed to set up "lessons and plans toward overcoming the
problems." For thirty years they had been busily solving a
problem on which Poremba had judged them to be failures.
In the long run, Poremba's argument would probably enable
the institution to strengthen its argument for more resources

and more control. Delinquency prevention would be another weapon in the arsenal of institutional management.

The delinquency-disabilities argument uses unverified assumptions to link two undefined problems in order to advocate an untested remedy. The diagnosis that can send a child to a try at gardening can also send his mother to the pharmacist for the child's supply of Ritalin; the sweet voice of reason that counsels "patient support and acceptance" of the learning-disabled child can also assign him to a lifetime of special classes. Using one test, for example, Berman concluded that of 50 "randomly selected delinquents," 18 suffered from "chronic, diffuse static cerebral dysfunction," 10 showed signs of "focal cerebral disorder [with] possible subconvulsive seizures" and 4 others were diagnosed as "peripheral neuropathy" or "borderline." Berman invoked Maurice Laufer's discarded concept of "hyperkinetic impulse disorder"—"hyperactivity, short attention span, poor powers of concentration, poor school work, unpredictable emotional reactivity, impulsivity, hostility, aggressiveness . . ."—to explain behavior over which, he suggested, the individual has "little voluntary control."[41]

> What happens is that children with these symptoms are often considered to be "just problems," who need only firm discipline. They often alienate teachers and workers by their hostility and aggressiveness, and are mistakenly judged as undesirous of changing. In reality they are frightened, lonely, somewhat depressed children, fighting to keep others from noticing how inadequate they feel they are. They need: (a) neurological, psychological and educational assessments to determine areas of deficit; (b) specific remedial programs to deal with learning disabilities; (c) medical consultant advice as to the desirability of medication to help with behavior control; and (d) an environment structured enough to help with controls but also accepting and supportive enough to help the child deal with his low self-esteem.[42]

Berman's conclusions were based on a twelve-hour battery of tests which he is trying to "hone down" to use as individual predictors "for an early diagnosis of delinquency and learning disabilities." Some children, he said, "are lucky enough to be in a school system where they can detect disabilities and deal with them; some bright kids with disabilities manage to make it because they are smart enough to compensate. The kids who don't make it are those from families and schools which can't detect the problem and don't know how to handle it." The theory is being tested in the Pueblo (Colorado) public schools which are operating a special program for "high-risk predelinquents." Supported by a $100,000 LEAA grant, the system is working with 56 children (of some 500 nominated by teachers and other school personnel) who have serious truancy records or other school problems. The heart of the program is intensive counseling directed to such things as "handling of frustration" and "appreciation of the national heritage." Bruce Burt of the state Division of Youth Services, who designed the program, thinks it is a model for all public schools. "It's become almost impossible," he said, "to separate education from treatment and treatment from education."

V

It is a moveable feast. What was established as sound education in one place becomes delinquency prevention in another and drug abuse control in a third. The methods adopted to "treat" delinquents in the detention center become the tools of prevention in the public school. The diagnostic screening program established in suburban Bucks County, Pennsylvania, to select students for "individualized teaching strategies" is recommended to the Governor's Council on Criminal Justice Planning in New Mexico as the ideal system to treat predelinquents; the project sold to the California Council on Criminal Justice as delinquency prevention is advertised among parents in Orange County as nothing but a system to help children overcome their academic problems. One can have it in any form. "Various studies indicate," says the flier from NIMH, "that young people who experience problems and failure in school, who have difficulties relating with parents, and who also have problems functioning in the community, are more likely to become involved with the juvenile justice system." The Center for Studies of Crime and Delinquency is supporting the PREP program (a school project for students with 'problems') "in the interest of developing preventive measures which can help children to develop effective academic, social and interpersonal skills, and thus to avoid serious future problems. In no way does this research support imply that students involved in this program are labeled or even considered to be pre-delinquent." The principal tells the parents that children who have been unable to keep up with their work or who "had some trouble getting along with the teacher or other students" will "practice self-control . . . which should help them learn to get along at school, and in the future, at work."[43] The agency says it is in the business of studying crime and delinquency. Either way it comes out as an attempt to manage and reform the behavior of children that the authorities consider problems.

Each "advance" in the field of delinquency flies the colors of liberal humanitarianism; each produces another increment of intervention and control; each gives work to a new squad of psychologists, social workers, teachers and consultants. When the first children's courts were established and the concept of delinquency was made popular, the ostensible purpose was to save juveniles from the invidiousness and harsh treatment of the adult criminal justice system, and to spare them the criminal record and public exposure suffered by adult offenders. Delinquency led to predelinquency, and predelinquency to diversion and early intervention. With each reform, the definitions became vaguer, the net wider and the individual's rights weaker, and while each category of crime and each new generation of intervention was advertised as more benign, each also carried with it the threat of more severe sanction. In theory a delinquent act was one which, if committed by an adult, would lead to criminal prosecution; in theory a predelinquent act was one which could only be committed by a minor (truancy, running away, "incorrigibility," "lewd and immoral conduct"); in theory, early intervention and treatment would spare the child the label of "predelinquent" (designed in turn to spare him the higher labels of "delinquent" and "criminal").[44] Each generation of preemptive labels requires less in the way of demonstrable acts, carries fewer legal protections and sanctions a wider and vaguer network of therapy and intervention.

What makes the medical model particularly attractive is that once deterrence and punishment are translated into treatment, civil liberties fly out the window. Behavior control in the name of delinquency may be suspect where the same control in the name of learning is welcome. The parent who objects to the LEAA-funded project for predelinquents in the local elementary school may be quite ready to enroll his child in precisely the same program if it promises to treat hyperkinesis, minimal brain dysfunction or some other "handicap." The point here is not that the cops have started to trade the blue uniform for the white coat (though in some cases they have) or that detectives appear in classrooms as "counselors" and teachers (though some do) but that the "disease" and the treatment in school, community and penal institution tend increasingly to reflect the same problems of behavior management, no matter how they are labeled.

The conventional wisdom that connects learning disabilities with delinquency is perhaps best summarized in a book called *Something's Wrong With My Child,* which has become a highly fashionable item on the disabilities circuit.[45] "Is there a link between learning disabilities and juvenile delinquency?" the authors ask. "The authors believe there is a relationship. Research has been limited. But signs do exist." Quotes are piled on quotes—cops, judges, probation officers, criminologists, psychologists, physicians—quotes from Camilla Anderson, the circuit-riding psychiatrist who believes that MBD is the cause of nearly all social evil and who goes about saying that the only real solution is to keep MBD carriers from having children; quotes from Dr. Frank Ervin, whom the authors describe as "a prominent researcher into causes of violence" without telling the reader that Ervin has also been one of the most prolific psychosurgeons in America ("We find that violence prone adults have a childhood history of hyperactive behavior. . . .") and without explaining that psychosurgery, as often as not, leaves its patients more incapacitated (though often more docile) than they were before; quotes from Saleem Shah of NIMH that "biological causes of violence are as important as the psychological or sociological ones."[46] Statistics follow statistics, extrapolating back (never forward) from crime to truancy to school failure to learning disabilities, from emotional problems to academic problems, from felons to dropouts, a great torrent of figures without a definition. If an attempt were made to reverse the projections, to carry them forward, the fallacy would be obvious. Most school failures do not become felons, and most hyperactive kids (no matter how defined) do not become killers or rapists. *Almost all delinquents are failures in school*, says the book with emphasis, but it does not point out that the same statement could undoubtedly be made about Appalachian coal miners, privates in the volunteer army and common laborers in the Department of Public Works.[47] In the context in which such statements are made, the confusion is further compounded by figures which lend an aura of scientific precision to the arbitrary terms that they purport to connect. The authors tell us, for example, that "ninety percent of 110 girls tested in a Tennessee state reformatory were from two to seven years below their grade level in reading."[48] The statement tells us nothing about why the girls were in the reformatory, what percentage of noninstitutionalized girls in Tennessee were from two to seven years below grade level in reading, or whether some third element—say a broken home or poor social skills or the fact that they were black—was a major factor in producing both the reading problem and the institutionalization in the reformatory. In another instance, they cite "a study of eighty-nine delinquents in California [which] revealed that 38 percent had learning disabilities [and that] an additional 20 percent were on the borderline."[49] Again there is no definition of terms and no indication that any control group was studied for purposes of comparison. But since the authors say elsewhere in the book that estimates of the percentage of children with learning disabilities in the population at large "range from 1 to 40 percent," the figures in the California study would make that group of eighty-nine a fair cross-section in some of the national estimates. In still another instance, they quote authorities to prove that "75 percent of the delinquents in New York are 'illiterate' " without so much as a clue as to their racial or economic background, the schools they attended or their intelligence.[50] (Since there are any number of studies to indicate that prisoners test below average in IQ, and since the authors of *Something's Wrong* define learning-disabled children as having "an intellectual potential that is usually normal or better," we may wonder whether IQ or LD or, quite possibly, something else is responsible.) Since virtually all studies of "delinquents" use institutionalized groups for their samples (institutions, of course, being a favorite hunting ground for social scientists), and since these groups are disproportionately composed of the poor and the black, one could just as easily conclude (as did most of the "authorities" of earlier days) that the poor and the black constitute the criminal class.

As used, the figures are, of course, meaningless: they connect undefined terms, reflect statistically biased samples and imply causality where none can be shown. In following their humanitarian inclinations to rescue "disabled" children from the horrors of the reformatory, however, the people who use such statistics manage to lend legitimacy to the very judgments which put those children there in the first place. It is only the category of "delinquent" which, in these links, supports the category of "learning disabled." If the first is arbitrary, then so is the second. In deploring the lack of medical and psychiatric attention given to children in the juvenile justice system, the advocates of treatment never raise the question whether the stupidity and callousness of the system comprise a vast spectrum of discrimination and arbitrary judgment involving every conceivable kind of case including thousands of kids who are not learning disabled (even by the widest stretch of definition) and who still shouldn't be there. The presentation of such statistics suggests the possibility, if not the likelihood, that the same prejudices and attitudes which create and impose the labels on one side of the equation also impose them on the other, that teachers and school principals impose the same demands and operate by the same standards as cops, probation officers and judges. Perhaps a hyperkinetic is a predelinquent because the same labels are imposed by similar people for similar reasons.

The effect of the argument is to reinforce the order of the school with the threat of the reformatory. It is not done (as it once was) with naked threats, invocations to behave, and maxims about character, but under the guise of an impersonal and objective science. Despite all the rhetoric about individualization, it is not the client who will be "individualized" but the treatment; the objective, training kids to conform to the system, is always the same. In such a process, the physical presence of the cop in the classroom, while symbolically revealing, is hardly necessary. The work will be done for him by those who would save the deviant from his clutches. In the happy society, none will be punished; all will be treated.

I V

Jerome Miller, Ph.D., sits in a cluttered cubicle on the tenth floor of a state office building in downtown Chicago contemplating the Bridgewaters of America. Miller, now the director of Family and Children's Services of the state of Illinois,

served from 1969 to 1973 as Commissioner of Youth Services
in Massachusetts. The Bridgewaters of America are the max-
imum-punishment detention centers and training schools to
which the most rebellious or "disturbed" juvenile offenders
are sentenced, what one study called "the final sanctions in
a graduated set of possible control measures to induce conformity by restrictions on freedom of movement, denial of
privileges, physical abuse, enforced idleness, silence, and ges-
tures of deference toward adult authorities."[51] Miller suc-
ceeded in closing down the original Bridgewater—formally
the Institute for Juvenile Guidance at Bridgewater, Massachusetts—and in initiating a set of extensive reforms that
replaced other institutions in Massachusetts with a spectrum
of alternatives from "community based treatment centers" to
outright release. The Massachusetts experiment generated a
furious battle between Miller and the state's corrections officers, probation departments and judges, threats of legislative
investigations and a series of incidents—fires, riots, escapes
—which Miller attributed to acts of sabotage by guards at
institutions scheduled to be closed.

The degree of Miller's "success" in Massachusetts is still
subject to debate; Miller himself decided early in 1973 that
the work he started could best be carried on by someone else
—presumably someone less controversial—and he resigned
to accept a similar mandate from Governor Dan Walker of
Illinois. But the theory is clear: "Until we've done everything
we can for the most unsalvageable we shouldn't try to deal
with the easy ones. If you take away the Bridgewaters, the
whole system begins to crack." The maximum-security institutions for hard-core offenders sustain the whole structure,
make all lesser impositions, threats and inducements to
"treatment" credible and legitimate, and sustain almost every argument for "prevention." "To the degree that you can
penetrate the deep end, the rest will take care of itself."

Forty minutes from Miller's downtown office, suburban
DuPage County recently opened its new Youth Home, a

$2 million detention center housing thirty adolescents in facilities so modern that the county and the architects distribute attractive little brochures to visitors:

> In the theme of the building, every effort has been made to preserve a residential and casual atmosphere consistent with the requirements of secure care. Wherever possible, materials that soften the institutional character are employed. Natural light is used discreetly through open courts . . . to relieve confinement. Decorative grilles provide protection to glazed areas without the adverse influence of barred enclosure. Natural materials in earth tones balance the gay cheerful paint colors and thread through the building to preserve continuity. . . . The child is accorded individual dignity and the opportunity to progress during his stay towards higher levels of responsibility as a prelude to eventual discharge from the influences of the court. . . . Maintenance and building control operation have been designed out to maximize opportunities for corrective programming for the individuals within the facility.
>
> In summation, the physical setting of the youth home is such as to provide a background for effective treatment with emphasis on constant direct visual and audio contact to maintain control rather than obvious physical restraints.

The "individuals within the facility" are kids between eleven and seventeen, the majority of whom committed no crime other than running away from home, and who are being held there for lack of alternatives. The "constant direct visual and audio contact to maintain control" includes wide glass partitions, electronically operated locks on all doors, "control stations" with banks of lights and switches, resembling a television station's control room, from which guards can monitor activity almost anywhere in the institution, and open microphones in all the cells. If a kid talks in his sleep, someone at a control station will be listening.[52] The director of the Youth Home, Merrill Moore, is also planning a token economy behavior modification system under which points will be awarded for good conduct; inmates will be promoted to higher levels of privileges (smoking, time to watch television, permission to stay up later) on the basis of points earned. At the top level, Moore said, the inmates will be allowed "coed privileges," which means permission to talk to inmates of the opposite sex, but "to maintain the top level, you've got to work your butt off." In this version of effective treatment, "obvious physical restraints" become unnecessary. Glass partitions, microphones and behavior modification arc better than clubs and bars.

"The question," said Jerry Miller, "is whether we can change the ideology before the technology overwhelms us." Gradually, the most obviously brutal juvenile prisons are being "reformed" or closed. In the summer of 1974, a federal judge in Sherman, Texas, ordered the Texas Youth Council to close down maximum-security centers for boys at Mountain View and Gatesville after uncontroverted testimony had revealed a pattern of brutality so vicious as to match anything in the history of American prisons.[53] Inmates were systematically beaten with sticks and fists; they were routinely forced to do meaningless work for six hours at a stretch (pulling blades of grass without bending their knees, shoveling sand from one pile to another), injected with powerful tranquilizers without medical supervision, forced to sign falsified incident reports to explain injuries inflicted by guards and locked in solitary cells for as long as thirty days on the whim of guards. Such institutions, said Judge William Wayne Justice, "are places where the delivery of effective rehabilitative treatment is impossible. . . . The court finds specifically that no reforms or alterations can rescue these institutions from their historical excesses."[54] He ordered the parties in the case—lawyers for several of the inmates, civil liberties groups, and the Texas Youth Council—to produce a plan for improved rehabilitation. The plan was to be based on a set of minimum standards which included provision of nonresidential community facilities, substantial upgrading of professional staff, employment of modern "diagnostic" tests to determine individual needs, and placement of clients in programs or institutions according to professionally assessed requirements.[55]

But the question of ideology remains. Miller was delighted with the Texas decision because it added to the legal weapons of reform the threat of closing down the most repressive institutions altogether. (Heretofore, "right to treatment" had been limited to judicial directives to improve services and facilities; all previous decisions had stopped short of an order to close an institution.[56]) But there was a better-than-even chance that despite the new weapon, "right to treatment" would sanction new styles of intervention which, if they were less brutal physically, might become more manipulative psychologically. It is the Bridgewaters, the Mountain Views and the Gatesvilles which make places like the DuPage County Youth Home appear enlightened and progressive and which, in turn, make "early intervention" by psychologists, teachers and social workers look like the very essence of liberal humanitarianism. "The corrections people are going to stand in line for behavior modification," Miller said, "because it will help them maintain the system; they'll have a whole new generation of professionals to front for them." The alternative, in his view, is to give the clients themselves economic and political power, enabling them to put pressure on the system and to choose placement and forms of "treatment." "In Massachusetts I had great hope in the possibilities of private care as an alternative to institutionalization; here in Illinois we have it, and it's as manipulative as anything else." The professionals become tools of the system, and the prime object of the system is to protect itself and maintain order. "The treatment options always condition the diagnosis; if you have a residential system, you'll get a lot of diagnoses oriented to residential treatment. The diagnostician always operates to eliminate his own risk. In one Texas institution for the so-called emotionally disturbed, 80 percent of the kids were sent home, and 80 percent of them are making it.

... The kid comes in as dependent or neglected; sooner or later you get him labeled as 'disturbed' or, if he's poor, as 'mentally retarded.' Eighty percent of the kids in institutions are there by court order because the social workers don't want to do the hard job of negotiating voluntary placements; if you had some real consumer muscle staffed by people who know the system, you could have some impact." One national survey concluded that the rate of recidivism in delinquency is higher for juveniles merely apprehended than for those who commit similar acts but are not apprehended, regardless of disposition.[57]

The technology is changing rapidly, the ideology hardly at all, and the consumers have yet to organize. Decisions such as that in the Texas case may give inmates and their lawyers a set of possible remedies against the overt abuses of the system, but they may also succeed in making the system more subtle and pervasive than it could have ever been before. As the Bridgewaters close, scientists replace brutes, and "direct visual and audio contact" is combined with behavior modification in the name of "individual dignity." Although "right to treatment" presumably implies a corollary right to be left alone, the reduction of overt brutality diminishes the reluctance of judges and social workers to enroll juveniles in whatever system replaces it. "There is some evidence," said a study of the Miller reforms in Massachusetts, "that referrals to the Department of Youth Services are increasing without compensating statewide reductions in commitments."[58] Obviously that wasn't what Miller intended, but it is the most likely way for the system to adjust.

The system creates the clients. In a book called *Radical Nonintervention,* sociologist Edwin M. Schur argues that "a great deal of the labeling of delinquents is socially unnecessary and counterproductive," and then continues to propose policies

that accept a greater diversity in youth behavior; special delinquency laws should be exceedingly narrow in scope or else abolished completely, along with preventive efforts that single out specific individuals and programs that employ "compulsory treatment." For those serious offenses that cannot simply be defined away through a greater tolerance of diversity, this reaction pattern may paradoxically increase "criminalization"—uniformly applied punishment not disguised as treatment; increased formalization of whatever juvenile court procedures remain, in order to limit sanctioning to cases where actual antisocial acts have been committed, and to provide constitutional safeguards for those proceeded against. . . .[59]

There is some leeway to influence the extent and forms of misconduct that prevail under a particular set of social conditions, but this influence can only operate as a consequence of efforts to shape the broader socio-cultural and definitional contexts that the behavior reflects. From this standpoint the specific youth "problems" we now experience have to be recognized as one of the prices we pay for maintaining a particular kind of social structure and dominant value system. We have to consider whether it is worth paying the price.[60]

The major developments of the late sixties and early seventies in the fields of delinquency and predelinquency indicate that the country is headed in quite a different direction, developing the appropriate technology and finding modes of control that will require very few Bridgewaters, if any, to make them appear credible. Increasingly, the new modes conceal the price, blur the distinction between "compulsory" and "voluntary" treatment and vitiate the line between crime and disease. Ideally clients will never know when they are being treated, or by whom.

SIX

The Dossiers of Children

Early in 1970, eight-year old David Isaacs was killed in a highway accident. In the course of the ensuing litigation, David's parents obtained a copy of the boy's "confidential" records from the suburban Philadelphia public school which he had attended since kindergarten. Like most such files, David's records were routinely available to school officials and, on demand, to other authorities, but neither the boy nor his parents had known what was in them before he was killed —they were not supposed to know. It took the efforts of a lawyer to pry them loose from the school. David's father, Mark Isaacs, at the time a visiting professor at Temple University, later described the experience of seeing his son's file —"startling reading," he said, "particularly to someone who knew him."[1]

> For example, he is described in several places as not being mature. "He can read and do numbers," according to one unsigned comment, "but is too immature." This was at the end of first grade.

I am not sure what the criteria of maturity are for a boy of six, but the year that followed was the year of the raisins. A few weeks after school started my wife noticed that David had suddenly begun to consume an unusual number of those individual boxes of raisins, the kind children put in their lunch kettles. David was averaging better than two boxes a day, five days a week, which is a lot of raisins even for a very active boy.

It turned out that he was feeding a special buddy at school. Buddy was undersized and came from a poor family. David had concluded that the reason Buddy was undersized was the fact that he was poor and therefore undernourished. Hence, the raisins.

But maybe warmth and concern for other people have nothing to do with maturity. At any rate the school could not find these qualities in David. In an undated "behavior description" he was given a rating of two under "concern for others." Two means "self-centered."

The fact is, David had almost too great a sense of responsibility for a small boy. I was free-lancing then, a mode of life that involved frequent plane trips. David was the one who did the most worrying about getting me to the airport on time. Sometimes I would josh him for acting like "a little old man." That would make him grin; he enjoyed being relied on.

Another anonymous comment: "Refuses to use left hand. Dislikes being reminded to try." Of course he refused. Of course he disliked nagging. He had an orthopedic problem on his left side and, as a result, there was a slight limp to his gait, although he could move like a flash, and a lack of agility and strength in his left hand.

An orthopedic surgeon had prescribed exercises and both the hand and the foot were improving, but David still worried about them and it bothered him to have other people call attention to them.

Possibly this suggests that there was no communication between home and school. Not so. My wife faithfully attended every parent-teacher conference that was scheduled—a total of six or seven on David.

My wife is an articulate woman and, in addition to

talking to David's teachers about his left hand and foot, she also discussed without reserve his attitudes and his work. The remarkable thing about the confidential file, however, is that not one word of what my wife said is reported. That's the convenience of confidential files. They don't have to be complete or even true.

Two months before he was killed David was given a standard psychological test. The results themselves are not significant—he scored average to high average—but the comments appended by the school psychologist fascinate me. And this time the comments are signed.

Subject boy had bad associates, the psychologist declared. The bad associates were his parents. Allow me to quote, correcting the misspellings and mistakes in punctuation: "Although David was generally cooperative, he became very argumentative and disrespectful when his date of birth was questioned. Although it was listed as 1-22-62 on the cumulative folder, he insisted it was changed to 9-4-61. David also gives one the impression that he had a feeling of superiority and perfection. He stated that his mother said he read well at home. Up to this point the parent-school rapport hasn't been too good. Perhaps David's feelings of superiority, if they do exist, are bolstered through parent attitudes. . . ."

My wife and I have tried to recall situations in which we had proved unmanageable. We have come up with three: (1) I refused to fill out a questionnaire from a commercial insurance company that had worked out a special accident policy deal with the school board; (2) I also refused to answer questions about my income in a survey designed to justify federal contributions to the district; and (3) My wife refused to go along with a teacher who wanted David punished on weekends by barring him from his two or three favorite TV programs—this when he did not do his reading to the teacher's satisfaction. My wife's answer in the third case was that she saw no virtue in ganging up on the kid.

My answer in the first instance was that I had been evading insurance deals for years and in the second that my income was not any of the school board's business. But

David was in tears when I refused to fill out the forms. He said the teacher would be very angry with him. I pooh-poohed that and told him to ask her or the principal to call me, if he were given a hard time. He was right and I was wrong.

But the appalling thing to me about this report is the psychologist's self-revealed insensitivity. Obviously, if a boy insists his birthday has been changed, there must be a reason. There was.

The Sunday before that school year started, David and I were working around the garage and he asked me if we could have another "man-to-man" talk (we had them once or twice a month). We got into the car, so we could be comfortable and undisturbed—and he poured his heart out to me.

He would be going into the third grade, he said, with the terrible handicap of being only seven, when everyone else would be eight. Although he was tall enough and strong enough to take care of himself, he would still be the youngest boy in class and everyone would be looking down on him until January, when he would become eight. Wasn't there anything I could do about it?

For some reason, the convention of the Queen's birthday popped into my head. Queen Elizabeth's actual birthday is in April, but the official one, the one at which honors are conferred, takes place in May or June, when the weather is better for a garden party. What was good enough for Her Majesty was certainly good enough for my son. I told him about the Queen and proposed that we shift his official birthday to the coming week.

David beamed in ecstasy, but there was one small cloud. Could we get away with it? Indeed we could, I assured him. After all, I was his father and his birthday would be whenever I said it was. But again, of course, he was right in his fears and I was wrong.

And yet I don't regret our subterfuge. We had a birthday party that first week in September and for the remaining five months of his life David was as happy an eight-year-old as I have ever known.

Why didn't the school psychologist call us to find out about it? I don't know. I can only suppose that, if he had, he might have compromised the security of that precious confidential file.

The experience of the Isaacs family was unusual in that they managed to see the file, all of it, presumably, and not just those portions that the school system saw fit to show them. Until recently most parents had no such access, no control over who saw the file, no check on what went into it, no opportunity to delete or correct misinformation, and, in many cases, no idea of the scope of the data collected. With the passage in 1974 of the so-called Buckley Amendment governing access to, and privacy of, school records (see pages 185–87), that situation may change for some parents and students, though it is unlikely that many will be affected. Yet the contents of David's dossier were in most respects typical, even benign, a common example of an almost universal tendency to collect not only the obvious data on school performance—grades, tests and, on occasion, anecdotal observations of conduct—but also a vast amount of medical and psychological information from counselors, disciplinary personnel, doctors, nurses, psychiatrists, social workers, courts and the police concerning the child, his parents, his siblings and his friends. The results of screens for LD, MBD and emotional disturbance become part of that record, as do psychological test scores, reports from welfare workers and material on family history derived from parent questionnaires and interviews. In New York, for example, a typical student dossier comprises a rainbow of variously colored forms which include:

A buff-colored, cumulative four-page record card that notes personal and social behavior, along with scholastic achievement. The card is kept on file for fifty years.

A blue or green test data card recording all standardized test scores and grade equivalents. That card is also kept on file for fifty years.

A white four-page chronological reading record.

An emergency home contact card.

A salmon-colored health record, one side for the information of teachers, the other for the school nurse and doctor.

A dental check card.

An audiometer screening test report.

An "articulation card" containing teachers' recommendations for tracking in the junior high school.

A teacher's anecdotal file on the student's behavior.

An office guidance record, comprising counselors' evaluations of aptitudes, behavior and personality characteristics.

A Bureau of Child Guidance file that is described (though not always treated) as confidential, and which includes reports to and from psychologists, psychiatrists, social workers, various public and private social welfare agencies, the courts and the police.

All disciplinary referral cards, recording every instance of punitive action by the school.

The record has room for nearly everything. In a survey conducted in the late sixties, a team supported by the Russell Sage Foundation discovered that three-fourths of all school systems kept personality ratings, samples of student work and autobiographies; one-third recorded the race and religion of students; nearly half noted nationality or national origin; and half kept photographs on the record form.[2] In New York City, one parent learned accidentally (from a friend in a school office) that his child's record contained the observation that the parent was "a black militant" and the daughter would therefore be a troublemaker; another stumbled on a notation that her child had engaged in "unauthorized distribution of a student rights handbook"; a third—again by accident—found an entry categorizing her son as "a real sickie—absent, truant, stubborn and very dull"; and a fourth, attending a routine parent-teacher conference about his teenage son, discovered that the boy had been cited as "strangely introspective" in the third grade, "unnaturally interested in girls" in the fifth and possessed of "peculiar political ideas" by the time he was twelve. There was no way for the parent to challenge, explain or amend the record. It was sheer coincidence that he even learned of it.[3]

Most parents never see the record, or see only those parts that the system, "in the interest of the child," chooses to disclose, and very few are informed that the files that they are not permitted to see are accessible to cops, juvenile officers, welfare workers and, in many instances, to employers and military recruiters. The Russell Sage study, conducted by David A. Goslin and Nancy Bordier, found that in more than half of the systems surveyed, juvenile courts, health departments and agents of the FBI and CIA can see student files on request (without consent by, or notification to, parents); that in more than a third, the local police had routine access, but that in fewer than 10 percent was complete access granted either to the students or their parents. "What is particularly significant," said Goslin and Bordier, "is the impression that school officials have strong reservations about giving parents very much information (other than grade reports and sometimes achievement test scores) about the content of evaluations that are continually being made of their children." In a followup study completed in 1972, the Russell Sage Foundation found that of a sample of some 450 schools, only 40 percent had, or intended to develop, written policies for records; one-third did not ask for any form of consent before collecting personality test data; nearly half did not obtain any form of consent before collecting information on a student's family background or outside interests; and 16 percent did not obtain any form of consent before submitting students to psychiatric examinations. The followup also indicated that a fourth of the schools surveyed never reviewed or destroyed records, that a fifth denied parents access to any part of their children's records and that less than half protected records from outside parties.[4] Even in those systems which try to institute policies of confidentiality, informal arrangements between school personnel and outside parties often maintain the flow of information. In one system visited by a Russell Sage researcher, the written policy had been drawn up by a committee of counselors. As a result, "the social worker thought the policy did not apply to her records; the mechanics teacher who had considerable informal contact with local employers thought that it applied only to formal requests handled by the registrar, and one of the principals regarded it as of the utmost importance to stay on good terms with local employers by telling them in detail of all the behavior problems potential employees had experienced while in school."

The outside parties depend on school records for information and are prepared to fight for the privilege, frustrating even the best-intentioned efforts of school administrations to establish some control. In 1970, partly in response to mounting public concern about privacy, the New York City Board of Education appointed a committee to review and reshape the system's record policies. The committee, composed of school officials and representatives of civic organizations, recommended that the system stop furnishing sensitive information about students to outside agencies until more restrictive policies could be adopted. The chancellor of the system, Harvey B. Scribner, a liberal with a reputation for concern for student rights, accepted the recommendation and ordered the schools not to furnish information to outside parties without the consent of students or their parents. Two weeks later he reversed himself and rescinded the order. In the interim, the Board of Education had been swamped by calls from 28 separate and distinct categories of outsiders complaining that their usual sources of information had been cut off. The complaints came from officials of the city and state civil service commissions, representatives of the Health Department, district attorneys, representatives of the Selective Service System, probation officers, the police, welfare workers, military intelligence officers and agents of the FBI.

In most instances, school administrators regard themselves as representatives of authority, not as advocates of children, and are therefore happy to furnish information to any official agent without a semblance of resistance. In what was perhaps the most flagrant violation of confidentiality ever recorded, and certainly the most visible, the U.S. Government Printing Office, late in 1970, published a report of a Congressional committee investigation of the Washington public schools which included 45 pages of absence sheets, test papers and documents concerning the discipline problems of certain specifically named students. The investigation had been conducted by a Special Select Subcommittee of the Committee on the District of Columbia (chaired by Representative John L. McMillan of South Carolina), and its report was routinely printed and offered for distribution by the committee. The report included 29 test papers—21 with failing grades—all with the names of students, as well as letters, memoranda and other documents—also with the names of students—which included allegations of sexual perversion, criminal violations and other forms of personal and social deviance. The documents had been furnished voluntarily by the school system; there had been no attempt to alert parents or students, no effort to obtain consent and no attempt to resist. Parents in the District sued the committee and the school system for an injunction to stop Congress from circulating the report, for an injunction prohibiting the schools from further disclosure of confidential information and for money damages from school and Congressional officials. In May 1973, after losing in the lower courts, the parents obtained a qualified decision from the Supreme Court remanding the case to the Circuit Court of Appeals, which had originally ruled that the Committee report was immune from legal action under the Congressional "Speech or Debate" clause of the Constitution. (The clause, originally drawn to protect legislative acts against executive or "royal" retribution, protects official acts of members of Congress against civil suit or criminal penalties.) The burden of the Supreme Court decision was that while the collection of personal information about Washington schoolchildren—as part of the investigation—was within the powers of Congress (and therefore privileged), public distribution of the report was not protected.[5] In the meantime, however, the issue of the records themselves had, in the view of the Court, become moot; the House Committee had already assured the courts that it planned no further distribution of the report (though copies were, in fact, still available from Congressional sources) and the school system had announced new policies purportedly designed to protect confidential information, leading the trial court (with the Supreme Court's concurrence) to conclude that "there is no substantial threat of future injury to appellants." In furnishing the information to Congress, the Supreme Court said, the school officials "were acting within the scope of their authority under applicable law." What that meant was that no school official would, or could, be held accountable for furnishing even the most damaging personal data to Congress.

Yet the circulation of "confidential" information to employers, to the police or to others may in fact constitute the most benign element of the process. The fact is that almost invariably the record is a weapon of control, perhaps the most significant weapon the schools now possess, particularly in those systems which are prohibited by law or ideology from more direct forms of retribution. Everywhere students are told—and told and told and told—that everything they do is being watched and recorded, that it will all go on that record and that the record is likely to shape their lives forever. Part of the object of those records is to make students *believe* that they will be seen by employers and other authorities. It is a process in which, as Edgar Friedenberg pointed out, students "learn that the most terrifying creatures are those whose bite passes unnoticed at the time and later swells, festers and paralyzes; they cannot defend themselves against the covert, lingering hostility of teachers and administrators."[6] And even where there is no hostility and no bite, the threat exists. Given the unlimited scope of contemporary school records, it is hard to say whether those most damaged are the conformists or the deviants.

Ever since the late sixties, mounting public concern about privacy has generated growing pressure on school systems, as on other agencies, to protect confidential records and to give the subjects of those records (and/or their parents) opportunities to inspect and correct them. The original Russell Sage study prompted the Foundation to publish a set of guidelines which have since become the bases of other efforts, local and national, to check school records abuses. The National Education Association and certain other professional groups have issued codes and drawn model policies for school records, and a growing number of state legislatures and local school systems have adopted regulations and issued policy statements purporting to protect confidentiality and guarantee access to parents or, if they are old enough, to the students themselves.[7] The most significant measure to protect student privacy, however, came in the summer of 1974 when Congress passed the Family Educational Rights and Privacy Act requiring all school systems receiving federal funds to give parents "the right to inspect and review any and all records, files and data concerning their children [and] to a hearing to challenge the contents." The legislation, sponsored by Senator James Buckley of New York, a conservative, came in the form of an amendment to extensions of federal aid-to-education bills, and also includes a prohibition against the release of student records or personal information, without written parental consent, to anyone other than school officials who have a legitimate "educational interest." Regulations issued by the Department of Health, Education and Welfare to implement the law (summer 1975) impose stringent requirements on schools receiving federal education funds. The schools must allow parents full access to all records maintained on their children, provide them with copies upon request and provide "an opportunity for a hearing to challenge such records on the grounds that they are inaccurate, misleading or otherwise inappropriate." The hearing may be quite formal, conducted by a disinterested third party, and must give parents "a full and fair opportunity" to present relevant evidence; a decision must be "rendered in writing with a reasonable period of time." Schools, moreover, may not release data about a student to any outsider, or give outsiders access to student records, without the written informed consent of parents specifying the records to be released, the reasons for such release and the names of the persons to whom such records are being released. On request, parents are to be given a copy of any record which they consent to release to outsiders.[8]

The act is likely to have an impact, particularly in suburban systems which are already responsive to middle-class parents; it may also make teachers and administrators more cautious about what they put in student records, and give parents a new weapon in demanding access to files. Yet the chances of rigorous enforcement are slim. Even in cases involving the most flagrant violations of civil rights laws and desegregation guidelines, the government has been reluctant to cut off funds to local schools. In the case of records, the chances are even slimmer, despite the stringent provisions of the regulations. Within a few months after the law's passage, school systems were finding ways to sabotage or circumvent its provisions. One, in the name of compliance, sent students home with forms asking parents to give blanket permission to release records to general categories of outsiders—"potential employers,""social agencies," "police authorities," or "all of the above." Others cleaned out—or hid away—their more sensitive files in preparation for parental requests to inspect; still others chose not to define as "records" student data they didn't wish parents to see or control.

Since the formal regulations were not issued until the end of the 1974–1975 school year, it will be some time before the full effects of the law are felt. The HEW regulations are explicit about what constitutes a "record," but schools in the past have been adept at redefining the term. Even in those systems which already have regulations guaranteeing parental access, there has never been agreement on which portions should be accessible to parents (or students) or under what conditions they may be inspected. Nearly half the states now have laws which provide that the files of school counselors —which include psychological test scores and observations —are privileged and that they should be treated like the records of physicians. The American Personnel and Guidance Association (APGA), the professional organization of school counselors, maintains that that privilege protects the client (i.e., the student) even against his parents, though in practice it often fails to protect him against other school officials. A California law on the books since 1959 gives parents the right to inspect their children's cumulative records, but local officials routinely limit their access to hard data kept on cards in the office, or simply refuse to comply at all. "Parents can get terribly upset about IQ scores," said the principal of a Beverly Hills school that otherwise works hard to cater to parents. "I would only reveal an IQ score if I decided the parent was the kind who should know it."

School psychologists, guidance counselors and deans have successfully maintained the position that their files, which usually include the most extensive personal information about individual students, are not part of the individual student's "record." Many systems, moreover, maintain multiple sets of files, particularly in those states and communities where some form of access is permitted, and that practice, in turn, is compounded by the highly sophisticated techniques of bureaucratic resistance and obfuscation which have developed in large urban systems.

New York, the only state where confidentiality and parental access regulations have been on the books for fifteen years, provides an example of the problem. In 1960, the New York State Commissioner of Education directed broad disclosure to parents of all records including "progress reports, subject grades, intelligence quotients, tests, achievement scores, medical records, psychological and psychiatric reports, selective guidance notes and the evaluations of students by educators."[9] "The parent," as a matter of law," said the directive, "is entitled to such information." A year later, a state court in Nassau County cited the Commissioner's order in directing a Long Island school system to give parents access to their son's records, and six months thereafter, the Commissioner specifically directed the New York City Board of Education to comply with those rulings.[10] New York City, however, defied the order, and, in 1962, issued its own regulations—both acts in flagrant violation of the law and the Commissioner's directives—which stated that although "upon request" a parent could inspect the official school record of his child, consisting of "the cumulative record cards, including the test data card," everything else, including "teacher notes, guidance notes, record books or other data" as well as "correspondence and reports of social agencies, clinics, doctors, psychiatrists, psychologists, hospitals" are "not part of the official school record" and are "therefore, not to be made available for the parent to inspect."[11] (The same city circular gave outside agencies the right to obtain "such information as may be deemed essential to the child's welfare"—in other words, *carte blanche* access, again violating state regulations.) In 1966, New York City updated its policies, but did nothing to conform to state regulations,[12] and its official flaunting of the law persisted, in spite of a precise and comprehensive definition of legal requirements in the state's *Manual on Pupil Records* and mounting pressure from citizens' groups, until 1972, when the matter of parental access to records again came before the Commissioner. The case involved a junior high school girl whose parents were told she could not attend graduation exercises because she was a "bad citizen." The parents wanted to know what she had done, and the principal replied that the school had an entire dossier on her "poor citizenship" which was confidential—they couldn't see it. It took a hearing and another ruling by the Commissioner, eight months after the graduation ceremonies, to restate the regulations that were already twelve years old. Sounding weary of repeating himself, Commissioner Ewald Nyquist ruled that refusing parents access to records "is unsound from an educational viewpoint and, in addition, violates the spirit of my decision [in prior cases]. . . . It has been argued that the school acts *in loco parentis* and may in the best interest of the student refuse to reveal information contained in his record to his parent. . . . There is no merit to this contention."[13]

New York City school administrators responded in form, arguing that parental access would create "serious problems for schools and for pupils," conjuring up visions of parents lining up for blocks to see their children's records, demanding use of overworked duplicating machines and closing down the system with their onslaughts. But that, too, was sheer obfuscation. For years, even the limited portion of the record that parents were permitted to inspect was subject to such cumbersome administrative machinery that the process remained practically unmanageable for most parents. The parents had to make an appointment weeks in advance, and they would then be shown the file, or portions of the file, in the presence of an assistant principal or other school official. The parents were not permitted to take notes, make copies or, in many instances, even to hold anything in their hands. The record would be "interpreted" for them by the official.

The argument of the school psychologists and counselors that they are protecting children by denying access to parents is nearly always pure wind. The real client is not the child but the school—the dean of discipline, the principal—and the measure of success, the thing that most counselors are rated on by their own superiors, is the record itself. (A "complete" folder is the mark of professional competence; a fat folder is an indication that the child is a problem.) There are instances where a child's remarks to a counselor can produce parental retribution if the parents were to hear about them, but that possibility does not affect the child's own right to know what's in the record. In practice, however, the counselors are as careful about keeping the dossier from the student as they are about keeping it from the parents, and many will admit that they do it primarily to protect themselves. "If there was ever a requirement to give parents access to those records," said one, "I'd keep them at home, bring in only those I need each day, and insist that they're my private files which don't belong to the school. Nobody wants to be spending half their time defending himself against people who don't agree with something they write in a case study, or maybe—who knows—face a lawsuit because some mother is angry and thinks you slandered her child." Such admissions are almost always accompanied by the assertion that the counselor will protect the student's privacy against anyone, that even teachers are not allowed to see the counselor's case files without a legitimate reason. Yet almost any teacher can get any record he wants, formally or informally, and the conclusions of those "confidential case files" routinely make the rounds of the teachers' room and frequently appear on other portions of a student's dossier. (For example, "John's emotional state is caused by contemporary negative family dynamics; the subject has aggressive feelings and behavior which are complicating his dyslexic state."[14]) The fact that those conclusions are often a mix of pseudo-psychology and pure gibberish, and that many of them are based on the observations of untrained personnel, or simply on hearsay, does not preclude their circulation.[15] In one instance, administrators of a public school in California announced publicly that a student facing suspension by the Board of Education had been guilty of "serious violations of manners, morals and discipline." The parents sued, and three years later the courts concluded that the public statement was based on nothing more than the allegations of the school superintendent, and the student was awarded damages. In another instance, a secretary at a private tutoring agency in New York City called a public junior high school principal to inquire about a child's reading level and was gratuitously informed that the child had a history of bed wetting, that his mother was an alcoholic and that a different man slept at the home every night. The disclosures were reported to the Board of Education, which promised to investigate; the principal, however, denied that the incident ever took place, and his superiors backed him up. In still another case, a private psychiatrist who had (with the parents' consent) voluntarily furnished a report on a student which he subsequently felt was inaccurate formally asked (again with parental consent) that the school remove the report from the student's file. The school refused, even after it was threatened with a lawsuit. What was in the record would always remain in the record. If it is subject to inspection, challenge or amendment, its usefulness as a weapon of intimidation is diminished. From the viewpoint of the school, perhaps the worst thing would be for parents and students to discover that the record contains little of substance that can be used against them.

I I

Billy Washington was sixteen when he dropped out of a San Francisco high school and nineteen when he found what he thought would be his first regular job. An assistant employment manager of the local branch of a department store chain had promised him full-time work as a "tire buster" changing tires in the automotive department, but on the day Billy Washington reported for work, he was told he had no job. Four years earlier he had been a passenger in a stolen car, had been questioned about the theft and then released by the police. No charges had ever been brought, but young Washington got a juvenile police arrest record in connection with the theft which did not indicate the disposition of the case. In theory that record was confidential, but the chain for which Billy thought he was going to work, like most large enterprises, has access to such files. It is easy.[16]

Harriet Mannheim was fifteen years old when she was arrested in a demonstration at a New York City high school. In the company of other students (and parents), Harriet had been manning a "grievance table" in the school lobby; they had been ordered by the principal to leave the table and warned that they would be suspended and arrested. Shortly thereafter more than fifty police officers arrived, escorted the students out and took them to the local precinct station. There Harriet Mannheim was told that she would not face formal charges but that henceforth she would have a juvenile arrest record. Ten days later, she and her father were called to a meeting at the police station where they were told that there was no way that the record could be expunged, that it "would remain for life." The charge was criminal trespass. In the process, she and her father learned that the record also contained information that she had attempted to enter a school during an illegal teachers' strike the year before. That, too, was part of the record.[17]

There is no way to know how many Harriet Mannheims and Billy Washingtons there are. Few ever learn why they are not hired, and some are not informed that a record even exists. (In Billy's case, the employment manager later denied that he knew anything about the police record, or that the company had access to such data. Billy, he said, had misunderstood what he told him; no job had ever been firmly promised.) What is certain is that more than ten million juveniles in America have police dossiers—the figure may be much higher—and that many private corporations and government agencies have access to that information. One study, published in 1967, indicated that 27 percent of all male youths in the country will have been arrested at least once by the time they turn eighteen; in addition, many police departments open a file on any minor who has had a "police contact"—as suspect, victim, witness or offender, or as an associate of a suspect or offender.[18] The record may indicate the disposition of the case, but frequently it indicates no more than the fact that the individual was referred to a court or to the juvenile authorities or that he was "counseled and released" by the police.

Given the scope of activities for which a juvenile can get a police record, it is hardly surprising that the data are often vague, misleading or blatantly false. In New York City, where the police file a YD (Youth Division) card for almost every minor who runs afoul of a policeman—at a rate of 60,000 a year—a study conducted by the city's Criminal Justice Coordinating Council concluded that nearly half are issued for behavior which, under a different exercise of police discretion, would have led to no action at all.[19] Included in that behavior were "loudness, boisterousness, use of obscene language, annoying people, throwing objects, causing crowds to gather, demonstrating, swimming, and refusing to move from a park." The study also found that:

In approximately 40 percent of the cases there is no check on the validity of the initial decision to classify the behavior as an offense.

YD cards found to have been issued in error—that is, the behavior was later found not to have been appropriately classified as an offense—are not removed from the data bank.

YD cards are filed for the victims of offenses although there is no evidence of improper behavior on the part of the victims. Yet such cards are, for many purposes, equated with the cards for offenders. . . . In one case, a youth was accused of hitting a woman with a stick. The investigator discovered that the complainant had lied and the complaint was unfounded. Yet the record remains. Similarly, when a youth is innocently involved, or when the initial issuance of a YD card is unauthorized, the offense report remains in the data banks.

Despite such handicaps, the record was found to be a major determinant in the disposition of subsequent charges. Minors with three or four entries on their YD cards were much less likely to qualify for probation or to have their cases dismissed than those with no record. Length, not content, appeared to matter most.

In theory, the records produced by police contacts are supposed to be confidential. Juvenile court proceedings are usually closed to the press and spectators to protect minors, and a few states have provisions allowing minors, when they reach the age of eighteen, to petition the courts to have their juvenile records legally sealed, thereby precluding their use in subsequent judicial proceedings. In practice, however, both police and court records, or portions thereof, find their way into other hands and continue to follow the individual into his adult life. In San Francisco, where Billy Washington tried to get his job, attorneys from the Youth Law Center occasionally call the Juvenile Division of the city's Police Department, identify themselves as the manager of a restaurant or other small business and ask whether a particular individual has a record. Usually they are told to come to the office, identify themselves and get the information. They have never been told that such information is unavailable. In San Francisco, the standing instructions on juvenile police records (issued in 1972 by the presiding judge of the juvenile court) provide that "law enforcement agencies in San Francisco County . . . may release any information in their files regarding juveniles to the following: California Bureau of Investigation and Information; all California law enforcement agencies; all California school systems; all California public welfare agencies; all California district attorneys' offices; California Youth Authority [and] any California court pursuant to subpoena from such court." The judge who issued those instructions regarded them as consistent with the most recent court decisions.[20]

In general, juvenile police records fall into four categories: the files of state youth authorities and correctional systems,

the files of juvenile courts and probation departments (including the growing files of diversion projects), the juvenile records of individual police departments and the extensive juvenile indexes maintained by state police agencies and county sheriffs' departments which list only name, certain vital statistics, "offense" and the name of the local police department from which the complete record can be obtained.
For the majority of the individuals on the index, the "offense" never led to formal court action, for many it may be nothing more than truancy or running away from home, hanging around a street corner, or "suspicion," and for many others the index will fail to indicate final disposition of the case. The index, therefore, is stuffed with the names of innocent children who have never been charged with a criminal offense. In Orange County, California, (which is largely white, suburban and affluent), the Central Juvenile Index maintained by the Sheriff's Department contains the names of 160,000 minors, roughly 30 percent of the total juvenile population.

Of all those police data systems, the juvenile index is the most porous. Because it is designed to be a common reference file through which one police department can learn about the existence of information on individuals in the files of other jurisdictions, it is open on a routine basis to personnel of different agencies: district attorneys, local police, military recruiters, military intelligence and the FBI. Most of the indexes are now computerized in such a way that officers of participating agencies can query the data bank either through local computer or teletype terminals or by calling a central telephone number, giving a departmental or individual access code number and furnishing the name and vital statistics of the person about whom the information is being sought. (If there is such information in the data bank, it will come back in seconds.) As a consequence, the information in the system is subject to the standards of confidentiality of dozens of different police departments and the varying scruples of thousands of cops and other officers. In Orange County, for example, Captain James Luxemburger, who runs the Central Juvenile Index for the Sheriff's Department, conceded that information sometimes gets into the wrong hands through "these mickey mouse police agencies, podunk police departments that'll pass it on to the mayor, who owns a store, or to somebody's cousin." Luxemburger insisted that the practice isn't frequent, that if anyone was found leaking information from the index "they'd be in for a lawsuit" and that, in any case, the CJI is only an index, not a complete record.

Others, particularly lawyers who regularly defend juveniles, aren't as sanguine. "The CJI," said one, "is like a sieve. Every department store and every insurance company hires moonlighting cops and ex-cops for exactly that purpose—because they or their buddies have access to the records. We've had any number of kids tell us that they were told they couldn't get some job because they had a record, even if the record only said they'd once run away from home when they were fourteen. You can never prove it because it's the kid's word against the employer's, and what employer is going to compromise his access to the files by admitting it?"[21] Most minors do not know that in some states they have a right to have their court records sealed when they turn eighteen, the lawyer said, but even if they did, it would not protect them against the separate files and computers of individual police departments or the data bank of the CJI. The fact that the index provides only limited information is no deterrent against bias by employers, military recruiters or insurance companies: the existence of the "record" is in itself usually enough to slam the doors, particularly if the individual concerned was once associated with a criminal offense. The central index provides access to the fact that there is such a record. It is therefore no longer necessary for those employers to have a source in every local police department; a few moonlighting cops may be enough for an entire region and, in a growing number of instances, for an entire state.

The declarations and promises concerning the confidentiality of juvenile records, as Justice Fortas noted in the *Gault* opinion (1967), have always been "more rhetoric than reality."[22]

> Statutory restrictions almost invariably apply only to the court records, and even as to those the evidence is that many courts routinely furnish information to the FBI and the military, and on request to government agencies and even to private employers. Of more importance are police records. In most states, the police keep a complete file of juvenile "police contacts" and have complete discretion as to disclosure of juvenile records. Police departments receive requests for information from the FBI and other law enforcement agencies, the Armed Forces, and social service agencies, and most of them generally comply. Private employers word their application forms to produce information concerning juvenile arrests and court proceedings, and in some jurisdictions information concerning juvenile police contacts is furnished private employers as well as government agencies.

Fortas's observations were borne out by a survey of appropriate state legislation which found (in 1974) that the majority of states have no laws which control or limit access to juvenile records in the possession of the police, and that only six make it a crime to "improperly disclose" information from juvenile records.[23] Fortas, however, was writing in the comparatively primitive days before most juvenile arrest and court records were computerized, before the advent of federally funded predelinquency programs and before the ideology of early intervention and treatment had been fully developed. Since then, technology and ideology have conspired to make the scope of the record and the spectrum of agencies with access considerably more inclusive.

The most extensive personal records within the criminal justice system are those maintained by courts, probation departments and diversion programs. Because those agencies have a mandate to regard the individual's attitude, family background and social situation as highly significant in making decisions for correction and "treatment," they include virtually every form of personal information as a relevant part of the record: the names and relationships of all people living in the child's home; family income; educational history; parents' education; reports from doctors, psychiatrists, clinics and other social service agencies; and extensive interview data on the social attitudes of the client and his parents. With the advent of automatic data processing, some courts began to create new rationales, if not reliable methods, whereby the old data could be used more extensively and systematically. In St. Louis, for example, the information is now analyzed through computers to indicate the "probability" that a certain course of correction will be successful.[24] The data on which that probability is based include the individual's prior police record, the names and court records of all his siblings, his economic and social background, psychological information and other items. These are compared with the past performance of (presumably) similar individuals in similar situations to determine the chances of "success for correcting a child with specific social, psychological, economic, personal, and referral characteristics." There is little evidence, of course, that such predictive methods have ever worked and considerable evidence that they do not, but they do offer another scientific rationale for collecting all that information and making it part of the record.[25] One indication of the confidentiality of that record is the fact that in the promotional literature of the firm which designed the system there are at least two examples of cases which include the real names, addresses and police records of boys sixteen and seventeen years old.[26] (The files of diversion programs are even more subject to abuse. Few programs have any provision for the destruction of records, and in some instances they have been used later in court, despite guarantees of confidentiality.[27])

Other agencies are catching up. As police departments become more "scientific" and as cops become more educated, and, in a sense, more socially conscious, their appetite for similar kinds of data grows in proportion. It is no secret that most large police departments and the FBI maintain files of political radicals and other "subversives" (including minors), but there are strong indications that many police agencies are also in the habit of maintaining separate files (as in Los Angeles) of "hard-core delinquents" and other minors regarded by the schools, the police or other organizations as potentially "violent" or otherwise troublesome.[28] Information about such individuals is routinely exchanged between police and schools, with appropriate notations recorded in the dossiers maintained by each of the participating agencies. At one meeting in a public high school in Hollywood, California, attended by police and school officials (according to a participant) "it was suggested that the different police departments and the different schools work together to build files on students who were either problems or potential problems—in school as well as out. It was further suggested that this information follow the student from one school to another and from one incident to another. The type of information was not listed in detail but was of a type that would be incriminating if and when the student were stopped by the police or wished to be transferred out of the school."[29]

The practices vary but the pattern is consistent. In New York City, the citadel of American liberalism, the police not only maintain those files of YD cards but usually issue YD identification cards to individual children, telling them that they now have a record and that the card must be carried at all times. (There is no provision either in the law or in police regulations establishing this self-incriminating requirement, but individual officers do it anyway.) In some communities, the police maintain files of "habitual truants" to check when they stop children on the streets during school hours; in others, schools notify the police when students are given disciplinary transfers from one school to another; and in most there are formal procedures to exchange information among schools, the police and the courts about students who have been arrested, who confront court action, who participate in delinquency diversion projects, or who enroll in a new school after being detained in a youth home or correctional institution. In many cities with a computerized juvenile index, kids stopped in high-delinquency neighborhoods are routinely checked through the computer to see if they have a police record. "Imagine you're a cop," said a police officer in New Orleans, "and you stop a juvenile who appears to be truant in a high-delinquency neighborhood. You have to make a quick decision on the scene; so you call in and find out who you're dealing with."

The appetite for information is voracious, particularly in those police departments which pride themselves on their modernity, and where they do not collect it on their own, computers are making it easier to obtain it from others. It is the mark of sophistication. "Information about a juvenile's home life, affiliations, and welfare status," wrote John C. Coffee, a New York attorney who tried (with only limited success) to attack the issuance of YD cards, "generally seems outside the proper concern of the police. Yet if the position of the police vis-à-vis the juvenile is similar to that of a welfare agency, then all data are potentially pertinent. To limit the data which the police are allowed to record it is first necessary to insist upon jurisdictional limits to their authority."[30] The pressure, however, is all the other way; technology and ideology have broadened those jurisdictional limits and fostered what Coffee called a "case attribute" approach in which "any fact is relevant: a youth's past sexual history, attitudes toward teachers, political outlook, social affiliations—all are presumed to be of value."

I I I

At the end of the line is the not-so-hypothetical data bank collecting everything about everybody. Although computer systems are limited in their capacity, particularly for handling anecdotal impressions, they increase the tendency to convert subjective observations of behavior into "hard" information, to turn the annoying behavior of a student into a manageable category like "hyperkinetic" or the routine arrogance of a sixteen-year-old into "predelinquency." The Security and Privacy Manual of one juvenile computer system, for example, attempts to protect minors against innuendo by requiring police who enter data into the system to indicate that "the minor was questioned for possible violation of a specified law; but not that he was stopped because of apparent belligerency."[31] That requirement, if followed, may preclude some belligerency entries altogether, but it may also result in transformation of things like "belligerency" into the "hard" terms of penal code violations. (The study of juvenile records in New York found that for some categories 44 percent of the offenses were improperly classified; the behavior described was not covered by the penal code violation alleged on the record.) Equally important, the very existence of electronic data processing capacity increases the temptation to collect whatever data the computer will accept, regardless of their relevance to the particular case, and to integrate one system with another. The computer describes individuals in terms of the labels for which the machine has been programmed.

There is no way to estimate how many information systems now exist which deal with the records and case histories of children, but they seem to grow exponentially, centralizing the records of police, schools, welfare agencies and medical programs, and exchanging that information with other systems and other agencies. They include state-wide medical data banks like that of Medichek in Illinois, which promises to "provide a permanent healthcare record and information and retrieval system for each person in the system," including data on the psychological problems of every juvenile Medicaid recipient in the state (and which will undoubtedly anticipate other state systems);[32] a growing regional computer system in eight Western states that stores data on all children and adults classified by any social agency as mentally retarded, including, among other things, information on the individual's tendency to use profane language, the frequency of his masturbatory activity and his "abnormal sexual practices." In Florida a state-wide computer stores information on all school pupils from the ninth grade up which includes social security number, grade, school, address, type of curriculum, extracurricular activities, nationality, sex, race, religion, marital status, health and physical disabilities, languages spoken at home, family background, academic record and test scores; and in Maryland a statewide system collects and computerizes the names and records of all children identified as "handicapped" by schools or other agencies, including everything from asthma to "emotionally handicapped" and "neurological problem (other or unspecified)." There are the central juvenile record systems and indexes maintained by police departments, among them computerized state-wide systems in Delaware, Maryland, Oklahoma, Pennsylvania, Nevada, Missouri, Minnesota, Kansas, South Carolina, South Dakota, Utah, Washington and the District of Columbia, and in most major metropolitan regions; juvenile court information and record systems like JURIS in St. Louis, AJJUST in Kansas City and PROFILE, which serves the entire state of Utah; central drug abuse registers maintained by public health departments which encourage—and sometimes, as in New York, require—teachers and others to report the names of all minors they believe to be "drug abusers," or which, as in Maryland, encouraged reports from all drug counseling agencies, including storefront crisis centers; and the centralized social service system and welfare client computers operated by most state welfare agencies. There have been frequent reports that information from juvenile record systems is furnished routinely to the FBI's National Crime Information Center, the Bureau's master index, but the FBI has consistently denied it. Many of the juvenile index computers, nonetheless, are compatible with the NCIC system, and the technical possibility for information sharing is therefore already in place.[33]

The information flows up, it flows sideways and it flows down: data from school systems, from screening programs, from local police departments and from clinics and social service agencies. In Maryland, for example, the Data System for the Handicapped (DSH) has collected the records of some 75,000 children, roughly 10 percent of the school age population (largely, it is said, to improve managerial efficiency, prevent duplication, produce reliable statistics and facilitate audits). The records, furnished by the schools, the Department of Juvenile Services, the Department of Mental Hygiene and similar agencies, include race and ethnic background, IQ level, grade level and "identified manifestations" of handicap. For children receiving some kind of aid from social service agencies, including neglected or dependent children, truants, runaways or children who have been detained by the police, the handicapping conditions can include the following (all quoted from the DSH manual):[34]

> Behavior Disorder—Unsocialized Aggressive: This is shown in covert or hostile disobedience, and is often directed against peers.

> Behavior Disorder—Group Delinquency: This is characterized by the acquisition and acceptance of values, behavior and skills of a delinquent peer group.

Sexual Deviation: This is characterized by individuals whose primary sexual interests are toward objects other than people of the opposite sex, or toward sexual activities under bizarre circumstances. . . .

Personality Disorder—Antisocial: This is reserved for those who are unsocialized and repeatedly in conflict with society. They are incapable of significant loyalty to anyone and do not feel guilt for their actions.

Personality Disorder—Schizoid: This is characterized by shyness, avoidance of close relationships, and an inability to express ordinary aggressive feelings.

For schoolchildren without records in the social service system, local school administrators are required to submit forms specifying the "identified manifestation" of handicap for each child receiving some form of special service within the school. Among those manifestations are "minimal brain damage (hyperkinetic syndrome)," "mild emotional handicap," "moderate emotional handicap," "severe emotional handicap," "profound emotional handicap" and "emotional handicap (other, or unspecified)." When DSH was first established, two suburban counties, Montgomery and Prince George's, refused to furnish information, but after they were threatened with a cutoff of state funds, they complied. The resulting publicity, however, produced assurances from DSH that individual records in the data bank would be identified only by a code number and not by name, that they would not be furnished to outside agencies, and that, in any case, they were being used for statistical purposes only. Promises were also made that the syndrome labels would be reexamined and that DSH might eventually consider replacing them with more precise categories specifying only the category of service required.[35] The existence of such labels indicated, nonetheless, the kind of diagnoses that school and social service agencies were recording in their own files, and the attitudes that informed their approach to "treatment."

*   *   *

There have been a number of recent studies which argue that computerization, despite all dire prophecies, has not produced "revolutionary new powers of data surveillance." In *Databanks in a Free Society,* for example, Alan F. Westin and Michael Baker suggest that those prophecies were founded on what one sympathetic reviewer called "the overly optimistic, self-promotional puffery of a succession of urban consultants, city managers and public relations specialists."[36] They also argue that the cost of comprehensive data banks was simply not justified by the limited uses to which the data could be applied, that most computer systems only lend themselves to internal use and that, in any case, they are more limited in capacity and at least as accurate as the paper files they replace. The computer, in short, is simply a faster and more efficient way for an organization to do what it had probably been doing anyway.

The argument begs all sorts of questions, most significantly those which arise from the comparison with paper files, a classic case, however unintended, of damning with faint praise. It is true, of course, that concern about computerization has obscured the continuing, and serious, problems of paper files. The paper files, however, tend to have a self-betraying modesty deriving from the literary limitations of those who fill them: the painful prose of schoolteachers or guidance counselors which purports to describe learning disabilities or hyperkinesis constitutes a reminder of the fallibility of the judgment. The computer, on the other hand, compresses volumes of anecdotal material into the same labels and categories, prints them out in crisp upper-case letters and creates a fantasy of objectivity. To take the "observations" of schoolteachers or social workers, run them through a scoring process, print them out with a machine and call the result a diagnosis is simply compounding the effects of bias with the illusion of objectivity.

What is most significant, however, is that arguments like

Westin and Baker's fail to distinguish between juvenile records and the general run of computer-processed data. A credit bureau, however prejudiced its decisions, is in business to make money and protect its clients against loss, not to treat, educate or rehabilitate its applicants; the police, in dealing with adults, don't pretend that they are collecting information for the benefit of their suspects. It is the juvenile (or the involuntary inmate of a mental institution) who is, ostensibly at least, in the system for his own benefit, and there is, therefore, virtually no limit to the kind of material for which the social service system can claim legitimacy. The child cannot escape the system but is forced into it by law; he does not volunteer information about himself but is tested, screened and observed whether he likes it or not. The credit system and the employer have to go out of their way to get the information (even if it only means calling the school office), and to some extent they depend on the collaboration of the people about whom they get it. In twelve years of schooling, however, the schools and the social service system get the most personal data as a matter of routine. The chances of resistance are minimal, and for most of the clients there are no alternatives. Children are rarely in a position to tell someone that it's none of his business.[37]

America is now growing its first completely dossierized generation. Previous generations had school records and, in some instances, juvenile court records or files in social agencies, but both the nature of the data and the limitations of storage and retrieval made them perishable. Belligerent boys grow up, but violations of the penal code, although unproven, can follow a person forever. The casual interchange and, in many instances, the identity of the theories, labels and characterizations of the educational, medical and juvenile justice systems have a powerful tendency to produce what may become, in effect, if not in actuality, a single dossier of quasi-synonymous labels—learning-disabled–hyperkinetic–predelinquent, or any combination of scores of others—all of them sanctified by "diagnosis," "screen" and medical test. At the same time, this generation is learning at a very young age that there is nothing unusual about being watched, questioned, tested, labeled and "treated," or about the fact that the results of all that watching and questioning are being stored and processed in machines over which the individual has no control.[38] It is hardly worth saying again that the existence of such a record can have a chilling effect or that privacy is "the right to be left alone." But for those who become habituated to such records and treatment from the age of five, that chilling effect may never occur because they have never been left alone, and they will therefore never suspect that there might have been another way.

SEVEN

Therapy,
Punishment, Control

Before the sixties were over, two decades of lovely dreams had come to an end, and by the time Richard Nixon was reelected in 1972, the general course of the national mood seemed clear. What was not clear was the extent to which the political and psychological events symbolized by Vietnam, Nixon and what later came to be known as Watergate had their corollaries in the schoolhouse, the local police station and the clinic, and how they found expression in a wholly new set of practices which sought to reimpose traditional standards of discipline—real or imagined—through a novel combination of force, technology and psychological manipulation. In some respects those changes, like those in the national mood generally, were obvious: where the rhetoric and interest of the fifties and sixties were concerned primarily with liberalized child-rearing and educational reform—integration, new programs, alternatives—the new emphasis was on delinquency, vandalism, school and community disruptions and the restoration of order. Nonetheless, the nature of the response was often subtle. It took place in individual schools and classrooms, in juvenile delinquency programs, in the offices of doctors and clinics and in the privacy of the home; it was often couched in the language of therapy, and it was usually discussed in the relatively inaccessible precincts of the professional journal, the medical report and the private meeting. The sixties had left social institutions a mandate for intervention far more extensive than any they had had before—almost every child and every problem was now a legitimate target—and there was little chance that the mandate could be substantially reduced. The new techniques and attitudes of child control showed every sign of being permanent. They would survive Nixon and Watergate

The form and style vary according to place, social status, budget, personnel and cultural fashion, but the arsenal is immense. By early 1975 all of the following were being used on children, sometimes in combination, in major American communities: drugs; behavior modification of all sorts; security guards, uniformed police and undercover agents in the schools; electronic surveillance with television cameras and microphones in corridors and classrooms; student informers; forced participation in predelinquency counseling and "treatment" projects; coerced "diagnosis" and "treatment" of learning disabilities and emotional problems; mass screening of preschool children; and, of course, the traditional methods of intimidation, suspension and corporal punishment (which remains legal in nearly all school systems and which is still used in many, even where it is illegal, particularly on black children). In general—and with exceptions—it is the large urban school systems which are most heavily committed to the "security" approach: in Chicago, every high school student is required to carry a laminated identification card with his photo and his complete class schedule; in New York, teachers in a growing number of schools carry pen-size sonic alarm devices which can be used to call for help; in Los Angeles, police undercover agents posing as students infiltrate high schools to look for drug-dealing teenagers. The prescription of psychoactive drugs and the concomitant invocation of "learning disabilities" is largely a white middle-class phenomenon (politically active black parents regard drugging as a form of genocide, a way of seducing their children into the drug culture) and behavior modification, often used as a sobriquet for every attempt to maintain control, follows no pattern whatever.[1] Yet it is behavior modification—as rhetoric and ideology, if not as practice—which offers perhaps the most revealing indication of the new patterns of child pacification and control.

It has been fashionably abbreviated to "behavior mod" and it has become an umbrella phrase covering virtually every form of "systematic" intervention used by anyone to try to shape someone else's behavior: aversive shock therapy, drugs, psychosurgery, gold stars, candy bars, token economies and, among other things, the use of electric gadgets, now commercially available, which ring a bell each time a child-to-be-trained soils his or her underpants. Long before Skinner's *Beyond Freedom and Dignity* was published, the conventional wisdom was hospitable to the idea that the technology for extensive behavior control was already in existence and that its implementation was blocked largely by an atavistic adherence to the illusion of freedom. "Means are being found," wrote Perry London in 1968, "that will soon make possible precise control over much of people's individual actions, thoughts, emotions, moods and wills. Never in human history has this occurred before, except as fantasy."[2] Aldous Huxley, in a novel called *Island* (1962), provided one version:

> Dr. Robert nodded. "It isn't hard. Particularly if you start early enough. Between four and a half and five all our children get a thorough examination. Blood tests, psychological tests, somatyping: then we X-ray their wrists and give them an EEG. All the cute little Peter Pans are spotted without fail, and appropriate treatment is started immediately. Within a year practically all of them are

perfectly normal. A crop of potential failures and criminals, potential tyrants and sadists, potential misanthropes and revolutionaries for revolution's sake, has been transformed into a crop of useful citizens who can be governed ... without punishment and without a sword. In your part of the world delinquency is still left to clergymen, social workers and the police. Nonstop sermons and supportive therapy; prison sentences galore. With what results? The delinquency rate goes steadily up and up. No wonder. Words about sibling rivalry and hell and the personality of Jesus are no substitute for biochemistry. A year in jail won't cure a Peter Pan of his endocrine disbalance or help the ex-Peter Pan to get rid of his psychological consequences. For Peter-Panic delinquency, what you need is early diagnosis and three pink capsules before meals. Given a tolerable environment, the result will be sweet reasonableness and a modicum of the cardinal virtues within eighteen months.[3]

The "means," particularly as applied to children, include not only drugs, conventional Skinnerian reinforcement techniques (food pellets for rats, candy bars for children) and ordinary psychotherapy, but also an extensive list of high-technology approaches ranging from psychosurgery to the electronic brain implantations that people like Jose Delgado of Yale University have used to manipulate the moods and behavior of their patients.[4] What they have in common is not any particular technology, nor, in many cases, any technology more modern than the rack; one might even argue that most of the things that Skinner knows about conditioning animals someone at Barnum and Bailey had known long before him. The common denominator of those techniques lies in their ideology and objectives; it is the fantasy which gives the technology its meaning. In its crudest expression, the fantasy says simply, "I can make him do what I want him to do."

Behavior modification, by whatever means, is concerned only with behavior, and not with internal states, ailments, diagnoses or etiology. Where the medical model imposes a two-stage process—from behavior through diagnosis to syndrome, and from syndrome to remedy—behavior modification goes directly from behavior to remedy. It is in that sense (as many of its proponents claim) less individuous and more honest than the kind of intervention which follows the medical model. It makes no assumptions about health or sickness, uses no labels and insists (sometimes with justification) that it makes no moral judgments. It is merely a technique which (at least in theory) anyone can use on anyone else. In its most common form, the "token economy," behavior modification amounts to little more than awarding points (or gold stars or pieces of candy) for appropriate behavior and allowing the subject to exchange those points for some desired privilege: a longer school recess; more time to watch television in a detention home; an extra thirty minutes to play pool in a drug rehabilitation program. At the Castro School in Mountain View, California, which operates one of the more complex token economies, first graders are allowed to bake cakes if they learn their quota of new words, and children in remedial reading classes earn points for each correct response which, in turn, can be cashed in for play time with tinker toys, a chance to help in the school office or, for 10,000 points, going to a swim party at the principal's home. In other classes, points are awarded for everything from smiles to "not coming up to the teacher" (i.e., not bothering her) to "extra fantastic work." Those points, in turn, can be exchanged for free time, "first to be dismissed," library privileges or an invitation to dinner at the teacher's house. In other programs the rewards are intangible—praise for good behavior, snubbing inattention for bad—and in almost all (again in theory) the intrinsic rewards of the desired behavior (better school work, for example) are supposed, in the long run, to replace the contingencies of gold stars, points and free time as the source of reinforcement. Although there are classic experiments—with autistic children, for example—in which positive behavior survived the reinforcement program, the theory is rarely borne out in practice. At best one set of contingencies replaces another (good grades for gold stars), but not even the optimistic claim that awarding gold stars to children who learn new words bears any relation to the love of literature. "You can train a pigeon to execute a complicated dance perfectly by the pure application of behavior modification techniques; indeed there is probably no other way to do it," said Edgar Friedenberg. "But such a pigeon cannot be said to have developed an interest in ballet."[5] In most institutional programs, however, the lack of any permanent effect is not regarded as a crippling drawback; they are concerned primarily with daily management and control, and not with education or therapy.

In the controversies about the ethics and political significance of behavior modification, one fact is generally neglected: in practice, behavior modification has been used largely on institutional populations—prisoners, mental patients and schoolchildren; it seems to require that the shaper have at least some control over the person or animal to be shaped before the process even starts—the more control the better—and that he is willing to change his own behavior in accordance with the program. A residential school is preferable to a day school, a prison to a school and any authoritarian institution to one in which either the inmates or the staff are free to follow their own impulses. One of the classic models was the "brainwashing" of American prisoners during the Korean War; their Chinese captors used pure Skinnerian principles to "educate" them.[6] It is unlikely that any similar program of education could be carried off successfully in an American public high school. The argument that behavior modification can be used by anyone for any purpose (and is therefore politically neutral) has to be qualified; it can be used by anyone, but the more the shaper can control the environment, the more successful he will be. In the scattered instances in which attempts were made to train inmates to condition their keepers, the results were, at best, modest. In one trial, for example, schoolchildren were trained to modify the behavior of their teachers (to make them more pleasant in class) by praising their "good" behavior and ignoring the bad; success depended on the children's willingness to modify their own behavior in accordance with the experiment and the conventions of the school.[7] The teachers did become more pleasant, according to the reports, but it is inconceivable that the children could have trained them to line up on the playground every morning or to take a cut in salary.

Almost all systematic attempts to control behavior presume inequality and prior control. In the growing number of applications using more powerful technology—chemotherapy, psychosurgery, aversive shock treatments and brain implants—the imbalance between shaper and shaped is unequivocal. It is clear who has and always had control: "scientific" behavior control is merely a way of converting, refining or extending it, or of making its use more subtle. The pill or the electrode replaces the straitjacket and the padded cell. But even where no such technology is involved, the imbalance is apparent. Would even the best of training enable the prisoners at Soledad or San Quentin substantially to modify the behavior of their jailers? "Boy, do we have this guy conditioned," says the rat in the classic behavior modification cartoon. "Every time I press the bar down, he drops a pellet in." Everyone knows which is the psychologist and which is the rat.

Because the debates about the political and ethical implications usually ignore the necessary imbalance, the defenders of behavior modification sometimes have an infuriating tendency to exaggerate their powers in one context and minimize them in another. What the Chinese did with American prisoners proves how powerful it is; what schoolteachers can't do indicates, in the words of one advocate, that "it is questionable that an individual will do anything contrary to his values to obtain a reinforcer."[8] Since one of the official concerns of education is the formation of values in children, and since those values are presumed to be weak, one would assume that behavior modification could be re-

garded as an appropriate method in their nurture (and that
even if it is not, it might have some incidental influence on
them). But here the argument becomes totally confused since
there is no place for "values" in a "science of behavior" and
since, in any case, the possibilities of the technique depend
in great measure on the power that the shaper already has
over his subjects.

Given the vagueness of the definition and the ambiguity of
the research, it is hardly surprising that "behavior modification" can be applied to almost anything (much to the chagrin
of the purists) or that the professional controversies have yet
to generate sufficient data to answer Chomsky's charge that
"one waits in vain for psychologists to make clear   . the
actual limits of what is known."[9] There are mountains of
reports about animals—Skinner's famous Ping-Pong playing
pigeons (which, of course, never could play; they merely
pecked the ball from one end of the table to another), Navy
dolphins trained to "attack" enemy ships with explosives
strapped to their backs, an army of rats pressing levers and
running mazes—and there are many clinical studies on toilet
training children, teaching the retarded to function and curing child molesters with aversive shock. But there are virtually no long-term controlled studies of large groups, no real
theory, no definition of "learning" and no agreement about
techniques. Within the field, for example, there is an ongoing
controversy about the relative merits of positive and negative
reinforcement—rewarding good behavior as opposed to pun-
ishing bad behavior. Skinner, among others, insists that punishment is generally ineffective and that, in any case, "direct
positive reinforcement is to be preferred because it appears
to have fewer objectionable byproducts" (rage, fear, anxiety.)[10] Ever since the mid-sixties, however, there has been a
sharp increase in the study of punishment which, in the
words of one of its academic advocates, "has widespread
humanitarian uses" and which "can effectively suppress behavior, provided it is sufficiently severe."[11]

The choice of technique, if it follows any pattern, depends

much more on a judgment of the severity of the problem and on the political and social context of the program than it does on scientific theory or experimental validation. Prisoners are more vulnerable than free men; institutionalized "severely disturbed" mental patients are more vulnerable than neurotic outpatients; children are more vulnerable than adults. Each degree of intervention is defended (often quite properly) as the preferable alternative: behavior modification is better than chemotherapy; chemotherapy is better than psychosurgery; psychosurgery is better than uncontrolled violence. What those defenses do not discuss are the assumptions which define the problem: institutional requirements of management and control, social definitions of the severity of deviance, the degree of parental or social willingness to tolerate a situation and support expensive remedies. The difference between an "autistic" child subject to an extended course of positive reinforcement and a "severely disturbed" back ward mental patient treated with electroshock may be nothing more than parental attitude or the availability of money. The difference between a public school relying on corporal punishment and one using behavior modification based on awarding extra playground time to cooperative students is more likely to lie in political attitudes than in anything related to science.

The new modes of control, whether or not labeled as "behavior modification," are part of a continuum linked by scientific pretension: the replacement of overt authority by technological, medical or psychological manipulation, and the use of scientific language to mask the imposition of social and institutional norms. Once that language is employed it can, like the language of pacification in Vietnam, be used to rationalize almost any practice.

In Jackson, Mississippi, Orlando J. Andy of the Department of Neurosurgery at the University of Mississippi Medical Center reports that he performed psychosurgery on more than thirty patients between 1961 and 1974. Nearly half were children, some as young as six, most of whom were labeled "hyperactive" or diagnosed as suffering from "maladjust-ment" and "aggression." The operations were done by drill-ing holes in their skulls, inserting electrodes into certain parts of the brain and burning out parts of the tissue. Among the cases for which Andy reported "poor" results was a fourteen-year-old who died three weeks after an operation "due to brain abscesses." Among those for which Andy re-ported "good results" was the following:

J.M., a boy of 9, had seizures and behavioral disorder (hyperactive, aggressive, combative, explosive, destruc-tive, sadistic). Pneumoencephalogram revealed bilateral marked dilation of the ventricles. EEG was abnormally slow. Mentally the patient was in the average range. Dilat eral thalamotomy was done, left (January 12, 1962) and right (January 30, 1962). Right thalamotomy was repeated on September 18, 1962. The patient's behavior was markedly improved and enabled him to return to special education school. After one year, symptoms of hyperirri-tability, aggressiveness, negativism, and combativeness slowly reappeared. A fornicotomy was performed on January 15, 1965. Impaired memory for recent events de-veloped and the patient became much more irritable, negativistic and combative. Consequently, a simultaneous bilateral thalamotomy was done one month later. . . . The patient has again become adjusted to his environment and has displayed marked improvement in behavior and mem-ory. Intellectually, however, the patient is deteriorating.[12]

Andy defended psychosurgery as a "treatment of last resort" for "behavioral problems which do not respond adequately to medical, psychiatric, psychologic and sociologic meth-ods." Psychosurgery, he said, "should be used for custodial purposes when a patient requires constant attention, supervi-sion and an inordinate amount of institutional care. . . . It should be used in the adolescent and pediatric age group in order to allow the developing brain to mature with as normal a reaction to its environment as possible." Psychosurgery, he argued in Congressional testimony, is preferable to "having a child with abnormal behavior continue under inadequate control during the formative and developmental years of his life."[13] Nowhere does he provide a medical definition of the problems he purports to cure.

In Grand Island, Nebraska, the Farrall Instrument Company manufactures a variety of electric shock instruments, among them the AR–5 Receiver-Shocker and Transmitter for "remote wireless shocking of humans." As advertised, the AR–5 can be used by a teacher or therapist to shock a patient each time he shows undesirable behavior in class, or on the playground, and thereby "extinguish" that behavior. The receiver is strapped to the patient (most commonly institutionalized mentally retarded children) and operated from as far as 300 feet.

> Those who feel it is morally wrong to give electric shocks [says the Farrall catalog] must forget the emotional content of the question and address themselves to the issue of the alternatives. Is it more humane for a self-destructive child to receive a few controlled shocks or to go through life in a straight jacket? Is it better to lock a sex deviant away as a criminal or treat him with aversive therapy so that he can become a productive member of society? It is true that in both examples . . . some cases would respond to prolonged conventional therapy; but in most institutions this is not possible because of the shortage of professional personnel. Probably the most valuable contribution therapy can make is the reduction of treatment time.[14]

William R. Farrall, president of the company, said more than 100 schools and other institutions are using the instrument, although none, to his knowledge, were being employed in regular classrooms. "I don't like to shock children either, but you have to consider the alternatives."

In Silver Spring, Maryland, Harold Cohen, James Filipczak and their colleagues at the Institute for Behavioral Research (IBR) are working, with grants from the NIMH Center for Studies of Crime and Delinquency now amounting to more than $900,000, to develop what the agency hopes will be model behavior modification programs for public schools.

One project, operated at Montgomery Hills Junior High School just down the road from IBR, was described in a grant application as "a program of interpersonal academic behavior development for predelinquent adolescents" who "are experiencing social or academic difficulty" and are considered disruptive to school life. (Published NIMH reports specifically deny that support from the Crime Studies Center in any way implies that the children are "considered to be predelinquent."[15]) Until 1973, when IBR moved its experiment to another school, the core of the Montgomery Hills program was a "Reinforcement Area" where children could spend points earned for good behavior and completed school work on soft drinks, candy and a pinball bowling game. The Reinforcement Area was monitored by an IDR worker with a closed circuit television system; the children requested their rewards from the unseen worker, who would push a button, causing a buzzer to sound. The children could then operate the machines which delivered the rewards. Time spent in the Reinforcement Area and in a "skills center" was recorded for each child (down to each one-hundredth of an hour) by requiring him to punch a clock as he entered and left the room. The program, according to an NIMH report,

> has brought modern technological techniques into a school facility. . . . This investment in money, time and concern for children has brought a short-term reward for students in terms of higher grades in all classes, better test results in English and math, and improved relations with teachers, parents and their friends.
>
> The long-range effect that this experience of success will have on the lives of these children cannot be measured as yet, but it is fairly safe to assume that the replacement of failure with a successful learning experience will have useful and rewarding ramifications for the child in particular and for society in general.[16]

In 1973, IBR moved its experiment to another school, and the local district took over the Montgomery Hills project. The soft drinks and candy were dropped, and the scope of the program substantially reduced, despite the reported success.

The program had cost about $3,000 per child in addition to the regular school budget. In the new school, located near Columbia, Maryland, the rewards were limited to encouragement from teachers, the opportunity to read comics and magazines in the reinforcement area, and a chance to go on class trips and become "helper of the day."

There is no way to know how many institutions—schools, detention homes, clinics—now employ some form of what they call "behavior modification," but their number has been growing dramatically, particularly in regions surrounding research institutions which specialize in it: IBR, the University of Kansas, the University of Washington, Western Michigan University and a handful of others. Its development, similar to that of pediatric psychopharmacology, began with animal research, moved to work with severely disturbed patients, particularly retarded and autistic children, and then spread into schools, detention homes and prisons. In general, the programs in prisons and detention homes are the most extensive; they involve every aspect of the subject's life. Those in public schools are necessarily confined to the activities and concerns of the six-hour school day. (In some school programs attempts are made to train parents to maintain token economies at home in which points awarded for responsible behavior; the completion of household duties or other tasks can be cashed in for television time or use of the family car.) What is particularly significant, however, is the growing fashion for relabeling almost any form of reward or punishment as "behavior mod" and backing it up with punchcards, rating sheets, "reinforcement schedules," graphs, charts and a growing number of gadgets—many now commercially available—which measure classroom noise, count disruptions or otherwise time, measure and record various forms of behavior. Most of it is harmless, though it may be expensive and time consuming; in some cases it may even make the system more reliable and less capricious for the inmates: a classroom decibel counter, for example, may reduce the outbursts of a hysterical teacher, and a point system may circumscribe the overt brutality of a prison guard. At the same time, however, it legitimizes the norms on which the hysteria is founded, contributes to the processes of mystification and enables the institution to conceal its standards behind a screen of objectivity. It is no longer a person who doles out the Cokes and candy bars (or the punishment), it is an electronic system.[17] (One of the checks on implementation of behavior modification in prisons—at least so far—has been the difficulty of reshaping the attitudes of the guards, many of whom are certain that only the threat or exercise of punishment will work. In that sense they do more honor to the will, character and dignity of the prisoners than the more "humane" behavior modifiers who see the prisoners as subjects to be conditioned and don't recognize will or character.)

What makes behavior modification particularly attractive to schools and other pediatric institutions is its comfortable consistency with a set of institutional objectives in which control often masquerades as education, rehabilitation or therapy, and where Pavlovian responses are commonly confused with learning. Whatever its moral or ethical implications, the notion of the student as rat is hardly novel, and anyone who has spent any time in a public school can probably recognize it. The average institution tolerates only a severely limited set of responses, most of them regurgitative, as legitimate indications of learning. They do not demand thought or imagination but repetition of clichés from the text or lecture. (How limited is not really the issue; the point is rather that legitimate learning is regarded as a closed system.) Cohen and Filipczak have written that the "basic premise" of their work "is that learning behaviors are related to their consequences, and that, by establishing specific learning procedures, environmental controls, and appropriate consequences for performance, those learning behaviors can be developed, maintained and extended."[18] The "learning behavior" demanded of the average student in the average classroom is very much like the education of a rat in a

Skinner box: it has always consisted of a predetermined set of "behaviors" bearing a strong resemblance to the consequences of operant conditioning in psychological experiments. Those experiments, by definition, reward only those forms of behavior which the trainer expects to develop; they are limited to his scenario. Presumably one could design a behavior modification program to reward the most sophisticated kind of activity (e.g., replication of Einstein's proof of relativity), but it is impossible to program outcomes beyond the imagination of the programmer.

In actual practice, all behavior modification, even at its best, is training and not education. That may be one reason why so many teachers have flocked to weekend institutes and summer courses in behavior modification: it puts control and training into a package called "learning" and gives it the blessing of science. The teacher no longer has to worry about the distinctions between teaching and classroom management; it has all become one. The sort of "learning behavior" it can reward validates the controls and schedules of the teacher or psychologist; it does not honor the mind and spirit of the subject. (Genuine learning, on the other hand, is by definition unpredictable and unlimited; it cannot be contained by preset programs.) More important, there is no way for the program to be self-conscious: neither the student nor the rat is encouraged to ask why he has to do his tricks, to challenge the validity of the "learning behaviors" that his trainers expect or to modify the objectives of the program. What children are commonly left with is the lesson that the price of a Coke is, on the one hand, completion of a mindless exercise and, on the other, the acceptance of authority. Behavior modification can make the effects of such authority more painless than, for example, the use of a club or the threat of punishment, but in its ideal form it will erase all awareness of its existence and thereby make it absolute.

I I

In all the debates about the strengths and failures of democratic education, the most significant virtue is almost always overlooked, and that is the weakness of the traditional methods. It does not require much imagination to comprehend what would have happened if the average school or the government had possessed genuinely powerful means of producing the "learning behaviors" that the teachers, the police or the community often desired. If one includes only Skinnerian reinforcement techniques, the means are still weak, particularly where the clients are subjected only to limited institutional control. But if one includes chemotherapy, psychosurgery and similar techniques, the technology is "at hand." The purists in behavior modification reject those techniques; those are precisely the things that they say they want to prevent. Yet if one accepts the rationale and objectives of one, one must necessarily accept the objectives of the other, because they are the same. Here again the severity of every form of intervention seems to validate every lesser form. "With all its problems of power and manipulation," writes Philip J. Hilts in a gee-whiz book called *Behavior Mod,* "it [behavior modification] is a pale threat alongside the butchery of psychosurgery and the personality distortion of psychopharmacology. In fact, looking at such things as hyperactivity, which has been attacked with each of the three psychotechniques, behavior mod seems the innocent, sensible and humane treatment."[19] He has, of course, already lost the argument. It is the "thing" called hyperactivity which raises the "problems of power and manipulation." If one accepts it as essentially a medical problem, the choice of treatment is a secondary issue limited only by the changes and effectiveness of the alternate technologies. If one accepts the terms of that choice, the legitimacy of the system which imposes it goes unquestioned.

The professional custodians of children—teachers, school administrators, probation officers and clinicians—have become particularly adept in exploiting and obfuscating the uncertain and often overlapping definitions of education, therapy, punishment and control. Each of the court decisions and legislative reforms which sought to clarify some of the distinctions—due process in juvenile court procedures and in school suspensions, "right to treatment" in juvenile corrections, directives regarding access to, and confidentiality of, records—has been met by a new round of professional efforts to redefine and replace overt forms of power and manipulation with covert "innocent, sensible and humane" means. The transformation of punishment into "therapy" which accompanied the establishment of the juvenile justice system at the turn of the century, and which was billed as a magnificent reform, removed minors from most due process protections and subjected them to indefinite prison terms. The prohibition of corporal punishment in the New York City schools in the early sixties immediately generated increases in arbitrary school suspensions and an inflationary expansion of school records (which replaced the stick not only as instruments of intimidation but also as vehicles of retribution). The *Morales* suit against the physical brutality in the Texas juvenile prisons prompted the institution of a behavior modification program called "positive peer group culture," which rewarded inmates for the good conduct of the group and which soon resulted in complaints that while fewer boys were being beaten by guards, more were being beaten by other inmates; the imposition of due process in school suspensions and juvenile arrests (and particularly the protection of *Gault* and *Miranda*) helped make the medical model fashionable and prompted the concomitant resort to psychoactive drugs, screening projects and predelinquency programs. Equally significant, many programs were susceptible to simultaneous redefinition: what is punishment within the confines of the institution becomes rehabilitation before a court of law; what is control in the classroom turns into therapy at the doctor's

office. When "therapy" comes in, due process goes out.[20]
Through all this torture of language, the constant is the
integrity of the institution. Each step of the treatment further
conceals and legitimizes institutional practices and authority, and each makes it harder for the client to strike back. The
behavior modifier knows no passions, no fear, anger, love or
joy, though he may employ them as contingencies or regard
them as problems; he is merely the operator of an impersonal
system. If one can define deviance as sickness, then by inference the norm becomes health and its defense merely an
invocation of the natural order. In that context all the pious
statements about the neutrality of science or the universal
availability of behavior modification become so much more
obfuscation, something akin to saying that research on chemical defoliants is neutral because someday the Vietnamese
might use them to destroy wheat in Kansas. Everyone knows
how such things are used: schoolchildren cannot coerce their
teachers to take psychoactive drugs, prisoners cannot
rehabilitate their jailers, and the school systems which, like
New York's, publish statistics on the number of assaults by
students on teachers do not even collect data on the number
of assaults by teachers on students. (Where such information
is reported, the system does its best to hide or deny it.) It is
the inmates who are screened, diagnosed and treated, not the
institution and staff.

The rationale for this treatment is a special version of what
William Ryan called "blaming the victim." ("First identify
a social problem. Second, study those affected by the problem and discover in what ways they are different from the
rest of us. . . . Third, define the differences as the cause of
the social problem itself. Finally . . . assign a government
bureaucrat to invent a humanitarian action program to correct the differences."[21]) There is, however, a difference: the
transparently soggy language of sociology ("cultural depri-
vation," "the Negro family") has been replaced by the more
intimidating hard language of science and medicine, and
bolstered by the testimony of psychologists, physicians and

chemists. By inference, the social order thus becomes an expression of the natural order, a system as immutable as the rotation of the earth or the movement of the tides.

I I I

Among the more important political developments of the sixties was the recognition of juveniles as a force in domestic life. Perceptions of that force varied, and they changed over time: Charles Reich's verdant dreams in *The Greening of America,* Spiro Agnew's warnings about permissiveness, the flower child at Woodstock, the Hell's Angel at Altamont. What was certain was that through some combination of social factors, children and adolescents appeared to shed some of their docility and to develop a form of citizenship apart from their parents and the institutions which had always purported to speak for them. Although political activism was short-lived, the psychological and institutional impact was permanent, even among those who never thought of youth as a sort of home-grown Vietcong hiding in every schoolyard and crawling out of every commune. The movement exacerbated the traditional ambivalence about children —a mix of love, resentment, ambition, pride, fear and envy —which could be contained only while it remained immune to excessive demands either from the children or the society at large. Economic scarcity had been a major disciplining force, the dream of success provided morale, and Social Darwinism was the abiding ideology of the school and marketplace: in combination they were sufficient to restrain deviance or to justify its expulsion. The affluence of the postwar years undermined that discipline, and the youth movement of the sixties, however defined, exposed and destroyed the atavistic moral defenses and disciplinary rhetoric inherited from another age. However brief, the movement left the elders vulnerable and looking for new weapons.

The normative assumptions and natural order invoked by the new modes of control are, in one sense, disciplinary replacements for Social Darwinism. Each in its own time was (or is) "scientific." But while Social Darwinism was almost entirely an economic "law" concerned with the individual's fitness for the labor market (and particularly the factory), its contemporary substitute is concerned with every aspect of the individual's life and, most particularly, with his potential as a client. The system no longer requires his muscle, but it needs his obedience. It no longer must train him to be a reliable worker, but it must condition him to be managed. If the public school of the 1890s or the 1920s was modeled (ideologically or architecturally) on the factory, and if the hickory stick was an extension of the doctrine of survival of the fittest, the contemporary school more nearly resembles Doctor Welby's hospital which, by training its clients to be good patients, also makes them better, happier and friendlier people. Take your pill and trust the doctor. Such an institution, by whatever name, can serve all the elements of the traditional ambivalence about children equally well—love, hate, ambition, fear; it can treat and punish, control and modify, all in the name of the best of care. Since children, by social definition, fall into a legal and social no-man's land in which education, training, treatment, punishment and management are vague, overlapping and often interchangeable, and since they are children, they are the most vulnerable and accessible targets of control. Yet inevitably, if they succeed, the new modes of therapy and management will produce adults fit only for perpetual dependence, a fixed, hermetic world where everything can and must be subject to management, where nothing is left to chance, where therapy or behavior modification obviate punishment and due process, and where civil liberties become superfluous.

I V

The greatest possibilities against the realization of that brave new hermetic world lie in the fact that the technologies of control are still relatively rudimentary and in the hope that sufficient personal, legal and political resistance will develop before they are perfected. We have, in a sense, been saved temporarily by the crudeness of the methods, by drugs with negative side effects, by behavior modification programs that show only marginal results and by other techniques either too crude and heavy-handed or too weak to make them universally acceptable and absolutely irremediable. But the critical point can't be far off, particularly if one considers the phenomenal spread of these techniques in the past five years, and the growth of the ideology which sustains them. Even if the technologies are not substantially refined to make them more effective, less obviously painful and "smoother," there is at least a chance that the society will be ready to accept them in a relatively primitive state.

The record is hardly reassuring. Before the mid-sixties few if any of those techniques were being used on the general population; now they are part of the landscape. More important, the ideology which sustains them has become endemic: every agency of education and social welfare is talking the language of screening, diagnosis and treatment. It is, as we have said before, a seductive and intimidating language, professedly humane, scientific and benevolent: who among us doesn't want to reduce crime, enable children to learn, and eradicate other social or psychological problems? Its effects, moreover, are subtle, and they are often felt only in the long run, if at all; "therapy" is the narcotic of politics. The temptation is to allow oneself (or one's child) to be treated, to be cared for, to be managed. We all want to believe that it's for our own good, and we are rapidly learning to mortgage the psychological and political future in return for a little momentary peace.

The race is between technology and ideology. If the techniques are recognized for what they are—as means of controlling and managing people—the political issues will be apparent and there will be a chance for individuals, organizations and communities to confront them in a legal and political context. If, on the other hand, the proponents—scientists, doctors, school administrators, the police, the drug companies and the federal government—continue successfully to present those technologies and ideas as therapeutic measures to "treat" individual children, then there will not even be a fight. More important, it is also a race against time and habit. The longer the fight is postponed, the more normative the various methods of manipulation will seem; the longer it is postponed, the more children there will be whose personalities have been reshaped and lobotomized for institutional convenience or who will have learned that they cannot get along without their chemical, institutional or psychological crutches. "Science" in that sense abolishes the Constitution —informally, gradually, subtly—and scientism becomes the instrument by which the individual is subsumed to the requirements and impositions of an orderly system. The country has probably not yet reached the critical point from which there is no return, but it is close.

APPENDIX

The Elements of Self-Defense

There are no assured means of resistance, no simple cures. Even the most comprehensive formal regulations assuring due process, access to records, confidentiality and other individual liberties are no guarantee against violations of privacy, subtle forms of manipulation or overt intrusions into the lives of children and their parents. As the techniques of control become more complex, "scientific" and "humane"—and as they become less overtly punitive—resistance will become that much more difficult. Where the institution (school, police, court) acknowledges that the objective is punishment or deterrence, formal modes of defense—lawyers, trials and hearings—are regarded as necessary and proper; where the objective is said to be "treatment," resistance becomes more difficult and the potential for manipulation more extensive. The rationale of therapy, education and rehabilitation almost inevitably clouds due process and individual liberties. It creates great opportunities for obfuscation and mystification: claims of expertise and the invocation of special knowledge (or the use of sophisticated technology) are no less intimidating than naked authority.

There are, nonetheless, certain techniques and resources which have been used successfully in the past:

1. The beginning of almost all resistance is demystification. Ask dumb questions, and be bold. What do the words mean? Is the person behind the desk talking about a real disease or is he merely using pseudo-medical terms to describe subjective impressions of behavior, to excuse pedagogical failure, or to conceal institutional biases and demands? Is there a remedy for this disease and what are its possible side effects? What, if anything, does the test or screen really measure? Does it have any validation, and if so is that

validation based merely on the biases of other "professionals" in other institutions? (The burden of proof is on the developer and user of the test and treatment, not on the subject.) What does the therapist (teacher, counselor) know about the instruments he is using and why is he really using them? Does he know and understand the literature? Of what use is the information being requested? Will it lead to genuine remedies, real individualization of program or other help, or will it merely produce an accumulation of labels in a child's file or (worse) serve as a rationale for failure in the future? A series of such questions may quickly indicate that under the guise of the kindly counselor there is just another administrator concerned about order and management or a bureaucrat protecting his own flanks. Such a revelation may not be very reassuring to a parent, but it will at least alert all concerned parties about the nature of the "problem" they are dealing with.

2. Don't let the old feeling of being a child take over when dealing with authorities, particularly in schools. Don't be brushed off or patronized. Agents of public institutions—welfare, police, schools, hospitals, courts—are often adept at patronizing or intimidating clients and at taking advantage of some primal feeling on the part of the client that he is The Child and that the man sitting across from him is The Principal. (Or criminal and cop, patient and doctor, examiner and applicant, IRS agent and taxpayer.) If you are sitting in an office waiting for someone to interpret a record, open the file and read it. Lightning will not strike, and only in a few school systems (such as New York's) have administrators been known to call the police when they have found a parent reading her own child's file.

3. Get everything in writing—laws, regulations, directives. Do not take the explanations of administrators as gospel. Take notes, insist on seeing everything in writing and keep copies. A contentious or litigious confrontation may not be necessary—nor is it conducive to the best relationship with authorities—but it is important to remember that it takes two parties to create such a confrontation, and that the client's fear of offending authorities is precisely the thing that many administrators count on when they try to patronize and intimidate. Some school administrators seem to have a natural tendency to treat everyone as a child; in general, the weaker their position, the more they will be tempted to bluster and bully.

4. Have as many weapons available as possible. In all large cities there are community groups with some experience in dealing with schools, welfare systems and the police. (We have provided a sample list below.) Some are engaged largely in gathering and disseminating information; others have been successful advocates for children and parents. Most should have some knowledge of the applicable law and regulations or, if not, be able to provide leads on where to obtain them. The important rule here is to disregard ideology; the local chapter of the American Civil Liberties Union and the John Birch Society may sometimes be fighting the same battle, particularly on such issues as privacy, screening, drugging and behavior control. One can't afford to be choosy in looking for help.

5. Stay on the side of suspicion. Even a parent who loves his child's school, teachers and administrators and respects their competence and concern is not assured that they will honor the child's privacy, or that they can. People are transferred, teachers change, administrators move on, but the system, the records and the child's life go on indefinitely. Such problems may be tempered by the nature of the system itself; in general small school systems are more candid, suburban systems more friendly, urban systems more bureaucratic and less responsive. Yet it may be the very friendliness or candor of a system that will make privacy more vulnerable. The warm treatment extended by the school to the parent may also be extended to the chief of police, to the owner of a downtown department store or to anyone who happens to walk into the office. Similar principles apply, of course, to courts, probation departments, police and clinics.

6. Act in advance. When your child is first enrolled in school, make it clear that you will be checking his record every few months, that you want no screening or testing unless you've given informed consent, in writing, for that particular test. Do not give blanket consent, either for screening or for the release of records. Put appropriate statements in your child's file, and send copies to the superintendent. Take along a copy of the Buckley Amendment, in case no one knows the law.

7. If a child is to be referred to a psychologist, physician, psychiatrist or other specialist, choose the practitioner yourself. The school (or the clinic, or the police) may have a list, but the chances are that the people on the list will be those that the institution

regards as most sympathetic to its purposes. That does not necessarily mean that all are drug pushers or that they are inadequate as diagnosticians or practitioners. Still, it is important to find one who is personally and ideologically in phase with your own interests. When consulting any specialist, remember point 1 (above). Ask dumb questions.

8. In all formal disciplinary confrontations with institutional representatives, and particularly with the police and juvenile authorities, get legal advice and, if possible, have a lawyer or lay advocate experienced in the field present at all meetings. That includes any school suspension hearing, any conference regarding delinquency, truancy or other violation of the law, or, indeed, any major situation that may affect a child's status, his record or his participation in a school program, a delinquency project or a course of "treatment." Not any lawyer or advocate will do: the highly paid counsel to a corporation doing a parent a favor may be a babe in the woods of a police station. A lawyer or even an experienced layman from an organization of community advocates is usually preferable.

In January 1975, the Supreme Court, in *Goss v. Lopez* (USSC 73-898), ruled that a child cannot be suspended from school, even for a short period of time, without "oral or written notice of the charges" against him, a "rudimentary hearing" that includes an explanation of the evidence against him, and an opportunity to present his side of the story. As a rule, the Court said, this notice and hearing "should precede removal of the student from school." Although the decision did not promise students suspended for less than ten days a full panoply of due process protections, the Court did say that if the disciplinarian finds "the existence of disputes about facts, and arguments about cause and effect" in the hearing, he might "then determine himself to summon the accuser, permit cross examination, and allow the student to present his own witnesses. In more difficult cases, he may permit counsel." The Court made it clear that its basic requirements applied only to routine suspensions of less than ten days. "Longer suspensions or expulsions for the remainder of the school term, or permanently, may require more formal procedures. Nor do we put aside the possibility that in unusual situations, although involving only a short suspension, something more than the rudimentary procedures will be required." Such protections may seem fragile to those in states like New York, where school administrators have been required for some years to provide much more extensive due process in suspending students. However, in a state like Ohio, where *Goss* originated, principals have by law been able to suspend students for ten days without a hearing of any kind.

The *Goss* decision—and student rights in general—were substantially strengthened by a subsequent Supreme Court Decision, *Wood v. Strickland* (USSC 73-1258), in which the Court ruled that students may sue for damages school officials who are guilty of "intentional or otherwise inexcusable deprivations" of student's constitutional rights. School officials who discipline a student unfairly cannot defend themselves against civil suit by claiming ignorance of the student's basic rights, the Court said, because "an act violating a student's constitutional rights can be no more justified by ignorance or disregard of settled, indisputable law on the part of one entrusted with supervision of students' daily lives than by . . . actual malice." Although the decision is too recent to have clear-cut effects in the schools, the rush of school boards to increase their liability insurance coverage and their complaints about this "perilous precedent" indicate that it will make a difference. For the first time parents and students have been given a genuinely powerful weapon in the enforcement of students' constitutional rights: the ability to sue for money damages and the chance to collect.

9. In every case, be certain that you obtain all applicable statutes and regulations and that you understand local practice, which may vary considerably from place to place. (Policy on school suspension, placement, truancy and related matters may vary not only from community to community, but from school to school within a community; police and juvenile probation practices are subject to similar differences.) In one community truancy laws are rigidly enforced; in an adjoining community they are neglected. One principal beats children (or has his assistants do it) while the principal in the school five blocks away does not. The employment of such practices may bear no relationship to the formal rules of the board of education.

10. In all cases involving the rights of juveniles, remember that prevention is probably the only remedy. The courts have been highly reluctant to award damages or order compensation to the victims of official abuse, and the administrators of public institutions—schools, hospitals and police—will almost never acknowl-

edge malfeasance on the part of their subordinates. Although there are exceptions, the general rule is that administrators know that there is very little they can do for which they may be punished later. This means that anything they want to do, they will do, unless they are stopped before they do it. Even in those cases where parents have proved that a school beating administered to their child resulted in a permanent physical injury, little or no compensation was awarded by the courts. Damages are sometimes awarded for neglect in violation of state school laws (e.g., injuries in an unattended gymnasium class) but not for acts committed in fulfillment of "official" duties.

One final note: individual bargaining power is almost always enhanced when the issue is punishment or institutional management; punishment is usually subject to some due process, but therapy is not. Despite the harsh connotations, and despite the temptation to play the sickness-and-treatment game with a friendly administrator or counselor, individual rights are subject to more respect when the institution concedes that the issue stems from infractions of the rules, a teacher's inability to deal with a child or just plain bad behavior.

There are a growing number of organizations which provide various forms of assistance to children and parents. Some specialize in the defense of individual cases; others are primarily engaged in political action; still others compile and disseminate information. Many, moreover, are short-lived, and most are overburdened, understaffed and underfinanced. The better ones, however, will at least know what sort of help may be available, even if they cannot provide it themselves. Here is a small annotated list of national organizations.

1. The National Committee for Citizens in Education, Suite 410, Wilde Lake Village Green, Columbia, Maryland 21044. NCCE maintains a hotline for inquiries with a toll-free number: (800) 638–9675 (NETWORK). The organization has specialized in the school records issue and was instrumental in getting Senator Buckley to sponsor his amendment on records; its publication, *Children, Parents and School Records* (1974) is the most comprehensive collection of state laws and regulations governing student records and includes lists of other available publications and local and national organizations concerned with records.

2. The American Civil Liberties Union (which has local chapters in all major cities) and, in particular, the New York Civil Liberties Union, 84 Fifth Avenue, New York, New York 10017, (212) 924–7800. NYCLU has developed considerable experience, particularly in school suspension cases, though it is now operating with only one person who specializes in student rights. ACLU also has a Privacy Project which collects and publishes information dealing with records and data banks: ACLU Privacy Project, 22 East 40 Street, New York, New York 10016. (212)725-1222.

3. The Children's Defense Fund, 1763 R Street N.W., Washington, D.C., 20009, (202) 483–1470. CDF has collected extensive data on everything from records to chromosome research and behavior modification; although it is engaged in litigation, it does not usually take individual cases unless they involve major issues of policy.

4. The Youth Law Center, 693 Mission Street, San Francisco, California, 94103, (415) 495–6420. The Law Center, staffed by capable attorneys, handles a broad spectrum of juvenile cases "on behalf of indigent youths." A major portion of its time and energy has been devoted to establishing procedural rights of juveniles, right to treatment in juvenile institutions and litigating "major educational law questions, bilingual education, special education, due process rights of students and similar issues."

5. The Medical Committee for Human Rights, P.O. Box 7155, Pittsburgh, Pennsylvania 15213, (412) 682–1200. MCHR deals with a range of issues including the use of drugs for social control, behavior modification, human experimentation and the misuse of psychiatry. There are local chapters in most major cities, including New York, Chicago and San Francisco.

6. The Student Press Law Center, Room 1316, 1750 Pennsylvania Avenue N.W., Washington, D.C. 20006, (202) 337–1113, an organization devoted to "explaining and protecting the rights of high school and college journalists."

7. The Harvard Center for Law and Education, Larsen Hall, 14 Appian Way, Cambridge, Massachusetts 02138, (617) 495–4666. The Center specializes in research on law and policy in education, student rights, tracking, testing and similar issues. It "promotes exchanges among academic researchers, attorneys, legislators, community and parent groups, and school people on education law matters."

8. Childhood and Government Project, Boalt Hall, University of

California, Berkeley, California 94720. Like the Center for Law and Education at Harvard, its primary focus is on research and policy studies; it does not litigate individual cases.

9. Privacy Review Office, Room 5660, Department of Health, Education and Welfare, 330 Independence Avenue, S.W., Washington, D.C. 20201, (202) 245–7488. This is the HEW office established to administer the Buckley Law. It can provide the HEW guidelines issued in conjunction with the law and has been designated to receive and investigate complaints.

There are, in addition, scores of local and state organizations active in law reform, defense of individual cases and the dissemination of data. Among the most active are the Massachusetts Advocacy Center, 2 Park Square, Boston, Massachusetts 02116, (61/) 357–8431; United Bronx Parents, 810 East 152 Street, Bronx, New York 10455, (212) 993–5300; the Education Law Center, 605 Broad Street, Suite 800, Newark, New Jersey 07102 (for New Jersey and Pennsylvania); the New York Public Education Association, 20 West 40 Street, New York, New York 10018; local chapters of civil rights organizations (e g, NAACP Legal Defense and Education Fund, the Mexican-American Legal Defense and Education Fund); the American Friends Service Committee; the League of Women Voters; and local public defenders' offices and legal services projects. It is important to understand, however, that in many communities (if not most) the juvenile division of the public defender's office may be ready to bargain away the rights of a client and too busy to provide an effective defense. In some areas, the local chapter of the Association for Children With Learning Disabilities (ACLD) may be helpful on issues of privacy, labeling and records.

In the search for resources, help may occasionally be available from journalists, legislators or others. Such help can take several forms: exposure through the media, legislative inquiries or simple exchange of information. Perhaps the best clearing center for information, and probably the most active defender of civil liberties in American journalism, is Nat Hentoff at *The Village Voice* (80 University Place, New York, New York 10003). Members of Congress who have been active in the area include Senator James L. Buckley (New York), 452 Old Senate Office Building, Washington; Senator Edward M. Kennedy (Massachusetts), 431 Old Senate

Office Building, Washington (on health and protection of human subjects in medical experimentation); Senator Barry Goldwater (Arizona), 440 Old Senate Office Building, Washington; Representative Edward I. Koch (New York), 1134 Longworth House Office Building, Washington; Representative Margaret M. Heckler (Massachusetts), 318 Cannon House Office Building, Washington; and Representative Barry Goldwater, Jr. (California), 1421 Longworth House Office Building, Washington.

BIBLIOGRAPHICAL NOTE

There are hundreds of books, journal articles and pamphlets available, and many are cited in the footnotes to the text. The following were chosen because they are relatively inexpensive and easy to obtain.

Children, Parents and School Records. Columbia, Maryland: The National Committee for Citizens in Education, 1974. This is the most comprehensive guide to state and local regulations and organizations dealing with school records. Copies are available from the committee, Suite 410, Wilde Lake Village Green, Columbia, Maryland 21044.

Alan H. Levine, *et al. The Rights of Students.* New York: Avon, 1973. This is one of a series of American Civil Liberties Union handbooks and is based largely on the experience of the New York Civil Liberties Union Project on Student Rights. It is well annotated with citations of pertinent legal cases.

Schools, Doctors and Drugs. Pittsburgh: The Medical Committee for Human Rights, n.d. This is an eight-page booklet summarizing the issues in the use of psychoactive drugs with school children. It is useful for distribution to parent and teacher organizations and school boards. Copies are available from MCHR, P.O. Box 7155, Pittsburgh, Pennsylvania 15213.

Guidelines for the Collection, Maintenance and Distribution of Pupil Records: Report of Conferences on the Ethical and Legal Aspects of School Record Keeping. New York: Russell Sage Foundation, (1970). This booklet is available from the Russell Sage Foundation, 230 Park Avenue, New York, New York, which published it. It has to some extent been superseded by the passage of the Buckley Amendment.

Norman E. Silberberg and Margaret C. Silberberg. *Who Speaks for the Child?* Springfield, Illinois: Charles C. Thomas, 1974. Parts of this book are devoted to low-key discussions of IQ, achievement and the meaning of "normal."

Edwin M. Lemert. *Instead of Court, Diversion in Juvenile Justice.* Rockville, Maryland: National Institute of Mental Health, 1971. This is a reasonable and balanced discussion about delinquency prevention, diversion and juvenile crime prevention.

Edwin M. Schur. *Radical Non-Intervention: Rethinking the Delinquency Problem.* Englewood Cliffs, New Jersey: Prentice-Hall, Inc., 1973.

Henry Lennard, *et al. Mystification and Drug Misuse.* New York: Perennial Library (Harper & Row), 1972. Probably the most intelligent book on the misuse of drugs.

"The Rights of Children," *Harvard Educational Review,* November 1973 and February 1974. Two issues devoted to major aspects of the rights of juveniles including a significant article by Lester Grinspoon and Susan B. Singer, "Amphetamines in the Treatment of Hyperkinetic Children."

Nora Klapmuts. *Children's Rights: The Legal Rights of Minors in Conflict With Law or Social Custom.* Hackensack, New Jersey: National Council on Crime and Delinquency, 1972. Pamphlet available from NCCD, Continental Plaza, Hackensack, New Jersey 07601.

NOTES

Chapter One: THE HUTSCHNECKER MEMO

1. "A Plan For Prevention Of Violent Crime." The undated memo from Dr. Hutschnecker was sent by Ehrlichman to Robert Finch, then Secretary of HEW, on December 30, 1969. We received a copy of the memo from a source at HEW. Hutschnecker relied on the predictive accuracy of older tests, and particularly on a scale developed by Sheldon and Eleanor Glueck of Harvard in the 1930s. By the time Hutschnecker made his proposal, the predictive value of such tests had been subject to serious doubt. See Chapter IV.

2. "Briefing Letter" and draft "Memorandum for Hon. John D. Ehrlichman" from Stanley Yolles to Finch, February 16, 1970. Copy from HEW source. The involvement of the National Institute of Mental Health in research on the use of psychoactive drugs and in the delinquency field has been extensive. See Chapters III and IV.

3. "To Move the Mountain." Address by James E. Allen, Jr., Assistant Secretary for Education and U.S. Commissioner of Education, before National School Boards Association, April 14, 1970, San Francisco. Ronald Moskowitz, education writer for the San Francisco *Chronicle,* who wrote the speech, said he had not been influenced by Hutschnecker's memo. Moskowitz and Allen had discussed the idea several months before the speech was delivered.

4. The San Francisco plan was embodied in a proposal submitted to the Ford Foundation by Steven P. Morena, Superintendent of Schools, November 30, 1973. Ford rejected the proposal but it generated interest at another foundation which promised support; it was scheduled for a test in the fall of 1975. The Illinois plan, called Medicheck, is described in Bruce A. Flashner, *et al.,* "Medicheck: State of Illinois' Approach to the Early and Periodic Screening of Title XIX Children," unpublished presentation at the American Public Health Association, November 15, 1972. Data on the number of children taking psychoactive drugs based on testimony before the Education Committee of the California State Senate, July 1974, by Thomas O. Boucher, Chairman of the Board, and Hugh D'Andrade, counsel, of CIBA-Geigy Corporation (manufacturers of Ritalin, the most frequently prescribed psychoactive drug) and on studies by Daniel Safer of the Johns Hopkins University School of Medicine, the Department of Health, Education and Welfare, and other sources. The figures are

discussed more extensively in note 2, Chapter III. For more extensive discussions of these proposals and programs, see Chapter IV.

5. Cesare Lombroso, *Crime: Its Causes and Remedies* (Boston: Little, Brown and Co., 1911), p. 306. Lombroso's original study of delinquent man was published in Italy in 1876.

6. *Ibid.*

7. *Ibid.*, pp. 371–372. For contemporary hypotheses reminiscent of Lombroso, see Camilla M. Anderson, M.D., *Society Pays* (New York: Walker and Co., 1970). Judith Rapaport, M.D., Patricia O. Quinn, M.D., and Friedhelm Lamprecht, M.D., "Minor Physical Anomalies and Plasma Dopamine-Beta-Hydroxylase Activity in Hyperactive Boys," *American Journal of Psychiatry,* Vol. 131, No. 4, April 1974. (See also Chapter V.)

8. William H. Sheldon, *Varieties of Delinquent Youth; An Introduction to Constitutional Psychiatry* (New York: Harper and Bros., 1949).

9. Sheldon and Eleanor Glueck, *Physique and Delinquency* (Cambridge: Harvard University Press, 1958).

10. *Ibid.*, pp. 268–269.

11. Lewis M. Terman, *The Measurement of Intelligence* (Boston: Houghton Mifflin, Co. 1916), p. 11.

12. Edward L. Thorndike, *Human Nature and the Social Order* (New York: Macmillan, 1940), p. 957; Thorndike, "How May We Improve the Selection, Training and Life-Work of Leaders?" *Addresses Delivered Before the Fifth Conference on Educational Policies* (New York: Columbia University Press, 1939), p. 32.

13. Lewis M. Terman, "The Conservation of Talent," *School and Society,* March 29, 1924, p. 363. For a general discussion of the social ideas of the pioneers in testing, see Clarence J. Karier, "Testing for Order and Control in the Corporate Liberal State," *Educational Theory,* Vol. 22, Spring 1972, pp. 155–180.

14. See, among others, Carl Senna, ed., *The Fallacy of I.Q.* (New York: The Third Press, 1973). For the more fundamental argument for disestablishing schools, see Ivan Illich, *De-Schooling Society* (New York: Harper and Row, 1971).

15. See, among others, John S. Werry and Robert L. Sprague, "Hyperactivity" in C. Costello, ed., *Symptoms of Psychopathology: A Handbook* (New York: John Wiley, 1970), pp. 397–412; Lester B. Grinspoon and Susan B. Singer, "Amphetamines in the Treatment of Hyperkinetic Children," *Harvard Educational Review,* Vol. 43, No. 4, November 1973; J. M. Wepman, W. Cruikshank, C.P. Deutsch *et al.,* "Classification in the Field of Learning Disabilities," *Task Force Report for the Project on Classification of Exceptional Children,* unpublished, 1973. (The report was drafted for the Secretary of Health, Education and Welfare.) Sam D. Clements, *Minimal Brain Dysfunction in Children: Terminology and Identification,* NINDB Monograph No. 3, U.S. Department of Health, Education and Welfare (1966); and Martin Bax, "The Active and Over-Active School Child," *Developmental Medicine and Child Neurology,* Vol. 14, 1972, pp. 83–86.

16. Camilla M. Anderson, "Society Pays for the Learning Disabled," unpublished address at symposium of the California Association for Neurologically Handicapped Children, Palo Alto, California, April 20, 1974.

17. The ideological rationale for the use of these techniques is, however, identical. All of them are defended as more "humane" than the alternatives. See, for example, the defense of psychosurgery by Dr. O. J. Andy of the University of Mississippi in *Hearings Before the Subcommittee on Health of the Committee on Labor and Public Welfare,* U.S. Senate, 93rd Congress, Part II, pp. 348–357.

18. See, among others, Camilla M. Anderson, *Society Pays;* Leon Eisenberg, "The Overactive Child," *Hospital Practice,* September 1973. A more extensive discussion of these symptoms and their uses will be found in Chapter II.

19. B. F. Skinner, *Beyond Freedom and Dignity* (New York: Alfred A. Knopf, 1971), pp. 149, 160. Skinner's argument, in a somewhat more tentative form, had already been published in his *Science and Human Behavior* (New York: Macmillan, 1953) but it received comparatively little attention. *The New York Times,* on the other hand, called *Beyond Freedom and Dignity* the most important book of 1971, and *Time* magazine ran a cover story on Skinner himself. Clearly something had changed which made Skinner's theories more attractive, if not more relevant, in the two decades since they were first published.

20. "Forecast for the '70s," *Today's Education,* January 1969.

21. Institute for Behavioral Research, *Programming Interpersonal Curricula for Adolescents,* Silver Spring, Maryland, 1971, p. v.

22. Sam D. Clements, *Minimal Brain Dysfunction,*

23. Noam Chomsky, "Psychology and Ideology" in *For Reasons of State* (New York: Pantheon Books, 1973), p. 363. Chomsky's critique of Skinner, which first appeared in abbreviated form in the *New York Review of Books,* is too extensive and elegant for summation. But his argument that Skinner "confuses science with terminology" is one that can be made about a great many practices and theories in the areas we are discussing. Like Skinner, the practitioners of screening and testing also manage to relabel the behavior of autonomous individuals, which makes them sound scientific without explaining anything that hadn't been explained before.

24. The Delaware Community School Corporation in Muncie, Indiana, in a project called Insight Unlimited. The director of the project told one of us that, "If a child gets through our screens, we'd call him Jesus Christ."

25. *In re Gault,* 387 U.S. 1. See Chapter V.

26. Alfred Kazin, *A Walker in the City* (New York: Harcourt Brace and World, Inc., 1951), p. 21.

27. Jacket copy for Milton Brutten, *et al., Something's Wrong With My Child* (New York: Harcourt Brace Jovanovich, Inc., 1973).

28. The research is being conducted at the Institute for Behavioral Genetics of the University of Colorado, Boulder, with support from the Spencer Foundation and the National Institute of Mental Health.

29. Ivan Illich, *Hygienic Nemesis,* Cuernavaca, Mexico, Cidoc Cuaderno No. 86, 1974, p. 77. (In press; New York: Pantheon Books, 1976.)

Chapter Two: THE INVENTION OF A DISEASE

1. The estimate is based on printouts of research project summaries and allocations compiled by the Smithsonian Science Information Exchange; most of those summaries include funding, though some do not. Figures for the number of children getting psychoactive medication are based on data discussed in Note 2, Chapter III.

2. Harold and June Shane, "Forecast for the 1970s," *Today's Education* (January 1969). The ideas were later incorporated in the proposal made by James E. Allen, Jr., the U.S. Commissioner of Education, to the National School Boards Association, which was discussed in Chapter 1.

3. National Institute of Neurological Diseases and Stroke, *Central Processing Dysfunctions in Children: A Review of Research,* Monograph No. 9, USGPO, 1970. The definition was formulated in the First Annual Report of the National Advisory Committee on Handicapped Children in 1968.

4. Nadine M. Lambert, Jonathan H. Sandoval, Wilson Yandell and Myra Windmiller, "Factors Associated With the Identification and Treatment of Children with Hyperactive-Learning-Behavior Disorders: Report of the Pilot Investigation," November 1, 1973. Research conducted at the University of California, Berkeley, School of Education under an NIMH grant. In 1965 a study found that intelligence test scores were unrelated to the activity level of preschool age children in a school setting: E. E. Maccoby, E. M. Dowley, J. W. Hagne and R. Degerman, "Activity Level and Functioning in Normal Preschool Children," *Child Development,* Vol. 36 (1965), pp. 761–770.

5. John H. Meier, "Prevalence and Characteristics of Learning Disabilities Found in Second Grade Children," *Journal of Learning Disabilities,* Vol. 4, No. 1 (January 1971).

6. Eric Denhoff, Peter K. Hainsworth and Marian L. Hainsworth, "The Child at Risk for Learning Disorder: Can He Be Identified During the First Year of Life?", *Clinical Pediatrics,* Vol. 11, No. 3 (March 1972).

7. The HEW figures come from the "Report on the Conference on the Use of Stimulant Drugs in the Treatment of Behaviorally Disturbed Young Children," Office of Child Development and the Office of the Assistant Secretary for Health and Scientific Affairs, HEW, January 1971. The higher figure has been used in a number of places, among them a staff report to Senator Albert S. Rodda, chairman of the Education Committee of the California State Senate on "Hyperkinesis Control in State Elementary Schools," July 1974.

8. R. Lapouse and M. A. Monk, "An Epidemiologic Study of Behavior Characteristics in Children," *American Journal of Public Health,* Vol. 48 (1958); and F. B. Stone, M. A. Wilson, M. E. Spence and R. C. Gibson, "A Survey of Elementary School Children's Behavior Problems," paper presented at the annual meeting of the American Orthopsychiatric Association, New York, 1969.

9. *Learning Disorders in Children: Report of the Sixty-First Ross Conference on Pediatric Research* (Columbus, Ohio: Ross Laboratories, 1971), pp. 24–25.

10. George F. Still, "The Coulstonian Lectures on Some Abnormal Physical Conditions in Children," *The Lancet* (April 12, 1902), pp. 1008–1012; (April 19, 1902), pp. 1077–1082; (April 26, 1902), pp. 1163–1168.

11. Samuel Torrey Orton, *Reading, Writing and Speech Problems in Children* (New York: W. W. Norton & Co., Inc., 1939).

12. *Ibid.*, p. 74.

13. E. Kahn and L. Cohen, "Organic Drivenness: A Brain-stem Syndrome and Experience," *New England Journal of Medicine,* Vol. 210 (April 1934), pp. 748–756.

14. Alfred A. Strauss and Laura E. Lehtinen, *Psychopathology and Education of the Brain-Injured Child* (New York: Grune & Stratton, 1947).

15. Alfred A. Strauss and Newell C. Kephart, *Psychopathology and Education of the Brain Injured Child*, Vol. II, Progress in Theory and Clinic (New York: Grune & Stratton, 1955), p. ix.

16. Maurice W. Laufer, Eric Denhoff and G. Solomons, "Hyperkinetic Impulse Disorder in Children's Behavior Problems," *Psychosomatic Medicine,* Vol. 19 (February 1957), pp. 38–49. Also Laufer and Denhoff, "Hyperkinetic Behavior Syndrome in Children," *Journal of Pediatrics,* Vol. 50 (April 1957), pp. 463–474. Lester Grinspoon and Susan B. Singer, in "Amphetamines in the Treatment of Hyperkinetic Children," *Harvard Educational Review,* Vol. 43, No. 4 (November 1973), pp. 515–549, describe Laufer's experiment: "In his experiment he established two groups of subjects from among the patients at a home for emotionally disturbed children. . . . The two groups were chosen solely on the basis of presence or absence of the clinically defined hyperkinetic impulse disorder. A history of factors considered capable of producing brain damage was not included in the criteria for selection. In fact, of those subjects identified as hyperkinetic, only 34 percent had such histories. Metrazol, a drug used to test the presence of brain dysfunction, was administered to each subject. For each child the amount necessary to evoke an EEG spikewave burst and a myoclonic jerk of the forearms in response to a stroboscope was determined. Analysis of the mean photo-Metrazol threshold for the two groups of children revealed that the threshold for the hyperkinetic children was significantly lower than the threshold for the nonhyperkinetic children. This was true regardless of whether the histories of the hyperkinetic children showed clear evidence of brain damage. Previously, H. Gastaut (1950), who developed the photo-Metrazol test for adults, had presented evidence for the theory that a photo-Metrazol threshold below a certain norm indicates damage to or dysfunction of the diencephalon. Thus, Laufer concluded that the hyperkinetic impulse disorder has an organic determinant, specifically a dysfunction of the diencephalon. Further support for the postulated organic basis of this clinical syndrome was derived from administering amphetamine to the hyperkinetic children and redetermining photo-Metrazol thresholds. Analysis showed the amphetamines increased the threshold of these children to a level characteristic of the nonhyperkinetic group. Unfortunately, in Laufer's experiment the effect of amphetamines on the photo-Metrazol thresholds of the *nonhyperkinetic* children was not determined. Nor was any effort made to correlate changes in photo-Metrazol thresholds with changes in behavior, even for the hyperkinetic children. Thus, the findings must remain inconclusive. . . ."

17. The hyperkinetic syndrome was, and, in some circles, still is, regarded as extremely rare. In one British study of 2,000 children published in 1970, nine were identified as suffering from neuroepileptic disorders, but only one was identified as hyperkinetic, and the researchers concluded that "the hyperkinetic syndrome is a decidedly uncommon disorder." And in another, which included all five-year-olds on the Isle of Wight—some 1,200 youngsters—not one case of hyperkinesis was found. M. Rutter, P. Graham and W. Yule, *A Neuropsychiatric Study in Childhood* (London: S.I.M.P. with Heinemann Medical, 1970); Martin Bax, "The Active and the Over-Active School Child," *Developmental Medicine and Child Neurology,* Vol. 14 (1972), pp. 83–86.

18. Sam D. Clements, "Task Force I: Minimal Brain Dysfunction in Children: Terminology and Identification," National Institute of Neurological Diseases and Blindness, Monograph No. 3, U.S. Department of Health, Education and Welfare, 1966.

19. *Ibid.,* pp. 6–7.

20. *Ibid.,* pp. 9–10.

21. In 1968, a followup study of all the 750 children born in one year on the island of Kauai, Hawaii, found that children who had a history of perinatal problems had no more difficulty in learning and no more behavior problems than those who had no such history, and that by the age of ten most of those who had suffered severe problems in infancy were doing well in school, a conclusion which called into question the assumption that perinatal "insult" was a factor in causing MBD. Emmy Werner, *et al.,* "Reproductive and Environmental Casualties: A Report of the 10–year Follow-Up of the Children of the Kauai Pregnancy Study," *Pediatrics,* Vol. 42 (1968), pp. 112–127.

22. Alexander Thomas, Stella Chess and Herbert G. Birch, *Temperament and Behavior Disorders in Children* (New York: New York University Press, 1968); Norman E. Silberberg and Margaret C. Silberberg, "Hyperlexia: The Other End of the Continuum," *The Journal of Special Education,* Vol. 5, No. 3 (Fall 1971), pp. 233–242; Norman E. Silberberg and Margaret C. Silberberg, "Case Studies in Hyperlexia," *Journal of School Psychology,* Vol. 7, No. 1 (1968–1969), pp. 3–7; Norman Silberberg and Margaret Silberberg, "Hyperlexia—Specific Word Recognition Skills in Young Children," *Exceptional Children,* Vol. 34 (1967), pp. 41–42; Donald K. Routh and Robert D. Robert, "Minimal Brain Dysfunction in Children: Failure to Find Evidence for a Behavioral Syndrome," *Psychological Reports,* Vol. 31 (1972), pp. 307–314.

23. Francis M. Crinella, Frances W. Beck and James W. Robinson, "Unilateral Dominance is Not Related to Neuropsychological Integrity," *Child Development,* Vol. 42 (1971), pp. 2033–2054; Francis M. Crinella, "Identification of Brain Dysfunction Syndromes in Children Through Profile Analysis: Patterns Associated With So-Called 'Minimal Brain Dysfunction'," submitted to the *Journal of Abnormal Psychology* (1972).

24. F. Beth Stone, "Assessment of Children's Activity Level," a paper presented at the 51st annual meeting of the American Orthopsychiatric Association, San Francisco, California, April 1974. Stone's quote is taken from T. McConnell, R. Cromwell, I. Bailer and C. D. Son, "Studies in Activity Level: VII. Effects of Amphetamine Drug Administration on the Activity Level of Retarded Children," *American Journal of Mental Deficiency*, Vol. 68 (1964), pp. 647–651.

25. H. H. Comly, "Cerebral Stimulants for Children with Learning Disorders," *Journal of Learning Disabilities*, Vol. 4 (1971), pp. 20–26.

26. L. Alan Sroufe and Mark A. Stewart, "Treating Problem Children with Stimulant Drugs," *New England Journal of Medicine*, Vol. 289, No. 8, pp. 407–414.

27. See also Nicholas Hobbs, et al., "The Futures of Children: Categories, Labels and Their Consequences," report of the Project on Classification of Exceptional Children, December 15, 1973. The report was commissioned in 1972 by Elliot Richardson, who was then Secretary of Health, Education and Welfare, and was the work of a large task force of doctors, psychologists, educators, lawyers and many of the major figures in the field of special education. The draft report, from which we quoted, generated a great deal of controversy among members of the group; by late 1974 it had not been released by HEW, but it was scheduled for commercial publication by Jossey-Bass, Inc., a San Francisco publishing house, early in 1975. It is to appear as two separate titles: Nicholas Hobbs, *The Futures of Children,* and Hobbs, ed., *Issues in the Classification of Children,* a two-volume collection of the background papers on which the original report was based. Together the three volumes constitute the most extensive and significant study on the labeling of children.

28. William M. Cruickshank, "Field of Learning Disability," *Journal of Learning Disabilities,* Vol. 5, No. 7 (August/September, 1972), pp. 6–7. The article was originally an address given at a learning disabilities symposium of the National Rehabilitation Training Institute at Miami Beach, Florida, October 26, 1971.

29. On chemical imbalance, see P. H. Wender, *Minimal Brain Dysfunction in Children* (New York: John Wiley and Sons, 1971); J. L. Rapoport, I. T. Lott and D. F. Alexander, *et al.,* "Urinary Noradrenaline and Playroom Behavior in Hyperactive Boys," *The Lancet,* Vol. 2, p. 1141 (1970); C. Kornetsky, "Psychoactive Drugs in the Immature Organism," *Psychopharmacologia* (Berlin), Vol. 17 (April 1970), pp. 105–136.

On megavitamin cures, see Abram Hoffer, *Megavitamin Therapy* (Denver: Aurora Book Companions, n.d.); Hugh W. S. Powers, Jr., "Dietary Measures to Improve Behavior and Achievement," *Academic Therapy* (Winter 1973–1974); William H. Philpott, "Biobehavioral Psychiatry and Learning Disabilities," a lecture given at the Association for Children with Learning Disabilities' international conference in March 1971; and Allan Cott, "Megavitamins: The Orthomolecular Approach to Behavioral Disorders and Learning Disabilities." An orthomolecular clinic at the San Bernardino, California, County General Hospital is testing out megavitamin therapy on learning-disabled children, as is Dr. Bernard Rimland of San Diego, California.

On genetic origins of MBD, see Daniel J. Safer, "A Familial Factor in Minimal Brain Dysfunction," *Behavioral Genetics*, Vol. 3, No. 2 (1973); J. Morison and M. Stewart, "A Family Study of the Hyperactive Child Syndrome," *Biological Psychiatry*, Vol. 3 (1971), pp. 189–195; D. P. Cantwell, "Psychiatric Illness in the Families of Hyperactive Children," *Archives of General Psychiatry*, Vol. 27 (1972), pp. 414–417. Researchers who hope to isolate the gene that causes reading disabilities are conducting a study to discover genetic patterns in this area at the Institute for Behavioral Genetics, University of Colorado, Boulder.

On allergy theories, see S. D. Klotz, "Making the Child Accessible for Teaching-Learning: The Role of the Internist and Allergist in Learning Disabilities"; Ray C. Wunderlich, *Allergy, Brains and Children Coping* (St. Petersburg, Florida: Johnny Reads, Inc., 1973); Robert D. Carpenter, *Why Can't I Learn?* (Glendale, California: Regal Books, 1973); Marshall Mandell, "Cerebral Allergy as a Major Cause of Learning Disabilities," an address given at the Association for Children with Learning Disabilities' international conference in March 1974 at Houston. Ben F. Feingold, emeritus chief of Kaiser Foundation allergy clinics, has proposed—based on a small sample he studied—that hyperactivity is an allergic response to food additives. This theory will be studied by C. Keith Conners, a psychopharmacologist now at the University of Pittsburgh, with a $59,896 grant from HEW's National Institute on Education.

On physical anomalies, see Mary F. Waldrop and Jacob D. Goering, "Hyperactivity and Minor Physical Anomalies in Elementary School Children," *American Journal of Orthopsychiatry*, Vol. 41 (1971), pp. 602–607; Mary Waldrop and Charles F. Halverson, Jr., "Minor Physical Anomalies and Hyperactive Behavior in Young Children," in *The Exceptional Infant*, J. Hellmuth (ed.), Vol. 2 (Bruner/Mazel, 1971); Judith L. Rapoport, Patricia O. Quinn and Friedhelm Lamprecht, "Minor Physical Anomalies and Plasma Dopamine-Beta-Hydroxlase Activity in Hyperactive Boys," *American Journal of Psychiatry*, Vol. 121, No. 4 (April 1974), pp. 386–390.

On fluorescent lighting as a cause of hyperactivity, see Joan Arehart-Treichel, "School Lights and Problem Pupils," *Science News*, Vol. 105 (April 20, 1974).

On the truancy-as-allergy hypothesis, see "Truancy May Be Allergy," *Academic Therapy*, Vol. 9, No. 4, p. 3.

30. Leon Oettinger, Jr., "Learning Disorders, Hyperkinesis, and the Use of Drugs in Children," *Rehabilitation Literature*, Vol. 32, No. 6 (June 1971), p. 165. When the CIBA officers testified before a Senate committee of the California Legislature in July 1974 on the efficacy of Ritalin in treating MBD, the only member of its contingent not employed by CIBA was Dr. Oettinger.

31. Camilla M. Anderson, "Manifestations of MBD," reprinted from *Society Pays* with permission of the publisher, Walker & Co., New York, pp. 61–62, 68–70. Distributed by CANHC, Mid-Peninsula Chapter.

32. Leon Oettinger, Jr., "Amphetamines, Hyperkinesis and Learning," distributed by CANHC Literature Distribution, P.O. Box 790, Lomita, California 90717. Conference programs often acknowledge the support of the drug companies.

33. Hobbs, *Futures of Children*, p. 125. Teacher preferences in labels are discussed in Stanley L. Hughes, "What Do Labels Really Mean to Classroom Teachers," *Academic Therapy* (Spring 1973), pp. 285–289.

34. Grinspoon and Singer, "Amphetamines," p. 539.

35. *The MBD Child: A Guide for Parents* (Summit, New Jersey: CIBA Pharmaceutical Company, 1972).

36. John E. Peters, Joanna S. Davis, Cleo M. Goolsby, Sam D. Clements and Tom J. Hicks, *Physician's Handbook: Screening for MBD* (Newark, New Jersey: CIBA Medical Horizons, Linden Medical Book Company, 1973).

37. *Ibid.*, pp. 1, 5.

38. The summary of Dr. Benvenuti's activities is based on interviews, on a memo he prepared for school officials, "Proposal for Program Design at Hillcrest Elementary, 1973–1974," on materials he employs to train school staff, which includes his "hyperkinetic syndromes chart," and on a three-page description of his work "Pre-delinquency Screening—The Beginning of Systems Therapy" which he prepared for us. The article from which the Benvenuti scale is taken is Mark A. Stewart, "Hyperactive Children," *Scientific American*, pp. 99–103.

39. Robert E. Valett, *The Remediation of Learning Disabilities: A Handbook of Psychoeducational Resource Programs* (Belmont, California: Fearon Publishers/Lear Siegler, Inc., 1967).

40. N. Dale Bryant, "Learning Disabilities: A Report on the State of the Art," *Teachers College Record*, Vol. 75, No. 3 (February 1974), pp. 401–402.

41. William H. Whyte, Jr., *The Organization Man* (Garden City, New York: Anchor Books, 1957), p. 436.

Chapter Three: THE SMART PILL

1. The story of Frank is based on our own research in clinics and doctors' offices. The story of John is from Francine Berlin, "Drugs and Hyperactive Children," unpublished, pp. 2–4; and the story of Shawn is from Daniel M. Martin, "Hyperkinetic Behavior Disorders in Children: Clinical Results With Methylphenidate Hydrochloride (Ritalin)," unpublished, p. 13.

2. Exact figures are difficult to establish. In the year ending September 1973, 623,000 prescriptions were written for Ritalin to treat MBD and hyperkinesis in children, according to the National Disease and Therapeutic Index (NDTI). This figure does not include prescriptions written in clinics where many difficult schoolchildren are referred. Size of prescription is also difficult to ascertain. According to one inventory, a typical prescription for Ritalin (20 milligrams) is for 78 tablets. Since the general pattern is for a child to take two tablets a day (but only on school days) such a prescription would last just under two months. If the child were taking the pills only in the morning—as about a third do—it would last almost four months. But since Ritalin was put under restrictions by the Bureau of Narcotics and Dangerous Drugs (in 1971) which prohibit prescription refills, many doctors are writing larger prescriptions, some for as many as 1,000 tablets. In 1971, Thomas O. Boucher, chairman of the board of CIBA-Geigy Corporation, testified before the Senate Judiciary Subcommittee to Investigate Juvenile Delinquency that two million patient visits a year involved Ritalin, and that "its use for hyperkinesis is approaching 60 percent . . . of production." Since then CIBA spokesmen have modified that estimate but have never provided a clear substitute. Donald K. Fletcher, a spokesman for Smith Kline & French Laboratories (which produces Dexedrine) testified in July 1974 before a California Senate Committee investigating hyperkinesis control in California elementary schools that his NDTI data showed that patient visits to private physicians involving prescriptions for hyperactive behavior came to somewhere between 850,000 and 875,000. Our own estimate, based on a study at a clinic in Iowa, is that patient visits and number of children medicated in any particular year correspond more or less evenly: one patient visit per year for every medicated child. The Iowa study, by Gerald Solomons ("Drug Therapy: Initiation and Follow-Up," *Annals of the New York Academy of Sciences.* Vol. 205, pp. 335–344) found that nearly half the cases sampled were followed up with less than two patient visits or *phone calls* in any six-month period, and that the average term of medication was nearly three years. Since the study was based on patients referred to private physicians by the leading clinic in the state, and since it was conducted in 1971, when experience with psychoactive drugs in treating MBD was relatively limited, it is unlikely that in current practice the number of patient visits for MBD problems averages more than one a year for each medicated child.

In the only recent attempts to pin down the prevalence of the use of stimulant drugs with schoolchildren, Daniel Safer of Johns Hopkins estimated in 1973 that 300,000 to 600,000 children were taking drugs. The study, based on projections from a sample in Baltimore County, also indicated that there had been a 55 percent increase in the previous two years. If that rate of increase continued, it would put the 1975 estimate at between 465,000 and 930,000. (A similar prevalence study in the Chicago area in 1971 would put the figure at between 500,000 and 1,000,000.) Safer also pointed out that while in 1971 Ritalin had only 53 percent of the market, its share had grown to between 80 and 88 percent by 1973. There is, of course, nothing like a perfect distribution of drug-taking children in the nation. In areas where prodrug doctors and clinics cluster, the percentage of children on these medications rises sharply. Dr. Eric Denhoff, a Providence, Rhode Island, pediatric neurologist who has been using the drugs with great enthusiasm for many years and who has been influential in their adoption nationally, states that in Rhode Island about 6,000 children are taking the drugs. He feels that only half as many—3,000— should be on them. If Rhode Island were typical, that would mean some 2.25 million children being medicated nationally; by his own estimates of what would be appropriate, the figure would shrink to 1.1 million.

3. See Lester Grinspoon and Peter Hedblom, *The Speed Culture: Amphetamine Use and Abuse in America* (Cambridge: Harvard University Press, 1975); Grinspoon and Hedblom, "Amphetamines Reconsidered," *Saturday Review,* July 8, 1972, pp. 33–46; and Gail Sheehy, "The Amphetamine Explosion," *New York,* July 21, 1969. According to federal accounts, the Department of Justice was unable to account for the sale of 38 percent of the more than 3 billion dosage units of amphetamines produced in this country in 1968 for domestic use. Although the official figure was something over 3 billion, a Congressional report put the production figure at 8 to 10 billion. See John Pekkanen, *The American Connection: Profiteering and Politicking in the "Ethical" Drug Industry* (Chicago: Follett Publishing Company, 1973).

4. For more discussion, see pages 86–88.

5. Christine W. Kehne, "Social Control of the Hyperactive Child Via Medication: At What Cost to Personality Development; Some Psychological Implications and Clinical Interventions," paper delivered at the annual meeting of the American Orthopsychiatric Association, 1974, p. 9.

6. *Federal Involvement in the Use of Behavior Modification Drugs on Grammar School Children.* Hearing Before A Subcommittee on Government Operations, U.S. House of Representatives, Ninety-First Congress, September 29, 1970, (Washington: U.S. Government Printing Office, 1970), p. 97. (Hereafter referred to as Subcommittee on Government Operations).

7. "When the MBD Child Goes to School," CIBA Pharmaceutical Company, Summit, N.J., May 1974.

8. Randall Richard, "Drugs for Children—Miracle or Nightmare?" *The Providence Journal,* February 8, 1972, p. 1.

9. Stanley S. Robin and James J. Bosco, "Three Perspectives on the Use of Ritalin: Teachers, Prospective Teachers and Professors: I. Description of Attitude, Knowledge and Role." The paper was part of the American Educational Research Association 1974 meeting's symposium on stimulant drugs and the schools. Part of this research was published in "Ritalin for School Children: The Teacher's Perspective," in *The Journal of School Health,* Vol. 43, No. 10 (1973), pp. 624–628; and James Bosco, "Implications of the Use of Stimulant Drugs for Educational Practices and Policies," paper presented at the annual meeting of the National School Boards Association, Houston, Texas, April 7, 1974.

10. Bosco, *ibid.,* p. 7. See also Edward L. Birch, "Development of a School District Policy on the Use of Stimulant Drugs for School Children," paper given at the American Educational Research Association, April 19, 1974, as part of the symposium on "Stimulant Drugs and the Schools: Dimensions in Remediation of Social Toxicity."

11. There is an elegant discussion of this issue in Henry L. Lennard, *et al., Mystification and Drug Misuse: Hazards in Using Psychoactive Drugs*

(New York: Harper & Row, 1972). Also, "Hazards Implicit in Prescribing Psychoactive Drugs," by the same authors, in *Science,* Vol. 169 (July 31, 1970), pp. 438–441.

12. Charles Bradley, "The Behavior of Children Receiving Benzedrine," *American Journal of Psychiatry,* Vol. 94 (November 1937), pp. 577–585.

13. Charles Bradley and M. Bowen, "Amphetamine (Benzedrine) Therapy of Children's Behavior Disorders," *American Journal of Orthopsychiatry,* Vol. 11 (January 1941), pp. 92–103; and Charles Bradley, "Benzedrine and Dexedrine in the Treatment of Children's Behavior Disorders," *Pediatrics,* Vol. 5 (January 1950), pp. 24–36.

14. Lester Grinspoon and Susan B. Singer, "Amphetamines in the Treatment of Hyperkinetic Children," *Harvard Educational Review,* Vol. 43, No. 4 (November 1973), p. 520.

15. Leon Cytryn, Anita Gilbert and Leon Eisenberg, "The Effectiveness of Tranquilizing Drugs Plus Supportive Psychotherapy in Treating Behavior Disorders of Children: A Double-Blind Study of Eighty Outpatients," *American Journal of Orthopsychiatry,* Vol. 30 (1960), pp. 113–129. Leon Eisenberg, Anita Gilbert, Leon Cytryn and P. A. Molling, "The Effectiveness of Psychotherapy Alone and in Conjunction with Perphenazine or Placebo in the Treatment of Neurotic and Hyperkinetic Children," *American Journal of Psychiatry,* Vol. 117 (1961), pp. 1088–1093. P. A. Molling, A. W. Lockner, R. J. Sauls and Leon Eisenberg, "Committed Delinquent Boys: The Impact of Perphenazine and of Placebo," *Archives of General Psychiatry,* Vol. 7 (1962), pp. 70–76. Leon Eisenberg, R. Lackman, P. A. Molling, A. Lockner, J. D. Mizelle and C. K. Conners, "A Psychopharmacologic Experiment in a Training School for Delinquent Boys," *American Journal of Orthopsychiatry,* Vol. 33, No. 3 (1963), pp. 431–446.

16. Ronald S. Lipman, "NIMH-PRB Support of Research in Minimal Brain Dysfunction and Other Disorders of Childhood," in *Psychopharmacology Bulletin,* Special Issue, Pharmacotherapy of Children (1973), p. 1.

17. Testimony of Thomas C. Points, Subcommittee on Government Operations, pp. 6–9.

18. Conners and Eisenberg, "The Effects of Methylphenidate on Symptomatology and Learning in Disturbed Children," *American Journal of Psychiatry,* Vol. 120, No. 5 (1963), pp. 458–464. Conners, Eisenberg and Lawrence Sharpe, "Effects of Methylphenidate (Ritalin) on Paired-Associate Learning and Porteus Maze Performance in Emotionally Disturbed Children," *Journal of Consulting Psychology,* Vol. 28, No. 1 (1964), pp. 14–22.

19. Conners, Eisenberg and Avner Barcai, "Effect of Dextroamphetamine on Children: Studies on Subjects With Learning Disabilities and School Behavior Problems," *Archives of General Psychiatry,* Vol. 17 (October, 1967), pp. 478–485.

20. Roger D. Freeman, "Review of Drug Effects on Learning in Children," in *Successful Programming: Many Points of View* (San Rafael, California: Academic Therapy, 1969), pp. 505–507. Roger D. Freeman, "Drug Effects on Learning in Children: A Selective Review of the Past Thirty Years," *Journal of Special Education,* Vol. 1, No. 1 (Fall 1966), pp. 17–44. Roger D. Freeman, "Review of Medicine in Special Education:

Another Look at Drugs and Behavior," *Journal of Special Education,* Vol. 4, No. 1 (Fall 1970), pp. 377–384. Roger D. Freeman, "Review of Medicine in Special Education: Medical-Behavioral Pseudorelationships," *Journal of Special Education,* Vol. 5 (Winter-Spring 1971), pp. 93–99.
21. See Paul H. Wender, "Some Speculations Concerning a Possible Biochemical Basis in Minimal Brain Dysfunction" in *Annals of the New York Academy of Sciences,* pp. 18–28.
22. See Leon Oettinger, Jr., "Learning Disorders, Hyperkinesis, and the Use of Drugs in Children," *Rehabilitation Literature,* Vol. 32, No. 6 (June 1971), pp. 162–167; Lester Tarnopol (ed.), *Learning Disorders in Children: Diagnosis, Medication, Education* (Boston: Little, Brown & Co., 1971) and Wender, "Some Speculations," p. 22.
23. Oettinger, *Learning Disorders,* p. 165.
24. Eisenberg, "The Overactive Child," *Hospital Practice* (September 1970). The article was reprinted and widely circulated at learning disabilities symposia by such groups of laymen as the California Association for Neurologically Handicapped Children. See also Eisenberg, The Clinical Use of Stimulant Drugs in Children," in *Pediatrics,* Vol. 49, No. 5 (May 1972), pp. 709–715.
25. See Grinspoon and Singer, "Amphetamines"; C. J. Weithorn, "Hyperactivity and the CNS: An Etiological and Diagnostic Dilemma," *Journal of Learning Disabilities,* Vol. 6 (January 1973), pp. 41–45; Barbara Fish, "The 'One Child, One Drug' Myth of Stimulants in Hyperkinesis," *Archives of General Psychiatry,* Vol. 25 (September 1971), pp. 212–227; J. S. Werry and R. L. Sprague, "Hyperactivity," in C. G. Costello (ed.), *Symptoms of Psychopathology* (New York: Wiley, 1970); Gabrielle Weiss, *et al.,* "Comparison of the Effects of Chlorpromazine, Dextroamphetamine and Methylphenidate on the Behavior and Intellectual Functioning of Hyperactive Children," *Canadian Medical Association Journal,* Vol. 104 (January 9, 1971), pp. 20–21.
26. T. Shetty, "Photic Responses in Hyperkinesis of Childhood," *Science,* 174 (1971), pp. 1356–1357.
27. Conners, "The Effect of Dexedrine on Rapid Discrimination and Motor Control of Hyperkinetic Children Under Mild Stress," *Journal of Nervous and Mental Disease,* Vol. 142 (May 1966), pp. 429–433.
28. L. Alan Sroufe and Mark A. Stewart, "Treating Problem Children with Stimulant Drugs," *The New England Journal of Medicine,* Vol. 289, No. 8 (August 23, 1973), pp. 407–412.
29. R. L. Sprague, *et al.,* "Methylphenidate and Thioridazine: Learning Reaction Time, Activity, and Classroom Behavior in Disturbed Children," *American Journal of Orthopsychiatry,* Vol. 40 (July 1970), pp. 615–628.
30. J. G. Millichap, *et al.,* "Hyperkinetic Behavior and Learning Disorders—III, Battery of Neuropsychological Tests in Controlled Trial of Methylphenidate," *American Journal of Diseases of Children,* Vol. 116 (September 1968), pp. 235–244.
31. J. G. Millichap and E. E. Boldrey, "Studies in Hyperkinetic Behavior: II, Laboratory and Clinical Evaluations of Drug Treatments," *Neurology,* Vol. 17 (May 1967), pp. 467–471.

32. Stephen I. Sulzbacher, "Psychotropic Medication with Children: An Evaluation of Procedural Biases in Results of Reported Studies," *Pediatrics,* Vol. 51, No. 3 (March 1973), pp. 513–517. Also, Sulzbacher, "Behavioral Analysis of Drug Effects in the Classroom," in Semb, *et al.* (eds.), *Behavioral Analysis and Education—1972* (Lawrence: University of Kansas, 1973).

33. Sroufe and Stewart, "Treating Problem Children," p. 410.

34. In a typical study, funded by NIMH and a drug company and reported late in 1972, the investigators found that among a group of children between six and eleven, 78 percent on dextroamphetamine lost appetite; 73 percent lost weight—an average of 3.2 pounds over eight weeks; 53 percent had insomnia; 49 percent experienced increased depression; 41 percent had headaches; and another 41 percent had stomachaches; 29 percent grew irritable and 23 percent complained of dizziness. In addition, one of the children on the amphetamines became "overtly psychotic," leading the authors to suggest that "the incidence of this serious complication may not be so small as was once thought." L. M. Greenburg, *et al.,* "Effects of Dextroamphetamine, Chlorpromazine, and Hydroxyzine on Behavior and Performance in Hyperactive Children," *American Journal of Psychiatry,* Vol. 129, No. 5 (November 1972), pp. 44–51.

35. D. S. Bell, "Comparison of Amphetamine Psychosis and Schizophrenia," *British Journal of Psychiatry,* Vol. 3 (August 1965), pp. 701–707. Bell notes that "amphetamine produces a 'model psychosis' that has a closer resemblance to schizophrenia than that produced by any other known hallucinogenic drug."

36. Philip G. Ney, "Psychosis in a Child, Associated With Amphetamine Administration," *Canadian Medical Association Journal,* Vol. 97 (October 21, 1967), pp. 1026–1029.

37. Alexander R. Lucas and Morris Weiss, "Methylphenidate Hallucinosis," *Journal of the American Medical Association,* Vol. 217, No. 8 (August 23, 1971), pp. 1079–1082.

38. Weiss, *et al.,* "Comparison of Effects," p. 24.

39. Daniel Safer, *et al.,* "Depression of Growth in Hyperactive Children on Stimulant Drugs," *New England Journal of Medicine,* Vol. 287 (August 1972), pp. 217–220.

40. Sroufe and Stewart, "Treating Problem Children," p. 409.

41. Mark Stewart, in telephone interview with authors.

42. Mark A. Stewart and Sally Wendkos Olds, *Raising a Hyperactive Child* (New York: Harper & Row, 1973), p. 135. The book contains a persuasive chapter, "Drugs and the Hyperactive Child," which warns parents to avoid medication except in the most desperate situations.

43. Sroufe and Stewart, *Treating Problem Children,* p. 410. Maurice Laufer, a pioneer in the field of stimulants with children, reported in the *Journal of Learning Disabilities,* Vol. 4 (1971), pp. 55–58, that a followup study of 100 former patients he had treated with drugs showed none of them had become addicts. However, only 57 of the 100 parents who were contacted answered the question about subsequent drug experimentation. Of those, 52 said their children were not experimenting with drugs, and

Laufer acknowledged, "Who knows how the nonrepliers might have altered the figures!" Stewart and Olds, *Raising a Hyperactive Child*, p. 240.

44. *Minimal Brain Dysfunction (MBD): Guidelines to Diagnosis/Guidelines to Treatment*, (Summit, New Jersey: CIBA Pharmaceutical Company, 1973).

45. Mauricio Knoebel, "Psychopharmacology for the Hyperkinetic Child," *Archives of General Psychiatry*, Vol. 6, pp. 198–202.

46. J. S. Werry, paper presented at the meeting of the American Psychiatric Association, Boston, May 13–17, 1968.

47. Robert M. Knights and George G. Hinton, "The Effects of Methylphenidate (Ritalin) on the Motor Skills and Behavior of Children With Learning Problems," *The Journal of Nervous and Mental Disease*, Vol. 148, No. 6 (1969), pp. 643–653.

48. Nat Hentoff, "Drug-pushing in the Schools: the Professionals (1)," *The Village Voice*, May 25, 1972, pp. 20–22.

49. Roger Rapoport, "To Keep The Kid Quiet?" *Los Angeles Times WEST Magazine*, April 25, 1971, pp. 38–42.

50. Subcommittee on Government Operations, p. 18. Ronald Lipman of NIMH testified that there was only one long-term followup of medicated children, and that was a study of 67 children then being conducted by Conners. Representative Cornelius Gallagher (New Jersey) wanted to know if there were "any dissenting studies going on, funded with federal money."

Dr. Lipman: Are there what?

Mr. Gallagher: Dissenting.

Dr. Lipman: Dissenting?

Mr. Gallagher: Dissenting. (Conners, he explained, "is obviously a dedicated scientist to his thing. Where do we have another scientist who may question this?") Lipman then went on to defend Conners as conducting studies that would "guard against biases that would creep in."

51. Daniel X. Freedman, *et al.*, "Report of the Conference on the Use of Stimulant Drugs in the Treatment of Behaviorally Disturbed Young School Children," sponsored by the Office of Child Development and the Office of the Assistant Secretary for Health and Scientific Affairs, Department of Health, Education and Welfare, Washington, D.C., January 11–12, 1971.

52. Much of the information which follows comes from memos, letters and other documents from FDA files which were given to us on condition that our source be kept confidential. We will cite documents where possible and identify those so obtained as "FDA Papers."

53. Three published reports connected with the Cylert studies have appeared: C. Keith Conners, "Psychological Effects of Stimulant Drugs in Children With Minimal Brain Dysfunction," *Pediatrics*, Vol. 49 (1972), pp. 702–708; Conners, *et al.*," "Magnesium Pemoline and Dextroamphetamine: A Controlled Study in Children With Minimal Brain Dysfunction," *Psychopharmacologia*, Vol. 26 (1972), pp. 321–336; and John G. Page, *et al.*, "Pemoline (Cylert) In the Treatment of Childhood Hyperkinesis," *Journal of Learning Disabilities*, Vol. 7, No. 8 (October 1974), pp.

42–47. The first two were based on the Conners project, the other on the multi-clinic study.

54. "Clinical Comparison of Dextroamphetamines and Cylert in Childhood Hyperkinesis: Eisenberg-Conners Study—Medical Officer Comments," FDA Papers, 1972. Similar conclusions were stated and restated in memos from Carol Kennedy to various officers of FDA written in the spring, summer and fall of 1972.

55. "Medical Officer Review," October 11, 1972; "Medical Officer Review," May 15, 1972, FDA Papers.

56. "Medical Officer Review," October 11, 1972, p. 2.

57. The reply letter, from Richard W. Kasperson, Abbott vice president for corporate regulatory affairs to the FDA, was dated June 21, 1972. The supporting letters were written between June 13 and June 18 and were all addressed to John G. Page, assistant medical director at Abbott.

58. "Task Force Evaluation of the NDA for Cylert," FDA Papers, p. 6.

59. Meeting transcript, September 29, 1972.

60. Letter from C. Keith Conners to Elmer Gardner, FDA, November 9, 1972; the letter included a 36–page attachment with detailed replies. FDA Papers.

61. Letter from Elmer Gardner, FDA, to Gerald Klerman, chairman of the FDA Neuropharmacology Advisory Committee, February 1973. FDA Papers.

62. "Report of the Ad Hoc Panel for Evaluation of NDA 16–832 Cylert," March 29, 1973. FDA Papers.

63. Page, *et al.,* "Pemoline." The article does not, of course, give any indication that all FDA reviewers and review committees had considered the study inadequate after examination of the raw data.

64. Food and Drug Administration: Minutes of the Neuropharmacology Advisory Committee, February 7–8, 1974, p. 3.

65. This statement, and those which follow, were made in telephone interviews.

Chapter Four: Screening for Deviance and Other Diseases

1. The literature on the Bucks County program includes two massive mimeographed books, *Bucks County Diagnostic Educational Grouping With Strategies for Teaching* (1970) and *Strategies for Teaching: Diagnostic Educational Grouping* (2nd edition, 1972). Both are published by Bucks County Public Schools, Intermediate Unit No. 22, Doyleston, Pennsylvania. There are also a number of journal articles, including Phyllis P. Green and Calvin Colarusso, M.D., "Grouping by Psyche," *Teacher* (February 1973), pp. 70–72, and Francis McGlannan, "Psychiatry—Classroom Groupings," *Journal of Learning Disabilities,* Vol. 6, No. 9 (November 1973), pp. 35–36. There are also a number of unpublished papers by Dr. William Stennis, the developer of the program.

2. We are concerned primarily with tests of development; to list all intelligence tests is impossible. The matter of straight intelligence testing, moreover, is a vast issue which doesn't require any additional elaboration here. It's our feeling that the attention focused on straight IQ testing has so far obscured what may be the far more significant issue of screening for "disabilities."

3. For the discussion on records, see Chapter VI.

4. The original legislation, amendments to Title 19 of the Social Security Act, was originally permissive, and later made mandatory. It is designed to provide screening, diagnosis and treatment to all individuals under twenty-one who are eligible for Medicaid. The states are to draw up plans to identify available services and make them available to all eligible individuals.

5. The plan for Medichek is described in Flashner, *Medichek*. The description of the program as implemented is based on telephone interviews with officials of the Illinois Department of Public Health.

6. California Assembly Bill 2008 (1973). The bill was sponsored by Assemblyman Willie Brown, a black and a liberal.

7. The original date for implementation of state screening programs for Medicaid clients was February 1972 (for those under 6) and July 1973 (for all others under 21). Since many states had failed to draw or implement plans for screening, Congress voted in 1974 to withhold a percentage of welfare funds from any state which fails to comply. The effective date was to be October 1, 1974, but it was clear that the date would not be met by many states and that HEW would not be rigid in enforcing it.

8. The definitions, as we have already pointed out, are often based on political or budgetary considerations rather than on medical distinctions. The Developmental Disabilities Act of 1970, for example, defines "developmental disability" as a condition "attributable to mental retardation, cerebral palsy, epilepsy or another neurological condition . . . closely related to mental retardation," thereby lumping palsied or epileptic children, some of whom may be quite bright, if not brilliant, with the retarded. Since the act provides funds for retarded children who had been politically neglected, there was no serious objection. The distinction between "mentally retarded" and "learning disabled" often depends on the race, class and economic status of the child, not on his medical or pedagogical condition (Hobbs, *Futures of Children*, p. 123).

9. William K. Frankenburg, "Evaluation and Screening Procedures," in A. Oglesby and H. Sterling, *Bi-Regional Institute on Earlier Recognition of Handicapping Conditions in Childhood* (Berkeley: University of California School of Public Health, 1970), p. 42. Frankenburg invented the Denver Developmental Screening Test, perhaps the best general inventory in the field; DDST simply provides the range in age when most children develop certain skills but it suggests no conclusions or "syndromes" for the child who falls outside the norms.

10. John Meier, *Screening and Assessment of Young Children at Developmental Risk*, Washington, DHEW Publication No. (OS) 73–90, 1973, p. 7.

11. *Individual Learning Disabilities Classroom Screening Instrument* (Evergreen, Colorado: Learning Pathways, Inc., 1970).

12. Meier, now regarded as one of the leading American authorities in

screening, developed an 80–item test based on material used in other screens, translated it into "teacher's language," and launched a study. He asked thirty teachers in Greeley, Colorado, to select those children in their classes who were having the most difficulty learning, eliminated those regarded as economically or culturally disadvantaged, and asked the teachers to try the 80–item screen on the eighty-odd children who remained. The results of the trial satisfied Meier that there was a significant statistical correlation between the test results and the teacher's individual assessments of the children tested. Subsequently, he further refined the language, called in a group of "experts" in the disabilities field, revised some of his items on the basis of their comments, and used the resulting instrument in a larger test involving some 284 children in eight Rocky Mountain states. The purpose of all these studies, financed by the federal government, was to determine the prevalence and characteristics of learning disabilities. On the basis of those studies, Meier and his colleagues decided that specific learning disabilities affected some 15 percent of the population. (They also announced that medical studies of learning-disabled children showed that 90 percent showed "soft" neurological signs, and that about 95 percent of them fell into the "organic brain syndrome category." At the same time, medical examinations of nineteen children in a control or normal group revealed that 75 percent of them showed "soft" neurological signs, and that 55 percent fell into the "organic brain syndrome category." After we queried him about these figures, Meier acknowledged that there was something peculiar about the results; although the data had been published in a number of journals and were used as the basis for any number of other studies and screening programs, no one had ever challenged the figures before. There was obviously an error, Meier told us, but he was unable to find its source.) John H. Meier, "Prevalence and Characteristics of Learning Disabilities Found in Second Grade Children," *Journal of Learning Disabilities,* Vol. 4, No. 1 (January 1971); Meier, *et al., Administration, Scoring and Interpretation Manual for the* ILD/CSI (Denver: University of Colorado Medical Center, 1970); *Technical Report: Individual Learning Disabilities Program Pilot Incidence Study,* Vol. II (Greeley: Rocky Mountain Educational Laboratory, 1970). The main reason, Meier said, that economically and culturally disadvantaged children were eliminated from the test is that they were covered by poverty programs and therefore excluded from the federal education grants which supported the Rocky Mountain Laboratory. The reason, in other words, was budgetary and bureaucratic, not scientific, and Meier readily admitted that the exclusion of those children substantially skewed the screen and the study. That concession, however, does not appear in the published literature cited above.

13. Marian T. Giles, ILDCSI *Administration and Scoring Manual With Remedial Suggestions* (Adolescent Level, and Pre-School and Kindergarten Level) (Evergreen, Colorado: Learning Pathways, Inc., 1973). The manual for each level contains a section called "Implications for Research" which outlines the validation studies for the screen. Meier said he would prefer that the tests had not been published and marketed; he was himself doubtful about their validity.

14. C. Keith Conners, "Rating Scales for Use in Drug Studies With Children," *Psychopharmacology Bulletin,* Special Issue (Rockville, Maryland: National Institute of Mental Health, 1973), p. 27. Conners said in an interview that he didn't "remember exactly" on what he based his conclusion. He had seen a "paperbound progress report" which he thought was "pretty good." What he had seen were the reports published by Meier and his colleagues and cited above.

15. Denhoff and Tarnopol, "Medical Responsibilities in Learning Disorders," in Tarnopol, *Learning Disorders in Children: Diagnosis, Medication, Education* (Boston: Little, Brown and Co., 1971), pp. 88–109. Denhoff is a pediatric neurologist associated with the Governor Medical Center in Providence and one of the most prolific writers on the use of psychoactive drugs in treating learning disorders. Tarnopol, a peripatetic operative, is a member of the faculties of psychology and engineering at San Francisco City College, has taught mathematics at Loyola University in Los Angeles and metallurgy at the University of Kentucky and served as a research associate in geophysics at Harvard. He has also edited two books on learning disabilities and conducted a delinquency prevention project for the Department of Health, Education and Welfare.

16. *Ibid.,* p. 109.

17. There are a number of studies purporting to show that teachers are effective predictors of learning disabilities, among them Mary Lu Cowgill, *et al.,* "Predicting Learning Disabilities from Kindergarten Reports," *Journal of Learning Disabilities,* Vol. 4, No. 9 (November 1973), pp. 50–54.

18. Like a number of other documents, this was given us in confidence. To protect the source and the boy, we chose not to name the school. We were told, however, that the second grade teacher was known as a political liberal in the school and that the fourth grade teacher was regarded as a conservative who kept an American flag decal on his car.

19. Stanley S. Robin and James J. Bosco (Western Michigan University), "Three Perspectives on the Use of Ritalin: Teachers, Prospective Teachers and Professors," unpublished (1973), pp. 5, 14; Thomas J. Kenny, *et al.,* "Characteristics of Children Referred Because of Hyperactivity," *Journal of Pediatrics,* Vol. 79 (1971), pp. 618–622; and Kenny, *et al.,* "The Medical Evaluation of Children With Reading Problems (Dyslexia)," *Pediatrics,* Vol. 49, No. 3 (1972), pp. 438–442.

20. James J. Gallagher and Robert H. Bradley, "Early Identification of Developmental Difficulties," in *Early Childhood Education, Seventy-first Yearbook of the National Society for the Study of Education* (Chicago: University of Chicago Press, 1972), pp. 87–122. The survey examines the literature and research validating a number of the most commonly used screens. Bailey Infant Scales: "predictions of later performance are uncertain with the exception of pathological cases"; Development Screening Inventory for Infants: "A substantial number of over-referrals"; Cattell Infant Intelligence Scale: "Limited predictive ability"; Gesell Infant Scales: "Criticized as subjective, spuriously high IQ in early months, poorly standardized"; Southern California Perceptual Motor Tests: "Little evidence of validity," and a number of others. The authors rate the Stanford-Binet test (and IQ scale) as "undoubtedly the best, most reliable measure" for young children in its ability to predict later academic success.

21. "Study of Early and Periodic Screening, Diagnosis and Treatment Programs," HEW Information Memorandum MSA-IM–74–11, February 21, 1974. The memo deplores the fact that of "abnormalities" identified in a pilot study, only 46 percent reached diagnosis and treatment. (Since learning disabilities were one of the conditions for which children were screened, it is hard to imagine what sort of treatment was anticipated.) Clearly, the answer for the problems of inadequate health care for poor people is to provide the care, through universal public medical programs, and forget the screen.

22. Hobbs, *Futures of Children,* p. 136. "Most developmental problems of serious nature get picked up in routine clinical practice or are identified by parents or other untrained observers, while mild and moderate problems (by far the largest number) are difficult to detect and assess even by well-trained professional people administering complete examinations with the best of equipment. The premature child is clearly at risk but is also readily identified at birth. So too are children with gross orthopedic handicaps, with Down's Syndrome, hydrocephaly, and other gross anomalies associated with mental retardation. . . . The conditions that go undetected by parents and by clinicians in routine examinations are the very ones that are difficult to detect. Most mental retardation, mild to moderate deficits in seeing or hearing, and mild to moderate emotional disturbance often go undetected for long periods of time. . . . Even systematic screening by competent clinicians turns up relatively few cases in total population studies." Head Start abandoned screening for dental defects because "it was much more efficient to assume that all the children in the population served are in need of dental care and to send them directly for treatment." Socio-economic status, Hobbs declares, is a far better index of need for medical and dental service than any screen.

23. The John machine is described in CANHC-GRAM, April 1974; the Ertl device in "Can a Machine Detect Learning Disabilities," *Los Angeles Times,* May 14, 1973.

24. Quoted in Meier, *Screening and Assessment,* p. 28.

Chapter Five: IN THE MATTER OF PREDELINQUENTS

1. The cases were drawn from the records of the project; they were made available to us by the director, despite the assurance of confidentiality given each client. We changed the names and other incidental details which could be used to identify the individuals.

2. See, for example, Edwin M. Lemert, *Instead of Court: Diversion in Juvenile Justice* (Rockville, Maryland: National Institute of Mental Health, Center for Studies of Crime and Delinquency, 1971); William H. Sheridan, "Juveniles Who Commit Non-Criminal Acts: Why Treat in a Correctional System?", *Federal Probation,* Vol. 31 (1967), p. 26; and James

F. Short and F. Ivan Nye, "Extent of Unrecorded Delinquency," *Journal of Criminal Law and Criminology*, Vol. 49 (1958), p. 296.
3. Lemert, *Instead of Court*, p. 11. "Court hearings," Lemert observes, "on many occasions are equivalents of degradation rituals in which probation officers recite in detail the moral failings or 'unfitness' of children, youth and parents. Hostile witnesses add to the condemnations, and judges often deliver sermon-like lectures, larded with threats, which confront children and parents with choices of reform or dire consequences. . . ." There is a vast amount of literature on the viciousness of the formal juvenile justice system. It's been our intention in this book, however, to focus only on the cases and practices outside the formal system and on children and adolescents who have not been successfully processed by courts. The story of juvenile probation, courts and corrections would fill volumes by itself. Among the most recent is Patrick T. Murphy, *Our Kindly Parent—The State: The Juvenile Justice System and How It Works* (New York: Viking Press, 1974). In 1970, when Murphy became chief attorney for the juvenile section of the Chicago Legal Society, he discovered that public defenders there had never appealed a juvenile court decision
4. *In re Gault*, 387 U.S. 1 (1967).
5. Harvey Treger, *et al.*, *Police Social Service Project* (Chicago: Jane Addams School of Social Work, University of Illinois at Chicago Circle, 1973), pp. 114, 112. It was Professor Treger who first designed the Wheaton project; in its initial three years of operation it was funded by the Law Enforcement Assistance Administration of the Department of Justice. Subsequently the funding was taken over by the city of Wheaton. The project has had a continuing relationship with the Jane Addams School.
6. Treger, *ibid.*, p. 117.
7. *Merriken v. Cressman*, U.S. District Court for Eastern Pennsylvania, September 28, 1973. *U.S. Law Week*, October 16, 1973, pp. 2203–2204.
8. The President's Commission on Law Enforcement and Administration of Justice, *Task Force Report: Juvenile Delinquency and Youth Crime* (Washington, D.C.: Government Printing Office, 1967), p. 16.
9. Youth Development and Delinquency Prevention Administration, *Better Ways to Help Youth* (Washington, D.C.: U.S. Department of Health, Education and Welfare Publication No. [SRS] 73–26017, 1973), p. i.
10. The quotes are from the official application for funds from the Bell Gardens Police Department to the California Council on Criminal Justice. The project was funded with LEAA money.
11. *Ibid.*
12. The estimates are based on extrapolations of representative project reports, budgets and other data derived from local agencies. Since the reports themselves are unreliable, the figures are subject to question. The figures do not include those reached by various "outreach" projects such as police counselors or teachers in schools, athletic programs or routine "friendly policeman" classes conducted by uniformed officers in schools.
13. U.S. Department of Justice, Law Enforcement Assistance Administration, *Fifth Annual Report of the* LEAA (Washington, D.C.: Government Printing Office, 1973).

14. California Council on Criminal Justice, *Delinquency Prevention in California* (Sacramento: CCCJ, 1973).

15. The applications are all on file at CCCJ in Sacramento. We attempted to visit the Orange County project, called "Behavior Assessment and Treatment Center," to determine whether the treatment promised in the application was being offered. Officials of the Probation Department, including Margaret Grier, chief county probation officer, and Rex Castellaw, her chief deputy, both insisted that the program was limited to "counseling" and that no chemotherapy or other "management of neurologically related behavior disorders" was being practiced, but while they permitted interviews related to other Orange County diversion programs, they adamantly refused permission to visit the Behavior Assessment and Treatment Center. The explanation was that personnel in the program were too busy. Individuals in the project also refused to be interviewed. Grier and Castellaw told us that they were forced to drop their plans for neurological therapy because funds were limited.

16. Such a "contract" is signed by every client of the project, and by the client's parents. A similar contract is used for truants referred by the school system. The directors of the program concede that the contracts are unenforceable but, they say, "if a kid breaks it and the police catch him doing something else, we'll really kick him in the ass."

17. Some police departments make assignments to a project part of the offender's terms of informal probation or "station adjustment"; instead of reporting to the juvenile officer (who normally sends him home after a short visit) he reports to the counselor.

18. Ramon J. Rivera, *et al., Juvenile Delinquency in Illinois* (Chicago: Institute for Juvenile Research, 1973), pp. 20, 38–39.

19. Rivera, *ibid.,* pp. 10–11.

20. *Delinquency Prevention in California,* p. 30.

21. The study was conducted by Public Systems, Inc., of Sunnyvale. It has not been published.

22. Eleanor Harlow, *et al., Diversion from the Criminal Justice System* (Rockville, Maryland: The National Institute of Mental Health, 1973), p. 25.

23. Ronald Filippi and Clyde L. Rousey, "Positive Carriers of Violence Among Children: Detection by Speech Deviations," *Mental Hygiene,* Vol. 55, No. 2 (1971), pp. 157–161. The article was immediately followed by a "reply" accusing Filippi and Rousey of a host of methodological fallacies and suggesting that the whole study was racially biased since, in the critics' view, people speaking "Black English" normally pronounced "bird" in the suspect manner.

24. Peter S. Venezia, "Delinquency Prediction: A Critique and a Suggestion," *Journal of Research in Crime and Delinquency,* Vol. 8, No. 1 (1971), pp. 108–117.

25. Venezia did not cite the Cambridge-Somerville Youth Study (see pp. 154–155) which did try to "capitalize on this skill" with dismal results. He did, however, express doubt that standardized tests "currently used as screening devices will prove valid in detecting predelinquents at an early age" (Venezia, p. 111). At the very moment he was writing, other attempts

were being made to use teachers to select children prone to delinquency.
26. Fred W. Vondracek, *et al., Project* CARES, University Park, Pennsylvania, College of Human Development, Pennsylvania State University, 1973. This report includes copies of a number of the forms used in the project and a fairly extensive description of how the system is used. A similar project was operated for several years by an organization called the Probation Service Institute in Boulder, Colorado. The head of PSI, Dr. Ivan H. Scheier, had contracted with courts in some fifteen states for his service. By 1974, however, a flurry of newspaper articles had generated sufficient public concern (including some attacks in Congress) to force Dr. Scheier to reduce his operation. He told us that he was still doing some evaluations for a handful of probation departments but that he was no longer using the computer. In the meantime, Dr. Vondracek told us that he was hoping to find new clients for CARES.
27. The study at Hopkins is discussed on pp. 155–156. The chromosome studies at the University of Wisconsin and the Educational Testing Service are described in grant announcements from the National Institute of Mental Health; the UCLA research is described in grant applications and related literature in the UCLA Center for the Study and Reduction of Violence; the work in Rhode Island is discussed more extensively on pp. 159–160; the Hamline project results were published by Betty Ruth Raygor in "Mental Ability, School Achievement, and Language Arts Achievement in the Prediction of Delinquency," *Journal of Educational Research,* Vol. 64 (1970), pp. 68–72; the New Mexico psychiatrist is Dr. William Stennis. His project, first developed in Pennsylvania, is described more extensively in Chapter IV.
28. The quoted definition is from Filippi and Rousey, "Positive Carriers," p. 159.
29. For discussions of the Kvaraceus KD scale see W. C. Kvaraceus, "Forecasting Juvenile Delinquency: A Three-Year Experiment," *Exceptional Children,* Vol. 27, No. 8 (1961), pp. 429–435, and John F. Feldhusen, *et al.,* "Prediction of Delinquency, Adjustment and Academic Achievement Over a Five Year Period with the Kvaraceus Delinquency Proneness Scale," *Journal of Educational Research,* Vol. 65 (1972), pp. 375–381. Kvaraceus himself warned that problems of validation in his study suggested caution in using the scale as a predictive instrument. The Feldhusen study raised further doubts about the scale's effectiveness. The Cambridge-Somerville study is discussed more extensively on pp. 154–155.
30. Sheldon and Eleanor Glueck, *Predicting Delinquency and Crime* (Cambridge, Massachusetts: Harvard University Press, 1959), pp. 114–115.
31. *Ibid.,* pp. 232–239.
32. There is a comprehensive review of the New York Youth Board Study and the Cambridge-Somerville study in Jackson Toby, "An Evaluation of Early Identification and Intensive Treatment Programs for Predelinquents," *Social Problems,* Vol. 13 (Fall, 1965), pp. 160–175.
33. Center for Studies of Crime and Delinquency, NIMH, *Active Research Grants* (1973).
34. Ashley Montague, "Chromosomes and Crime," *Psychology Today,* October 1968.

35. See among others, "Maryland Tests for Criminal Potential," *Washington Daily News,* January 22, 1970, January 30, 1970, February 3, 1970, February 6, 1970, February 13, 1970, May 4, 1970, May 8, 1970, and June 20, 1970. We verified the details in interviews with Diane Bauer, now at the Children's Defense Fund in Washington, D.C., with officials at NIMH and with officers of the Maryland Chapter of the American Civil Liberties Union.

36. The XYY anomaly was first reported in Great Britain in 1961. Since then there has been a series of studies, including W. M. Court-Brown, "Males With an XYY Sex Chromosome Complement," *Journal of Medical Genetics,* Vol. 5 (1968), p. 341; P.A. Jacobs, *et al.,* "Aggressive Behavior, Mental Subnormality and the XYY Male," *Nature,* Vol. 208 (1965), p. 1351; W.H. Price, *et al.,* "Criminal Patients With XYY Sex Chromosome Complement," *Lancet,* Vol. 2 (1966), p. 641; and T.R. Sarbin and J.M. Miller, "Demonism Revisited: The XYY Chromosomal Anomaly," *Issues in Criminology,* Vol. 5, No. 2 (1970).

37. The Violence Center has been a hot political issue both in California and in Washington. Its applications for funding have gone through several phases; they have included proposals to study "Hormonal Aspects of Violence in Women," studies of violent sex offenders, "Chromosomal Factors and Violent Behavior," and "Estimation of Probability of Repetition or Continuation of Violence." Civil libertarians in Southern California, activist students at UCLA, the Children's Defense Fund of Washington, D.C., and organized groups within professional societies, particularly in the American Orthopsychiatric Association, campaigned extensively against LEAA funding for the Center. After LEAA's announcement of its new policy against behavior modification, it was assumed that the Center's prospects for major federal funds had seriously declined. The critics warned, however, that the Center would attempt to continue its work with University funds and with support from other sources. They also charged that the Center, despite its denials, was planning to conduct experiments in psychosurgery. In January 1973, the director of Center, Dr. Louis J. West, requested use of an abandoned Army Nike missile base in the Santa Monica Mountains for a research facility. In a letter asking the support of California state health officials in obtaining the site, West wrote that "comparative studies could be carried out there, in an isolated but convenient location, of experimental or model programs for the alienation of undesirable behavior." The state's director of health turned the request down. The subject, he said, was too "delicate."

38. See, for example, Alfred O. Holte, "Learning Disabilities and Juvenile Delinquency," talk given to the Orton Society, March 27, 1971; William Mulligan, "Dyslexia, Specific Learning Disability and Delinquency," *Juvenile Justice,* November, 1972. Holte is a juvenile court judge; Mulligan is chief probation officer in Sonoma County, California. Both texts are sold as reprints by the California Association for Neurologically Handicapped Children.

39. Allen Berman, "Delinquents Are Disabled," unpublished paper obtained from the author, p. 5.

40. The statement, along with related data, appears in a flier issued by the Education Section of the Colorado Division of Youth Services, "Statistics on the 444 Students Received—1 July 1972 to 1 May 1973."

41. Allen Berman, "Learning Disabilities and Juvenile Delinquency: A Neuropsychological Approach," paper presented at the Regional Conference of the Association for Children With Learning Disabilities, Los Angeles, February 2, 1973, pp. 1–2.

42. *Ibid.,* pp. 10–11.

43. *Helping Schools Help Children,* Research Report—2. Center for Studies of Crime and Delinquency, NIMH, 1974.

44. Even where the criteria are defined by law, however, the walls between them remain porous. In 1966, for example, juvenile courts in California sent eighty minors to the Youth Authority by reclassifying them from Section 600 of the Welfare and Institutions Code (neglected, dependent) to Section 602 (delinquent) without calling them back to court for a rehearing (Lemert, *Instead of Court,* p. 17). Many courts have also made it a practice to escalate the charges against "predelinquent" recidivists from "predelinquency" to "delinquency." A child accused of being "incorrigible" and charged as a "predelinquent" may be charged as a delinquent if he repeats the same act. "A boy may take leave from a ranch school because of problems beyond his power to solve. Yet the court typically defines such actions as 'failures' or disobedience of its orders, which become legal justification for more severe measures whose effect is to move a minor further along the road to correctional school" *(ibid.).*

45. Milton Brutten, Ph.D., Sylvia Richardson, M.D., and Charles Mangel, *Something's Wrong With My Child* (New York: Harcourt Brace Jovanovich, Inc., 1973).

46. *Ibid.,* pp. 164–180.

47. The authors conceded in a footnote that "the fact that some learning disabled children have become delinquents does not mean it will happen to your child. Neglected or abused learning-disabled children typically are the ones who get into serious trouble." They then proceed blithely on to make their argument.

48. *Ibid.,* p. 167.

49. *Ibid.,* p. 170.

50. *Ibid.,* p. 167.

51. Lloyd E. Ohlin, *et al.,* "Radical Correctional Reform: A Case Study of the Massachusetts Youth Correctional System," *Harvard Educational Review,* Vol. 41, No. 1 (1974), p. 82.

52. Showers are also controlled by guards, gas-chamber style, from outside the shower room. This, we were told, was to keep the inmates from "scalding themselves."

53. *Morales v. Turman,* Civil Action No. 1948 (E.D. Texas, Sherman Division), 1974.

54. *Ibid.,* pp. 171, 175. "If ever confinement in an institution constituted a form of cruel and unusual punishment," the Court added, "Gatesville and Mountain View fully meet the applicable criteria. . . . The confinement of juveniles in a facility that compares unfavorably with one of the most notorious prisons in America is shocking and senseless." The comparison was with Angola Prison in Louisiana.

55. *Ibid.,* p. 163–187. The decision instructed the Texas Youth Council to "cease to institutionalize any juvenile except those who are found by a responsible professional assessment to be unsuited for any less restrictive, alternative form of rehabilitative treatment."

56. "Right to treatment" is founded on the principle that "any non-trivial governmental abridgement of liberty must be justified in terms of some permissible governmental goal . . . the juvenile [in this case] must be given treatment lest the involuntary commitment amount to an arbitrary exercise of governmental power proscribed by the due process clause. . . . The government must afford a *quid pro quo* to warrant the confinement of citizens in which the conventional limitations of the criminal process are inapplicable." In legal theory, all juvenile cases are civil cases founded on a *parens patriae* theory.

57. M. Gold and J. R. Williams, "National Study of the Aftermath of Apprehension," *Prospectus,* Vol. 3 (December 1969), pp. 3–12.

58. Ohlin, "Radical Correctional Reform", p. 99.

59. Edwin M. Schur, *Radical Nonintervention: Rethinking the Delinquency Problem* (Englewood Cliffs, New Jersey: Prentice-Hall, Inc., 1973), p. 23.

60. *Ibid.,* p. 167.

Chapter Six: THE DOSSIERS OF CHILDREN

1. Mark Isaacs, "Secret Dossiers vs. Parents' Right to Know," *Philadelphia Inquirer,* March 13, 1972, p. 11.

2. David A. Goslin and Nancy Bordier, "Record Keeping in Elementary and Secondary Schools," in Stanton Wheeler, ed., *On Record* (New York: The Russell Sage Foundation, 1970; distributed by Basic Books), pp. 29–65.

3. Information on school records in New York is derived largely from cases handled by Diane Divoky while she worked on the staff of the Student Rights Project of the New York Civil Liberties Union. Divoky also served on the Board of Education committee to revise school records policies and practices.

4. The study is unpublished. It was done by Vivian Stewart and David Goslin for the Russell Sage Foundation.

5. *Doe v. McMillan,* 41 LW 4752 (May 29, 1973). The appeals court decision is at 459 F.2d 1304. The Supreme Court opinion focused on the issue of what was privileged under the Speech or Debate clause, and hinged largely on the *Gravel* decision (*Gravel v. United States,* 408 U.S. 606) in which the Court ruled that Congressmen and their aides were immune from civil or criminal liability within their "legislative sphere" and in pursuit of legislative acts, but not beyond: "The Speech or Debate Clause (Art. I, Sec. 6 of the Constitution) was designed to assure a coequal branch of the government wide freedom of speech, debate, and deliberation without intimidation or threats from the Executive Branch. It thus protects Members against prosecutions that directly impinge upon or threaten the legislative process." In *McMillan,* the Court ruled, public circulation of the school report was not part of that process, although collection of the data and circulation within Congress were.

6. Edgar Z. Friedenberg, *The Vanishing Adolescent* (Boston: Beacon Press, 1969), p. 68.

7. The Russell Sage Guidelines are in *Guidelines For The Maintenance and Dissemination of Pupil Records,* (New York: The Russell Sage Foundation, 1970). It includes model forms and letters to be used in connection with the collection and circulation of pupil records. The National Education Association policy is in *Code of Student Rights and Responsibilities,* Washington, NEA, 1971. The most comprehensive collection of guidelines, state by state, complete with relevant statutes and other data, is in *Children Parents and School Records,* available from the National Committee for Citizens in Education, Suite 410, Wilde Lake Village Green, Columbia, Maryland.

8. Schools must also notify parents "at least annually" of the types of records that they maintain and the kind of information they contain; "of the name and position of the official responsible for the maintenance of each type of record, the persons who have access to those records, and the purpose for which they have access"; the procedures that have been set to allow parents to inspect records; the policies of the school for reviewing and expunging records; and the rights of parents and children under the law. Schools must provide an assurance that they are in compliance as part of any application for federal education funds. Moreover, any educational institution which receives U.S. Office of Education funds must guarantee that any other agency to which it makes those funds available is also in compliance. HEW has established an office and review board to investigate, process and review violations and complaints. A school failing to comply after reasonable notice and an opportunity for a hearing will lose its federal funds. The Buckley Law is PL 93-380; the complete regulations are available from HEW. (See Appendix.)

9. *Matter of Thibadeau,* New York State Education Department Report 607 (September 20, 1960). See also *Manual of Pupil Records,* published by New York State Education Department, Albany, New York, 1965.

10. *Van Allen v. McCleary,* 211 N.Y.S. 501 (1960).

11. Board of Education (New York) Special Circular No. 63, 1961–1962 (May 8, 1962).

12. Board of Education Special Circular No. 55, 1965–1966 (February 18, 1966).

13. *Matter of Wilson,* New York State Education Department Report 208 (February 22, 1972).

14. The quote is from a student's record in Martinez, California. It was obtained for us by a teacher. It is relatively easy, even for persons unknown to a school system, to get such information from members of the school staff.

15. Professional certification requirements for school counselors vary: in

some states they include a master's degree and specified courses in counseling; in others they stipulate only that the counselor have a teaching certificate.

16. Billy Washington is a pseudonym. The case comes from the records of the Youth Law Center in San Francisco, one of the few legal defense organizations in America which specializes in juvenile cases. Banks and all agencies of federal, state and local government regularly obtain adult criminal records of all job applicants. Banks are required to do so by the regulations of the Federal Deposit Insurance Corporation; the regulations, however, do not apply to juvenile records which, in theory, are not to be used to judge the trustworthiness of adult job applicants or (again in theory) for any other purpose after the individual turns eighteen.

17. The Mannheim case is discussed in an affidavit filed by Mannheim in *Cuevas v. Leary,* USDC for the Southern District of New York, 70 Civ. 2017, in which a group of minors and their parents sued the New York City Police Department to prohibit the police "from transferring the contents or otherwise indicating the existence of [juvenile police records] to other public agencies and from continuing to maintain such files or to register youths as delinquent." The records of the suit also include affidavits from several others—minors, parents and lawyers—with similar stories.

18. The estimate on juvenile arrests is from Alfred Blumstein, "Systems Analysis and the Criminal Justice System," *American Academy of Political and Social Sciences,* Vol. 374 (1967), pp. 92–100. The estimate on the number of juveniles with police records is based on arrest data and projections from figures obtained from local police record systems.

19. "A Qualitative and Quantitative Analysis of YDI Cards Issued in 1969," Appendix A to the *Staff Report of the Special Committee on the YDI System of the Criminal Justice Coordinating Council,* July 1, 1971. The report was unable to verify the accuracy of the behavioral anecdotes contained in the YD records. The analysis was based only on the contents of the records themselves. Comparisons were possible, however, in those cases where there were records of a followup investigation. In 1969, the New York police issued 53,000 YD cards. By 1974, attorneys defending minors in New York estimated that the figure was in excess of 60,000.

20. Rules circulated to law enforcement agencies and other organizations by Francis W. Mayer, Presiding Judge, Juvenile Court, for the City and County of San Francisco, January 3, 1972. It was filed as an exhibit in a lawsuit seeking expungement of certain juvenile records in San Francisco (*Doe v. Scott,* USDC for the Northern District of California, C–74–0231, 1974).

21. The source of the quote is Laurence Smith of the Juvenile Division of the Los Angeles Public Defender's Office.

22. *In re Gault,* 387 U.S. 1 (1967), p. 24–25.

23. Michael L. Altman, "Juvenile Information Systems: A Comparative Analysis," in *Computer Applications in the Juvenile Justice System,* (Reno: National Council of Juvenile Court Judges, 1974), pp. 6–7.

24. The description of the St. Louis system is based on internal documents, and particularly "St. Louis Juvenile Uniform Referral Information System (JURIS), Display and Report Examples" (December 1973), and

promotional literature circulated by Lawrence-Leiter and Co., the Kansas City management consultants who designed the software for the system.
25. Much of this was discussed in Chapter IV. For additional data, see D.M. Gottfredson, "Assessment and Prediction Methods in Crime and Delinquency," *President's Commission on Law Enforcement and Administration of Justice, Task Force Report: Juvenile Delinquency and Youth Crime* (Washington, D.C.: Government Printing Office, 1967); Altman, "Juvenile Information Systems,"; and Ernst A. Wenk, *et al.,* "Can Violence Be Predicted?" *Crime and Delinquency* (October 1972), pp. 393–402.
26. The record for the 16–year-old includes "stealing under $50," "runaway" and "burglary"; the record for the 17–year-old includes theft, auto theft and truancy. The records of both appear in the company's sales literature, along with addresses, the names of parents and, in one case, the telephone number. We phoned the number and spoke to the boy's father. In the other case, the number was unlisted, but the telephone company confirmed the existence of the listing for the name and address on the court record
27. A legislative report on delinquency diversion programs and predelinquency projects in California concluded that "there are no provisions for destruction of records after the programs are terminated." The "Report on Pre-Delinquency Programs Funded by the California Council on Criminal Justice" of the Joint Legislative Audit Committee (July, 1973) also noted that records and information from at least one "voluntary program outside of the juvenile court system have been used in subsequent dispositional hearings in juvenile court."
28. The Los Angeles Police Department made a public announcement that it was listing 793 minors as "hard-core delinquents" and confirmed, in public hearings before a state legislative committee, that in at least one area of the city the police were maintaining a list of names submitted by teachers, school bus drivers and others of "violent" minors. No investigation or verification was required before names were put on the list.
29. Quoted from a description of the meeting which we received from a person who attended.
30. John C. Coffee, "Privacy Versus Parens Patriae: The Role of Police Records in the Sentencing and Surveillance of Juveniles," *Cornell Law Review,* Vol. 57 (1972), pp. 612–613. Coffee was one of the attorneys in *Cuevas* (see note 17); as a consequence of the suit, the New York Police Department agreed to limit circulation of youth records and to expunge the records of most minors after their seventeenth birthdays.
31. "MYSIS (Michigan Youth Services Information System): Security and Privacy Manual," (Lansing: Department of Social Services, 1974), p. 4.
32. Medichek is discussed more extensively in Chapter IV. The federal guidelines for medical screening programs include a provision that records be available for inspection by the Department of Health, Education and Welfare. Since all states are required to operate screening programs for children eligible for Medicaid, the Medichek system will undoubtedly represent a model for other states
33. A number of juvenile court data systems are discussed in *Computer Applications in the Juvenile Justice System.* Data on juvenile po-

lice record systems come largely from an LEAA report, published in 1970, listing all police data banks then in existence. The Maryland drug abuse reporting system was modified in 1973 to make it optional: after promising confidentiality, the state's Drug Abuse Administration discovered that there was a police agent working under cover in the DAA offices, apparently looking for drug abuse among the staff. The reporting requirement is now optional and, according to John Roemer of the Maryland chapter of the American Civil Liberties Union, most agencies no longer file reports. In New York, drug abuse reporting continues, though a proposal to give all secondary school students periodic urine tests has been abandoned. For an example of the reports about information sharing with the FBI, see "The FBI's Big Brother Computer," *Washington Monthly,* September 1972, p. 28. The Bureau insists that it only processes records of those juveniles who are included in local records for adult offenders. There have been instances where those include fourteen-year-old shoplifters, but there is no way to know how many such cases there are.

34. "The Maryland Data System for the Handicapped, Instruction Manual," issued by the Department of Juvenile Services. The collaborating agencies include the State Department of Education, the Department of Mental Hygiene, the Mental Retardation Administration, the Preventive Medicine Administration and the Social Services Administration. The categories for public school students come from a similar document circulated by the Maryland State Department of Education. DSH is operated by the State Department of Education.

35. A citizens' committee on privacy was appointed in 1974 to make recommendations to modify the system. The committee was assured that individual records could be identified by name only by the agency which submitted the record.

36. Alan F. Westin and Michael Baker, *Databanks in a Free Society* (Chicago: Quadrangle, 1972). The book appears, in part, to be an attempt to refute the warnings contained in Arthur Miller's book, *The Assault on Privacy: Computers, Data Banks and Dossiers* (Ann Arbor: University of Michigan Press, 1971).

37. Where persons are institutionalized in the name of treatment or education, and not, after due process, for punishment or the "protection of society," the privacy issue should, in theory, become more sensitive. Common institutional ideology, however, runs the other way. Where the object is "treatment" or education, privacy considerations vanish, particularly where children are concerned. In an unpublished paper Michael Baker, Westin's collaborator in *Databanks,* points out "that children are not taken terribly seriously with respect to matters of privacy" (Michael Baker, Charles Lister and Raymond Milhous, "Privacy and Exceptional Children: Issues of Recordkeeping, Access and Confidentiality").

38. The student guide of a New York City high school warns incoming freshmen: "*Long after you have been graduated,* inquiries concerning your record are answered by consulting your record card. *This is a truly permanent one. Make it a good one.*"

Chapter Seven: THERAPY, PUNISHMENT, CONTROL

1. There is no way of knowing the racial proportions of children on drugs. There are communities—Columbus, Ohio, for example—where large percentages of black children are drugged, but nearly all the centers in which the prolific prescribers are located are surrounded by relatively comfortable or affluent white middle class communities, and the clients of prodrug doctors are nearly all white.

2. Perry London, *Behavior Control* (New York: Perennial Library, Harper and Row, 1969), p. 4.

3. Aldous Huxley, *Island* (New York: Harper and Row, 1962), pp. 175–176.

4. Delgado has elaborated some of his Faustian expectations in *Physical Control of the Mind: Toward a Psycho-civilized Society* (New York: Harper and Row, 1969). The idea of monitoring and controlling parolees or other potentially "dangerous" individuals through remote control brain stimulation is also discussed in Burton Ingraham and Gerald Smith, "The Use of Electronics in the Observation and Control of Human Behavior and Its Possible Use in Rehabilitation and Parole," *Issues in Criminology*, Vol. 8, No. 2 (1972).

5. Edgar Friedenberg, "Is the Pigeon Always Right?" *Ramparts*, December 1974/January 1975, p. 59.

6. There is a discussion of the Chinese "brainwashing" in Donald Whaley and Richard Malott, *Elementary Principles of Behavior* (New York: Appleton-Century-Crofts, 1971).

7. One experiment was carried on in Visalia, California, by Paul Graubard, Harry Rosenberg and Martin Miller. It is discussed in some detail in Philip J. Hilts, *Behavior Mod* (New York: Harper's Magazine Press, 1974), pp. 54–58.

8. John D. Nolan, "The True Humanist: The Behavior Modifier," *Teachers College Record*, Vol. 76, No. 2 (1974), p. 342.

9. Chomsky, "Psychology and Ideology," p. 365.

10. Skinner, *Science and Human Behavior*, p. 192.

11. Barry F. Singer, "Psychological Studies of Punishment," *California Law Review*, Vol. 58 (1973), pp. 414–415. The history of the idea of punishment as therapy is discussed in Thomas Szasz, *The Manufacture of Madness* (New York: Harper and Row, 1970). "The pious inquisitor," Szasz wrote, "would undoubtedly have been enraged at the suggestion that he was the heretic's foe, not his friend. . . . The inquisitor [would have asserted] that his ministrations—including burning the victim at the stake—were aimed at saving the heretic's soul from eternal damnation." Benjamin Rush, the "father" of American psychiatry, was even more explicit. The only remedy for the disease of lying, said Rush, is "bodily pain, inflicted by the rod, or confinement, or abstinence from food." Terror was also a good treatment, for "it acts powerfully upon the body, through the

medium of the mind, and should be employed in the cure of madness."
(Rush, *Medical Inquiries and Observations Upon the Diseases of the Mind*
[New York: Hafner, 1962], pp. 265–266 and 175. The book was originally
published in 1812.)
12. O. J. Andy, "Thalamotomy in Hyperactive and Aggressive Behavior,"
Confinia Neurologica, Vol. 32 (1970), p. 324.
13. "Quality of Health Care—Human Experimentation," Hearings
Before the Subcommittee on Health, U.S. Senate, 93rd Congress, Part 2,
pp. 348–357. Andy testified before the subcommittee, chaired by Senator
Edward M. Kennedy, on February 23, 1973. In the past five years there
has been extensive legal and medical debate about the use of psychosurgery, aversive therapy and terror drugs among prisoners and involuntary
mental patients. To meet the argument that inmates submit to such treatments "voluntarily" it has been argued (and the courts are beginning to
concur) either that prisoners and involuntary patients lack the capacity for
informed consent or that their status is inherently coercive and that they
are therefore always under duress in submitting "voluntarily." (There is
an extended discussion of those issues in Michael H. Shapiro, "Legislating
the Control of Behavior Control: Autonomy and the Coercive Use of
Organic Therapies," *Southern California Law Review,* Vol. 47 [1974], pp.
237–356.) Among the cases in which this view has been adopted is *Kaimo-
witz v. Department of Mental Health,* Civ. No. 73–19434–AW (Wayne
County, Michigan, Cir. Ct., July 10, 1973). The court held that "it is
impossible for an involuntarily detained mental patient to be free of ul-
terior forms of restraint or coercion when his very release from the institution may depend upon his cooperating with institutional authorities and
giving consent to experimental surgery." The argument could be applied
to all institutionalized minors, including schoolchildren (though it has
not). It may even be possible to maintain that parental authority to permit
irreversible procedures affecting mentation can be circumscribed by invocation of the child's inalienable rights against such a form of involuntary
treatment.
14. Farrall Instrument Company Catalog F–72 (P.O. Box 1037, Grand
Island, Nebraska). The catalog lists a number of shockers and other behavior modification instruments. Farrall also publishes *Behavioral Engineering,* a "mini-journal" which reports on "behavior modification techniques
using instrumentation."
15. *Helping Schools Help Children,* Research Report–2. (Washington,
D.C.: Department of Health, Education and Welfare No. [Adm] 74–33,
1974), p. 6. IBR has published a number of monographs and a film on its
behavior modification programs. The most comprehensive of these publications is PICA, *Project Three: A Laboratory Model,* (Silver Spring, Maryland: Institute of Behavioral Research, 1971).
16. *Helping Schools,* pp. 5–6.
17. A number of behavior modifiers, if not most, defend it as the most
"humanistic" of the available options because it replaces punishment with
rewards, and because it rewards all subjects, not just the most successful,
for appropriate behavior. See, for example, Nolan, "The True Humanist,"
pp. 335–343.

18. *PICA,* p. v.

19. Hilts, *Behavior Mod,* pp. 168–169.

20. *Morales* and *Gault* are discussed in Chapter V. *Miranda v. Arizona* imposed on police and prosecutors the duty to inform all defendants on arrest that they had a right to remain silent and to obtain counsel, and that if no such warning were given at the time of arrest, any subsequent conviction might be legally tainted and thrown out by higher courts. The right, of course, had always existed; what *Miranda* imposed was the duty to inform defendants of it. It therefore tended to extend some additional protection to the poor and the legally unsophisticated, including juveniles, who were routinely questioned without any warning.

21. William Ryan, *Blaming the Victim* (New York: Pantheon Books, 1972), p. 8.

Index

About the Authors

Peter Schrag is the author of many books, including *Test of Loyalty* and *The Decline of the Wasp.* He was an editor at *Saturday Review* and *Change* magazine, and is now a contributing editor to *MORE,* the journalism review.

Diane Divoky is one of the editors of *Learning* magazine, and has written a book on the rights of students. She has also been a teacher and a newspaper reporter.